REGENERATIVE POLITICS

NEW DIRECTIONS IN CRITICAL THEORY

NEW DIRECTIONS IN CRITICAL THEORY

Amy Allen, General Editor

New Directions in Critical Theory presents outstanding classic and contemporary texts in the tradition of critical social theory, broadly construed. The series aims to renew and advance the program of critical social theory, with a particular focus on theorizing contemporary struggles around gender, race, sexuality, class, and globalization and their complex interconnections.

For a complete list of books in the series, please see the Columbia University Press website.

REGENERATIVE POLITICS

EMMA PLANINC

Columbia University Press
New York

Columbia University Press
Publishers Since 1893
New York   Chichester, West Sussex
cup.columbia.edu

Library of Congress Cataloging-in-Publication Data
Names: Planinc, Emma, author.
Title: Regenerative politics / Emma Planinc.
Description: New York : Columbia University Press, [2024] |
Series: New directions in critical theory | Includes bibliographical
references and index.
Identifiers: LCCN 2024003377 | ISBN 9780231215824 (hardback) |
ISBN 9780231215831 (trade paperback) | ISBN 9780231560993 (ebook)
Subjects: LCSH: Political culture—Europe. | Political culture—
United States. | Democracy—Philosophy. | Liberalism—Europe. |
Liberalism—United States. | Europe—Politics and government. |
United States—Politics and government.
Classification: LCC JN94.A91 P52 2024 | DDC 306.2094—dc23/eng/20240205
LC record available at https://lccn.loc.gov/2024003377

Cover design: Emma Planinc and Milenda Nan Ok Lee
Cover image: Rich Fowler, Eco Owl Press

Je veux un monde nu d'univers non timbré / I want a naked world of unstamped universe.

—*THE REBEL*

CONTENTS

REGENERATIVE POLITICS

1

NO HUMANS LEFT

There are no humans left in politics. I do not mean by this that our politics are inhumane or that our politics lacks a kind of behavior befitting of humanity. I mean this quite substantively: there are no humans left. The rest of this book will be an attempt to persuade you that this is true, to explain why this is a dire situation for modern liberal democracies, and to offer a vision of how we might bring humans back into our political world.

For many, however, this claim will not be a surprise. Trenchant critiques of liberal democracies are issuing from those dismissive of the dominant liberal worldview and its foundation in a certain conception of the human being. Far Right thinkers demand change and a reconstitution of the current monolithic liberal world order, battling against a vision of today's political world as stagnant in its universalizing tendencies. This critique is reflected in their opposition to the human rights regime, the bureaucracy of democracies, the dulling qualities of the media, the notion that all people are equal, and the one-worldism of cosmopolitanism. The liberal, global order of human rights, and its accompanying Enlightenment-rooted universalism, is for thinkers like Guillaume Faye and Alain de Benoist the cause of the deracination of the human spirit in the modern world.[1] For them, there are no humans in politics.

Guillaume Faye writes in *Why We Fight*, for example, that "Europe today is the victim of an ideology that she herself created—one that began with the Eighteenth century philosophy of the Enlightenment and culminates in what one calls 'Western ideology' or 'globalist ideology.'"[2] Faye sees the Enlightenment values of this ideology in the contemporary commitment to "absolute individualism," the "hypocritical affirmation of the equality of all human beings," the "rejection of the divine," and the "cult of endless progress."[3] So, too, does Faye root this "Western ideology" in the "philosophy of 'human rights' . . . [which is] hegemonic, totalitarian. It tolerates no challenges."[4] A founding member of the Nouvelle Droite ("New Right"), Alain de Benoist similarly deplores "the ideology of human rights" along with its attendant Enlightenment values,[5] and he rejects the modern "linear notion of a goal-oriented history, having an absolute beginning and moving toward an unavoidable end; a notion which, starting with the eighteenth century, will give birth to all modern forms of historicisms, as well as the ideology of progress."[6] As the Far Right Arktos author Daniel Forrest writes, the modern, liberal West has precluded human beings from acting on their capacity to be the "creator[s] of a new future" and thus does not allow humans to be self-determining agents.[7]

But it is not only those on the Right who hold this critical position. The more damning critiques of liberalism and the Enlightenment vision of the human being have always come from progressives, who, while approaching from the opposing political position, nevertheless share many of the same commitments. Also locating the abstract "Man" in the Enlightenment and in rights-based discourse, critical theorists on the Left hold the universalization of the idea of the human being accountable for the injustices of the modern age. In *The Order of Things*, Michel Foucault locates the creation of Man in the eighteenth and nineteenth centuries, thus claiming (as is often quoted by those on the critical Left) that Man "is only a recent invention."[8] This invention and dominating acceptance of Man has put us into what Foucault calls an "anthropological sleep" that precludes all possibility of thinking the human anew.[9] Sylvia Wynter draws on Foucault in her critique of the "liberal monohumanist conception of being human,"[10] arguing that the Man of our current epoch, or historical understanding, is an Enlightenment inheritance that must be left behind in order to imagine a "new humanity";[11] "the West, over the last five hundred years, has brought the *whole* human species into its *hegemonic* . . . model of being human," which implicitly rejects different "discursive formations" of what it means to be a human being.[12] Following Frantz Fanon, Wynter writes that "what is to be done is to set man free," to demand an entirely new "question of *who we are as human*."[13]

Zakiyyah Iman Jackson has written recently that we must focus on "modes of being/knowing/feeling that gesture toward the overturning of Man," toward a "different 'genre of the human.'"[14] For Jackson, it is necessary to question "the universal liberal project," which masks Black subjection with claims about the human and "'the universal' subject of rights."[15] This perspective is shared by Angela Davis, Ta-Nehisi Coates, Rinaldo Walcott, and Achille Mbembe.[16] Walcott writes that "the very idea of the human requires rethinking in order for an authentic freedom to emerge for Black people,"[17] and in his *Necropolitics*, Mbembe lays out the many forms the "critique of Western humanism" has taken to "demystify the universalist pretensions" of the modern Enlightenment idea of the human being.[18] In the postcolonial critique, the liberal conception of the human is the source of not only a false kind of abstraction but also the colonial violence and injustice that was committed in its name. As Aimé Césaire writes in *Discourse on Colonialism*, "One of the values invented by the bourgeoisie in former times and launched throughout the world was *man*,"[19] an idea that was only ever a "pseudo-humanism"—"narrow and fragmentary, incomplete and biased and, all things considered, sordidly racist."[20] Kenan Malik claims in *The Meaning of Race* that "the distinction between the West and its Other is, for many contemporary theorists, implicit in the categories of Enlightenment universalism."[21] Malik cites Stuart Hall's "The West and the Rest":

The "West and the Rest" discourse greatly influenced Enlightenment thinking. . . . In Enlightenment discourse, the West was the model, the prototype and the measure of social progress. It was Western progress, civilization, rationality and development that were celebrated. And yet . . . without the Rest (or its own internal "others") the West would not have been able to recognize or represent itself as the summit of human history. The figure of the "Other," banished to the edge of the conceptual world and constructed as the absolute opposite, the negation, of everything which the West stood for, reappeared at the very center of the discourse of civilization.[22]

For both the Left and the Right, it is the success of modern humanism and its attendant liberal political worldview that is the cause of all our ills. The foundational claim of this liberal humanist position is that human beings transformed into agents of their own political fates, and of their own identities, at some pivotal point in the modern revolutionary era. This is located in an Enlightenment way of thinking about the human's place in the world—the rise of what Carl Becker described as the desire for "progressive improvement" rooted in the belief that "the salvation of man must be attained . . . by man himself."[23] While critics of this foundational claim might differ in integral respects, they share an account of our dilemma: that this largely accomplished vision of Man as individualistic and perfectible is problematic, either for its vacuity or its exclusionary injustice. The West accepted and perpetuated a conception of the human as an individual, active, and self-determining agent that, through its dominance, employed a feigned similarity and universality in order to efface difference. It is a view that attributes the human to some, bought at the exclusion of others.

Liberalism thus stands accused of dehumanization, and the proposed rectification of this injustice involves the abandonment of the tool that has committed the most heinous crime: the very idea that there is a human nature at all, reified in the universalism of rights. The Enlightenment is blamed for this creation of Man, a concept seemingly designed from its inception to establish its own exclusions rather than facilitate inclusive belonging. Today's critics of liberalism, and of its reliance on the assertion of human rights, tend to see only one solution: to discard rights and the modern view of the human person altogether in favor of a regenerated future.

From the Right we see calls to abandon liberal commitments like liberty, equality, and rights in favor of more ancient and hierarchical ways of being[24] or a Nietzschean desire to celebrate the strength of powerful geniuses.[25] Battling against a vision of the Left as banal, vacuous, and unmoving, the regenerative goal of the Far Right envisions a rebirth of human beings through political transformation, often declaring open war against defenders of liberalism and human rights. Forrest sees a choice between the stagnation of present-day life and a changeable, regenerated future: "Today's alternative is between globalization, entropy, and narcissistic consumerism, in a scenario of ever more dehumanizing effects—and the possibility of a community deciding to take charge of its own destiny and to regenerate humankind, reaching ever higher forms of life."[26] He argues that human beings must be reminded of, and awaken to, their "historical consciousness," which will open a new "unknown destiny—*the regeneration of history*."[27] The entries in Guillaume Faye's "metapolitical dictionary" present *human rights* and *egalitarianism* in the same light. Egalitarianism, Faye writes, "is the trunk root of the dominant ideology. It is the source of all modern totalitarianisms, as well as the decadence of so-called liberal, democratic societies."[28] Rooted in the Judeo-Christian tradition, this "dogma . . . claims that all men are in essence equal, atoms of moral, political, and social equivalence."[29] Human rights, "the cornerstone of the modern ideology and individualistic egalitarianism," are founded on "a synthesis of Eighteenth-century political philosophy"; "the 'human' in human rights is nothing but an abstraction, a consumer-client, an atom."[30] In his entry for *history*, Faye claims that we must see that the "future remains open . . . in order to regenerate history."[31]

From the Left we see a desire to move beyond "liberal monohumanism"[32] toward "versions of humanity unburdened by the shackles" of the Enlightenment's conception of Man.[33] "Eurocentric humanism" is grounded in the domination of others by a universal humanity, which cannot be overcome simply with a "fuller recognition within liberal humanism's terms."[34] Queer theorists like Dean Spade and Lee Edelman similarly see no possibility of living full self-determining queer lives within the liberal rights framework.[35] Like those on the Right, these figures on the Left are drawn to regenerative ideas—that is, visions of the remaking of the human being that will occur through the remaking (or, in the words of Frantz Fanon, the "restructuring") of the political world and the self. Mbembe casts this as a "transfiguration" of "becoming-human-in-the-world"[36] and Walcott as "a reorientation of the planet and all modes of being human on it." "With such an accounting," Walcott writes, "new registers of life would appear";[37] "in a world where Black people have been ejected from the category of the human and have struggled both to enter and to reanimate what it might/ can mean, rethinking the human is central to any notion of freedom for which we do not have the words."[38] Citing Césaire, Wynter imagines a "counterhumanism" that will be "made to the measure of the world."[39]

For these thinkers, the regeneration of the human being can occur only along with the abandonment of the Enlightenment legacy, embodied particularly in the concept of human rights. As Jackson writes in *Becoming Human*, there may be "a desire for, perhaps, a different 'genre of the human', or . . . an urgent demand for the dissolution of 'human' but, in either case, it is not simply a desire for fuller recognition with liberal humanism's terms";[40] " 'the universal' subject of rights and entitlements assumed a highly particularized subject that is held as paradigmatic, subjugating all other conceptions of being and justice."[41] Jackson's demands "emerge from a different way of being/knowing/feeling existence than the ones legible and codified in law and in the dialectics of Man. Their contestation invests in speculation and expressive culture as a site of creativity."[42] In its assertion of a falsely universalist conception of rights, the liberal world denies the creative and self-regenerative capacities of human beings. Walcott wants us to face up to the "ongoing brutality in the face of human rights discourse."[43] Ta-Nehisi Coates also rejects the liberal rights-based order: today's problem of race, he writes in *Between the World and Me*, is only the latest iteration of a "history of civilization [that] is littered with dead 'races' [Frankish, Italian, German, Irish] later abandoned because they no longer serve their purpose—the organization of people beneath, and beyond, the umbrella of rights."[44]

In many ways, these positions of the Right and Left are mutually exclusive, and the arguments of the one are inevitably rejected by the other. But taking them together, they say something extremely important: challenges to liberal democracy are not coming from a place of *politics* but from the question of *what it means to be human*. They attack not our political structures but the very notion of human rights and the question of the human in modernity. The challengers are severe precisely because their foundational premise is that today's politics say nothing to them about what it means to be a human being in the world, except that they do not belong in it—and we are increasingly seeing these positions gain more real-world traction in polarizing political parties, especially in the rise of the Far Right in Europe and in the United States.

These critics are typically cast as dangerously illiberal, as threats to the liberal democratic world that must be suppressed and defeated.[45] I argue, however, that it is time for us to take these critiques seriously as claims against liberalism and liberal democracies that speak not from a position outside liberalism but directly to the internal incoherence of our regime: that liberal democracies are not living up to their humanist commitments.

It is not that liberal democracies are failing to adhere to their own principles in an unjust or unequal fashion (that some are free while others
are not, for example) or that liberalism's success *is* its failure (as the new
postliberals argue, that rampant individualism and the fragmentation of
society are working against human interest).[46] My contention is that in
these growing critiques and political extremes we are facing not the dwin-
dling success but the ongoing and perpetual failure of modern humanism essentially from its inception—resting on its foundational idea of the
self-determining, rights-bearing subject.

My view of our predicament is that when modern politics became
reliant on the self-evident assertion of the rights-bearing—and ostensibly self-determining—person, there was no longer room for humans
to truly determine themselves; that is, the question of what it means to
be human was closed. Rights as we currently understand them eliminated the possibility of any redetermination of the human being, and the
question of the human being *was determined* with a political edifice built
on its base. This is the structure of Hobbes's and Locke's social contract
theories, which establish basic, rationally deducible, and self-evident
natural rights and which have been retroactively appropriated, especially
in Locke's case, to the project of establishing the history and perpetuation of liberalism.[47] This liberal politics is built on the foundational and
unshakable support of rights that are presumed to be universal.[48] The
determination of human nature, therefore, is not in question; the manner
in which that determined nature is organized, controlled, and officiated
is the political game. This is not a self-determining subject but a self that
is a determined subject.

It is a common presumption in political theory that liberal theories
grounded in natural right and law initiated a modern politics in which
human beings maintained a detachment from the artifice of political construction through the assertion of inalienable rights. Human nature was
here reconceived on apparently stable and minimalist universal ground
and was used to bolster a conception of politics in which the human being
maintained a freedom from collective definition. The human, in this view,
was seen to be protected from the determination of others by holding on
to a right of freedom or self-determination outside the state. My argument
is that the result was the inverse: these states of nature, and affirmations
of natural or self-evident rights, in fact eliminated the capacity for human

beings to determine themselves in the world. The political theories of the so-called founders of liberalism rest on states of nature, and visions of the human being, that construct closed loops, inextricably connecting human beings to their political regimes. If the state falls apart, according to Hobbes and Locke, human beings return to "nature" and to the same rights and laws that they possessed before the institution of the state. But so, too, are these rights and laws meant to result in the erection of an identical political structure in perpetuity if we recognize our self-evident rights, binding forever the image of the rights-bearing individual to one vision of politics. These rights thus served only to close, instead of open, the question of the human being, and their claims to maintain a place for human beings outside politics forever contained them in it.

The self-constituting, free human seen to have been born in early modern revolutionary periods, or in the Enlightenment, is not present in this conception of rights. If the liberal democratic world, then, is reliant on the self-determining individual—as Alan Ryan writes, the essence of all forms of liberalism is "that individuals are self-creating"[49]—there has never truly been a liberal democratic polity.[50] I believe that we are now witnessing the desire for self-determination, and the desire to be truly capable of deciding what and how one is in the world, bursting through from the extremes in calls for regeneration in the redetermination of the self. The critiques from both the Left and the Right reveal that at the core of the modern liberal idea of the person is a conceptual trick: premised on the novel superiority of the vision of a self-determining modern human being, the liberal democratic world does not actually leave open the question of how humans can determine themselves. The very rights that are there to secure our material well-being simultaneously prevent us from ever circumscribing for ourselves what it means to *be human*. With the liberal worldview itself not living up to its own apparently foundational demand that humans be entitled to determine themselves, neither the challengers nor the challenged, neither the excluded nor the included, have any real claim to be properly self-determining or self-defining. There are no humans left in today's politics.

Two routes out from similar kinds of dire assertions about the character of modernity or liberalism have been offered before: looking behind or looking forward. The first path is to claim that there is a prior vision—a more ancient, nonmodern one—that offers a properly human alternative.

Here company is kept among political philosophers such as Pierre Manent, Alasdair MacIntyre, and Leo Strauss,[51] all of whom think something went wrong in the modern project and that the solution lies in a more classically informed and robust conception of human nature. The second path, which we might describe as postmodern in contrast to the first (whether overtly or covertly) conservative view, is to turn against any universalizing claims about the human being, embracing the ways in which the human is constructed. This second, nonessentialist position is shared by the likes of, for example, Judith Butler, Michel Foucault, and Donna Haraway and perhaps originates, or is most forcefully expressed, in the philosophy of Friedrich Nietzsche.[52] The first path typically claims to resolve modernity's missteps by establishing and reaffirming an essence to the human being, something unshakable in the face of historical transformation. The second path denies any such unchangeable character, relying instead on the prospect of a future in which the human being is freed from the shackles of universalism and any conception of a unitary, unconstructed human nature. The first path digs into a conception of human nature or natural law that opposes itself to historical reconstitution—denying the self-determinative project of liberal modernity and imagining a political world set on a firmer foundation. The second path does the opposite: embracing only the changeability of historical and social contextual identities, there is no place for any universal conception of human nature, and any such conception is seen to do violence to the diversity in the world or to the foundationally creative capacities of human beings.

Neither of these approaches, however, can accommodate the fact that a clear assertion of universality is common to today's challengers of the liberal democratic vision in the belief that human beings have both a regenerative desire and a need to determine themselves in the world that is not currently being met. This conception of human self-determination relies on the capacity to change and so cannot be described as fixed or firm. It is thus not entirely the antimodern human nature imagined in the ancient mode, which is usually founded in a teleological conception of the human good. And while a desire or need for self-determination depends on the ability to historically reimagine the human being, it is also at its core a claim about a universal nature that is being denied and thus is not reducible to the commitments of the more postmodern or constructivist position.

Today's challenge is to somehow configure, accommodate, or understand this seemingly paradoxical idea of a human nature that is both universal and malleable. One temptation might be to shrug off these claims as illogical—or, as many do, to reject them as dangerously illiberal. No person, so this objection might go, who would argue for casting off rights and all their progressive successes in favor of such an incoherent self-conception is worth the time of day in a liberal democracy. This belief is dangerously naive, and we take this position at our peril. The claim to universal self-determination is not only a challenge to liberal democracies from what appears to be the outside but is the challenge liberal democrats must face in themselves, confronting the perpetually failed self-determinative promise of their own project and their own vision of humanity. For human beings to determine themselves in politics, politics must itself be open to the redetermination of what it means to be a human being. If the human is predetermined, then the capacity to *be human* is lost—and citizens are starting to notice.

This, I am sure, is starting to sound like a radical political argument. While it may share some premises with thinkers on the far academic Left,[53] the argument I will offer is also antiradical, tethered as it is to a substantive assertion of a universal human nature and, most importantly, committed to defending and resuscitating the core principles of modern liberal democracies, in particular the idea of human rights. Here, too, I will depart in one integral respect from the critics of the liberal democratic project that I have discussed: I will show that the ideas of human nature and human rights born in the French Enlightenment can themselves be the source of the very self-determinative claims challengers are making and that they want to see fulfilled. A polity founded on rights need not preclude the emergence of the truly self-determining human being; rather, the polities we currently have founded on and with a particular conception of rights are maladies of our making and can be undone in order to be remade.

The historical argument of this book is that at the inception of the idea of universal rights in the French Revolutionary period we see a much different conceptual universe from the rights-grounded liberal democracies we have today. In the French Enlightenment and French Revolution, rights were not self-evident. Philosophers and citizens alike saw that if a human being as a rights-bearer was to be in the world, man must recreate the world and thus also recreate himself as—that is, into—a rights-bearer in the process.[54] The term they used for this self-creating and world-creating process was *regeneration*. The self-regenerative human being, who gave rise to the Declaration of the Rights of Man and of the Citizen, existed precisely in this paradoxical liminal space between the universal claim to a human good and the contextual or historical claim about the malleability of human nature. It was only because the human being was able to regenerate or change himself that he was able to fashion himself anew in the image of what he believed himself to be by nature. In the efficiency of the self-determinative action, the human being truly became a rights-bearer and rights-maker: the regeneration, and thus the change or transformation, of the self was simultaneously the enactment of the universal natural right to do so. This was itself the source of the declaration of universal right: as Rabaut Saint-Étienne stated in the National Assembly on August 18, 1789, if "we want to regenerate ourselves; the declaration of rights is therefore essentially necessary."[55]

In this book, I am calling for a reinvigoration of this regenerative conception of rights against the grain of current rights discourse. Contemporary scholars increasingly favor seeing rights to freedom and equality as things that "humans *make happen*,"[56] that are "not detected but created."[57] But for these scholars, along with this notion must go any universalizing conception of the human being. As Marie-Luisa Frick writes, "Humans have no universal or permanent nature,"[58] and Anne Phillips, "We have to abandon a search for properties that belong to human beings."[59] In affirming the "essential contingency" of human rights, Mark Goodale claims we must take "leave, once and for all, of any remaining attachments to . . . the quasi-biological claim that human rights are '*natural rights . . .* [that] are natural in the sense that their source is human nature.' "[60] Echoing the perspectival divide that exists between the Left and the Right in their challenges to liberalism, this contextualist, or anti-essentialist, view is matched with more conservative counterarguments for the necessity of affirming a human nature, usually through appeals to moral codes or natural law. Pierre Manent writes, for example, that the "doctrine of the rights of man . . . [affirms] a humanity that begins in a freedom that ignores all law."[61] Manent wants to recall the "authority of nature" and human nature against modern thinkers who condone the emergence of "new 'form(s) of humanity' " in the invocation of rights.[62]

But the choice does not have to be between the historical/contingent and the natural/unchanging conception of rights and the human being.[63] The idea of universal rights in fact came into being precisely to accommodate the coexistence of the historical and the natural registers of the conceptual understanding of humanity.[64] This new language of natural right adumbrated the competing compulsions of the politically active human being: the ability and desire to regenerate oneself, and the awareness that the capacity for self-regeneration was a fact of one's universal nature. In this sense, rights are things that humans make happen, but only because human nature facilitates their making. The self-regenerative human being is naturally historical, determining himself in concert with others doing the same. This origin of the concept of rights, which can accommodate human change and self-determination, did not reject but affirmed a robust conception of human nature—and it offers us the vision of a new natural right on which to build a regenerative politics.

This natural right emerged in the strange and vibrant philosophic context of eighteenth-century France and was the generator of the philosophic principles contained in the Declaration of the Rights of Man and of the Citizen—the first political proclamation of a universal human right. In the natural philosophy of eighteenth-century France, a novel vision of nature emerged, and with it came a distinctive account of the human's place within it. The natural scientist Georges-Louis LeClerc, comte de Buffon, author of the enormously popular *Histoire naturelle*, established in France a vitalist conception of nature in which all natural things were embedded in a historical natural world in motion. Composed of motive organic particles, living things shared a substantive essence through which one could witness the universally renewing principle of nature. But each living thing—each species—also had what Buffon called an original prototype, or a form from or toward which individuals could degenerate or regenerate over time. The human remained embedded in this natural-historical universe but also stood apart in one fundamental respect: humans were the uniquely *self-regenerative* agents of this otherwise universal natural principle. It was only the human being, according to Buffon, that was able to regenerate itself, striving away from degenerations toward a vision of its original prototype.

This self-regenerative ability did not, however, detach the human from nature; rather, it made the human being the exemplar of the vitalism of the natural world. As Buffon wrote, the rights given to all of nature were to "alter, change, destroy, develop, renew, and produce,"[65] and by regenerating their own moral and political conditions, human beings were enacting the creative, regenerative power of nature to change itself.[66] Another natural scientist, Charles Bonnet, gave this power its explicitly regenerative language, culminating in his 1770 work *La palingénésie philosophique* (*Philosophical Palingenesis*).[67]

While the natural scientific works were highly influential, it was really in the work of Jean-Jacques Rousseau that this novel vision of nature, and the regenerative vision of the human being, acquired its most potent political force. Rousseau also saw the human as a unique natural creature in possession of the faculty of *perfectibility*, which consisted in the ability to change the world, changing both the human being and its conditions in the process. Although Rousseau located all of humanity's miseries in this changeable capacity and thus lacked the more robust optimism of his natural scientific interlocutors, he also offered accounts of how human beings might harness perfectibility to their advantage through education and political reconstitution. He did this by presenting an image of natural freedom and equality—the natural man of his *Discourse on the Origin and Foundations of Inequality Among Men* (also known as the *Second Discourse*)—that could become an aspirational object for political change when enacted through the political reforms in *Of the Social Contract*.[68]

For the revolutionaries putting together the Declaration of the Rights of Man and of the Citizen, the natural freedom and equality about which Rousseau spoke in the *Second Discourse* did not accord with the inequalities of their present-day reality. In regenerating the state through revolution and calling on Rousseau's *Social Contract* for inspiration, revolutionary actors saw themselves as regenerators. Political reconstitution would make them free and equal in accordance with a nature that they had that did not at present exist—and that they thus had to bring into being through self-transformation. The revolutionaries in France saw clearly the seemingly paradoxical role of human nature in this transformative discourse. The human being as a rights-bearer was both the beginning (origin) and the end (purpose) of political regeneration, and it was human nature itself—the capacity for self-regeneration—that facilitated the coming-into-being of the rights of man. Only in the tension between affirming a universal nature and asserting the need for conventionalist reconstitution was it possible to maintain a genuine sense of self-determination—of keeping the human being at the center of his own sense of self-making, and his political fate.

I reconstruct the historical genesis of the Declaration to show that another way of thinking about rights is possible; in fact, it was how the universality of rights was originally conceived. The regenerative conception of rights keeps the human being in politics, allowing for people to truly determine themselves while determining the world in which they live. These are not the rights we think of ourselves as having today. Rights today are presumptions, things that we possess. They are understood as what Ronald Dworkin terms individual trumps against collective political will.[69] Libertarians like Robert Nozick see our rights as "entitlements"; as Alan Ryan writes, here "the individual is the owner of his or her person and abilities; so viewed, our rights have two sources only—our initial ownership of our own selves and capacities, and the claims on whatever resources and abilities other people have freely agreed to transfer us. The state, if legitimate at all, may do no more than secure these rights."[70] Even critical theorists such as Jürgen Habermas and Rainer Forst—who take a more constructivist approach to the understanding of rights and liberal regimes—see rights and sovereignty as at the very least co-original and thus morally binding; as Forst writes, there can "be no absolute claim to sovereignty according to which imperatives of sovereignty trump human rights."[71]

Though I reject the idea of rights as self-evident trumps or universal moral (or extra-political) imperatives, I do not believe we need to abandon claims to universalism. In fact, I argue that a universal conception of human nature is necessary for the regeneration of the liberal democratic world because it is the only thing that will unite the claims of the Left, the Right, and the rest of our liberal democracies. The universal conception I offer here is the self-regenerative human being: a natural, not a moral, standard that comes with its own reconception of our natural right to make and remake ourselves and the world. In this view, all human beings are, by nature, capable of regenerating themselves, and are also capable in potentiality of changing the world around them. I also believe that all human beings, no matter how philosophical their orientation, at some point in their lives recognize that this is their desire as a person living in a world they did not create and which they will someday leave behind.

Every person will confront the world as refracted through the political context in which they find themselves and will see, to paraphrase Rousseau, that the ills they face when they confront inequalities or exclusions are not of their own making. Liberal democracies, founded on a vision of the self-determinative person, must be made open to the genuine redetermination and regeneration of human beings and the world(s) they construct. Only in a regenerative politics will we be able to bring humans—all humans—back into politics.

I anticipate already the forceful objection that this suggestion is too dangerous, particularly for rights themselves. In the historical case, of course, this objection is made for us: as I discuss in chapter 4, the regenerative enterprise of the French Revolution culminated in Robespierre's Reign of Terror and ultimately a rejection of universal right, resulting in centuries of the political and historiographical condemnation of regenerative politics. Robespierre and his followers famously installed the Fountain of Regeneration during the Terror, the radical aesthetic of which inextricably bound their regenerative politics to future fascistic rhetoric and ideology. Roger Griffin ties regenerative rhetoric explicitly to what he calls the "fascist minimum":[72] the line that must be crossed to label politics *fascistic*. Employing the Greek roots of *regeneration*, Griffin labels this type of politics "palingenetic." Palingenesis, Griffin writes, invokes "the myth of renewal, of rebirth. Etymologically, the term 'palingenesis,' deriving from *palin* (again, anew) and *genesis* (creation, birth), refers to the sense of a new start or of regeneration after a phase of crisis or decline, which can be associated just as much with mystical (for example the Second Coming) as secular realities (for example the New Germany)."[73] In modernity, regenerative thinking is tied to forms of "ultra-nationalist" politics that thrust toward "a new type of society."[74] Much of the historical work that I do in this book is to show that the inclination to see palingenesis only in its most radical, or fascistic, form is misplaced. Regenerative rhetoric was invoked by moderates and radicals alike in the French Revolution to describe political reconstitution and was used in relation to the genesis of universal human rights as much as—if not more than—it was used in support of terror or "ultra-nationalism."[75]

But the more moderate or liberal regenerative argument still might not answer the objection that the danger of regenerative politics lies in its instability, whether or not we are dealing with a palingenetic fascism. A regenerative politics can lead just as much to the abandonment of rights as to their preservation. The very virtue of liberal democracy and its reliance on self-evident rights, one might also say, is its relative stability and its minimalist capacity to allow human beings to live basically free and unencumbered lives without the threat of constant upheaval. Broadly speaking, this is the account of liberalism that we get in works as varied as Helena Rosenblatt's *The Lost History of Liberalism*, Judith Shklar's *After Utopia*, and Samuel Moyn's *The Last Utopia* and *Liberalism Against Itself*.[76] In these accounts, at some point in history there was a turn away from revolution and revolutionary freedom and from what Isaiah Berlin would come to call "positive freedom" toward the safer "negative freedom" of today's liberal democracies.[77] With so many examples of the terrifying excesses of regimes embracing positive freedom—what Berlin, in Rosenblatt's words, considered the "totalitarian kind of liberty" promising "collective self-direction" and "self-realization"[78]—in our political pasts, the desire seems to have been to foreclose the potentiality of their reemergence through mechanisms such as the protection of basic rights and a foundation in individual, rather than collective, ways of being. The presumption is that this more basic and undemanding foundation would keep future Robespierres or Hitlers from emerging.

I broadly agree with these accounts of a push toward a liberal minimalism, and in chapter 5 I track how, in the wake of the response to the French Revolution, there was a widespread condemnation of regenerative politics as dangerous and antithetical to the true principles and foundation of liberal polities, which were designed to protect rights and freedoms. Regenerative politics thus became bifurcated in its essence from liberal democracy, causing the calcification of liberalism and rights and foreclosing future self-regenerative possibilities. Whatever is left in today's conception of liberalism, the truly self-determining human being is no longer present, and this, I argue, is a consequence of the rejection of the regenerative political mode. With the presumed stability of liberal calm, the human lost its connection to politics, and rights claims thereby lost all of their vitalism. When there is no connection between the determination of the self and the determination of the political world in which one lives, a regime such as a liberal democracy—which ostensibly relies upon a self-determinative conception of the human person—lacks its own life force, its own motive and self-sustaining power. If we want to achieve genuine human self-determination in politics, then the regimes with which we have grown so comfortable will have to be refounded.

This refounding may indeed prove to be more unstable than the political world in which we now live. But the alternative to this, I believe, is much graver: a regime in which rights recede without the possibility of their redetermination or a leader who imposes a definitive vision of the human person upon his subjects. The most pressing lesson we might learn from opening ourselves up to thinking about modern politics as regenerative is in fact that this instability—the risk of losing everything a liberal democracy promises—has always been present. A truly regenerative politics would force us to look this reality in the face, constantly confronting the political truth of a self-determinative regime: nothing, not even the idea of what a human being is, can ever be taken for granted. While this idea might be destabilizing, it is the openness to the human question that maintains a reserve against anyone who might presume to foreclose the question altogether. The threat of the closed futures imagined by the most extreme exemplars of the Far Right, who seek to end the dynamism I am describing here, is the more dangerous force in today's political world. Far from being the harbinger of a fascistic palingenetic mysticism, the embrace of regenerative politics is precisely what might keep these possible futures at bay through a full openness to change and reconstitution.

My diagnosis of the dangers and potentialities of modern liberal democracies shares much with the work of Chantal Mouffe and Claude Lefort.[79] Mouffe, for example, writes in *The Return of the Political* that "democracy is something uncertain and improbable and must never be taken for granted. It is an always fragile conquest that needs to be defended as well as deepened."[80] Mouffe wants to reformulate, rather than reject, certain core democratic principles, perhaps including rights; the democratic project must be reconstituted as a space of open conflict, informing the "very possibility of a pluralist form of human existence in which rights can exist *and* be exercised."[81] In *Democracy and Political Theory*, Claude Lefort claims that the defining feature of the modern democracy is the "dissolution of the markers of certainty. It inaugurates a history in which people experience fundamental indeterminacy as to the basis of power, law, and knowledge."[82] Mouffe and Lefort claim as

I do that we ought to embrace the instability of our regime in order to preserve its potency. Mouffe, however, also claims that "the reformulation of the democratic project in terms of radical democracy requires giving up the abstract Enlightenment universalism of an undifferentiated human nature."[83] The agonistic conflict she imagines in a healthy radical democracy cannot be premised on an essentialist claim about human beings—everything has to be up for debate, up for grabs, and subject to the political sphere.[84] As I discuss in chapter 6, this argument is problematic. Without a conception of the human being, or of human nature, that might ground the desire for self-determination in the world, the political becomes the absolute determinant of all claims, even in a fascistic regime—and here, too, we can see in sharp relief the consequences of Mouffe's commitment to a Schmittian position.

This is precisely why I maintain that a conception of human nature is necessary. It is only through this connection to something not fundamentally reducible to the political that we can maintain the dynamism of the political world itself. The openness of a regime to the regeneration of the human being, and of the political order, does not entail the absolute reducibility of the human being to the political order in all things. It is precisely this reduction that led us into the condition in which we now find ourselves, with no humans left active in our liberal democracies, having been defined in their essence already by the regime itself. Rights claims, if properly reconceived, maintain the tension between our natural and our historical modes of self-understanding; they are not, as in the theories of Hobbes and Locke, the means to eradicate it. It is only in losing the very things we think protect us from being determined by others—inalienable and self-evident rights—that we will cease to be determined by others. It is thus only by placing the human being—and what I call the "first right" of human beings to constitute themselves and the world—truly outside of any political definition that human beings may, once again, be political. To put humans into politics, we must properly and comprehensively leave them out of it, free to do with it what they like and to make of themselves what they will. The reparation of the fissure between what we are (by nature) and what we are (in the world) is, strangely and yet necessarily, constituted in the first premise that the human is not ever reducible to, or solved by, the political sphere or any regime absolutely.

Understanding the historical coming-into-being of the conception of the regenerative human being and its relation to politics is important to the argument that modern universal rights were originally conceived as facilitators of transformative self-determination, and is also integral to what I will call (for lack of a better word) the method of my argument. The two camps of critique of the modern project in the twentieth century that we have considered—the ancient and the postmodern—rest on a kind of consensus position that there is something limitless about the modern self-determining subject. Although those who want to recall more telic visions of the human being are critical of this vision of the human being, and postmodern thinkers want to embrace the supposed limitlessness of human capacity, the two groups generally agree that to be modern is to be self-creating, or untethered to any limitation of nature.

The regenerative conception of the human being does not cohere with this view. My claim is that the idea of regeneration offers a uniquely *modern telic* view of human nature that is both bound by a commitment to a belief in a universal human nature and in practice continually open to being unbound by a future regenerative claim or reformulation. Importantly, this vision of the human being is *not progressive*.[85] Here I agree with Amy Allen that it is really the confidence in progress with which we must part most definitively[86]—not because it is impossible to better the conditions or conception of the human being, but because even if it were possible to do so, whatever progress we might be able to achieve can never be secured. Whatever can be regenerated can just as easily be degenerated. A regenerative politics is thus both presentist and cyclical but nevertheless tied indefinitely to the future and to the visions of a better future, which drive the ability and will of human beings to change themselves and their conditions. In this sense, the regenerative view is simultaneously ancient and modern. In its commitment to both an account of human nature and the prospect of a future remaking, regeneration preserves the dynamism and vitality of human life—most importantly, of the human lives that are present and contingently in the world together. Any political suggestion that demands a determined future vision is one of which we ought to be suspect; a regenerative politics, on the other hand, in being open to all new determinations, depends on remaining in motion. This motion is what would facilitate a constant renewal of the capacity of human beings to genuinely make themselves in a regime such as a liberal democracy.

There is a second sense in which this argument is not progressive. Regenerative politics as it is conceived here relies on refashioning how we understand rights and rights claims in contemporary liberal democracies. I am not following the many current critics of liberal humanism who advocate for a new future for humanity by looking forward, progressing beyond what is perceived to be an oppressive order of rights and of the conception of Man. Mine is not a politically transhumanist argument. This does not mean, however, that my argument is inherently conservative either; neither am I following those who want to look backward to a more robust conception of the human being in the ancient world or to former ways of life. Instead, to breathe new life into liberal democracy, we must practice what a truly regenerative project preaches: we must regenerate our present conceptions, looking toward the possible betterment of the future. Here I see us using a tool of modernity—the idea of human rights—to begin refashioning our political existence, but only if we remake how those rights are conceived.[87]

This follows from what I would call a conceptual materialist argument, grounded in the presumption that we do not need to convince people that rights exist. Rights are for the most part intuitively accepted, even by those who think they must be abandoned—the concept of rights is sociomaterially present in the liberal democratic world. If our rights-based polities are to survive, however, those rights need to be reimagined as opening up, as opposed to foreclosing, the question of what it means to be human. This reimagining requires that humans be brought back into politics and that the question of how one determines oneself in the world is fully brought to bear in the political sphere. To be human is to have a vision about the good for oneself, certainly, but, more importantly, it is about the capacity to have and change that vision. Rights must again be seen as aspects of the human identity that are made and remade through regenerative reconstitutions—they are a good to be achieved by humans desiring to give themselves rights in the world, and so, too, must they be vigilantly regenerated if they are to be kept alive.[88]

To transform rights from a stagnant to a regenerative conception, however, we need to be aware of the reality that rights are things that can easily be lost. Further than this, my claim is that we will have to *lose* our rights in order to gain them.[89] For rights to become the active claims of self-determining beings, their existence and survival—our "progress"—can never be presumed or assured. If liberal democracies are to be regenerated, liberal democracy must itself be the constant subject of its own commitment: it can only be one vision of the good. For it to truly facilitate the claims of the self-regenerative human being, it must be foundationally open to redetermination. As in the case of rights that we presume to be self-evident, so, too, have liberal democracies succumbed to the fallacy that their norms and values are self-evidently good.[90] The challenges to liberal democracies illuminate for us that this is simply not the case. Arguments from Black and queer scholars and advocates, Indigenous communities, right-wing populist movements and postliberal thinkers, and the European and American Far Right make it clear that the question of the human being, and the manner in which human beings ought to be determined in the world and in politics, is far from self-evidently settled. Taken together, these critics' arguments indicate a deep feeling of disenfranchisement—not from the political order but from involvement in the determination of what one *is*.

A liberal democracy thinks it promises human self-making, but in fact that is what it seems to fail most of all at facilitating.[91] I offer an account of how we might bring humans back into a shared political project grounded in self-determination. It is an argument for the possibility that the liberal democratic vision may yet survive if it is itself remade—if it no longer rests on the self-evidence of rights but sees rights, freedom, and equality as regenerative, active commitments of human beings in a world that provides no assurance that rights, freedom, or equality won are ever guaranteed to be maintained. The human question is never settled, precluding future contestations and recreations. Vitalism requires vigilance, and self-determination requires the active determination of the selves involved in the shared political world. While it is not without risk, regenerative politics is the only way for liberal democracies to resist the increasingly extreme challenges to the legitimacy of rights by remaining perpetually open to the full reconstitution of all rights and freedoms and aware of the omnipresent possibility of their loss. While a commitment to rights remains one possible future for human beings, however, the dynamism of a truly regenerative politics is contingent on remaining open to all political futures, including those that desire the elimination of rights altogether. There is an ineradicable uncertainty to rights in the face of all self-determinative human claims to make and remake the political order.

My argument is therefore that liberal democracies must open themselves up to their most extreme critics, recognizing their regenerative arguments as human claims rather than rejecting them as inherently illiberal and thus illegitimate. Liberals must themselves share the commitment that, in the words of the Black Studies scholar Rinaldo Walcott, "the question of the human is not settled,"[92] and they must heed the words of the Far Right author Daniel Forrest that the world is one of the "dehumanizing effects" that foreclose "the possibility of a community deciding to take charge of its own destiny and to regenerate humankind."[93] While it may be unsettling to allow these kinds of claims into our politics, it is only the dynamism and open-endedness of self-determinative and interacting human claims that will prevent a degenerating, and degenerative, political world. Without any genuinely self-determinative commitment of the self to liberal democracy, the push against it will get stronger, and citizens' attraction to increasingly undemocratic political movements will grow. Lacking a regenerative and vital account of rights, the rights that citizens perceive as shallow will dry out completely, left with no defenders and no connection between the political apparatus of liberal democratic regimes and the human beings who live within their borders.

This is a concern I share with many others. Wendy Brown writes of the "remains" of the hollow neoliberal worldview, concerned that today's nihilism, in which Man has lost meaning, is a breeding ground for attraction to the Right.[94] She also writes that the "task of the Left today is compounded by [the] generalized collapse of faith in the powers of knowledge, reason, and will for the deliberate remaking and tending of our common existence."[95] Opposite to the general or civilizational despair of the modern world is the idea that "another world is possible," and reigniting this hope is the work of the Left—work that "carries no guarantee of success."[96] Helena Rosenblatt concludes *The Lost History of Liberalism* with a similar call to future liberals against the pessimism of the modern age: "We often hear that liberalism is suffering a crisis of confidence, a crisis made more intense by the recent rise of 'illiberal democracy' around the world. It is suggested that the problem could be solved if only liberals would agree about what they stood for and have courage in their convictions. Liberalism, there are those who say, contains within itself the resources it needs to articulate a conception of the good and a liberal theory of virtue. Liberals should reconnect with the resources of their liberal tradition to recover, understand, and embrace its core values."[97] Rosenblatt sees resources for us in liberalism's history, which she roots in a more robust conception of democratic coexistence beginning in the French Revolutionary period. In *Liberalism Against Itself*, Samuel Moyn concludes with a similar plea to liberals: to find the resources in their own history and tradition to save liberalism from itself and from its deracination in the Cold War; to "make it credible enough for salvation."[98] Brown, Rosenblatt, and Moyn thus join the late Charles Mills in seeing the possibility for a "liberalism that should have been"—a liberalism that could be "retrieved for a radical agenda."[99]

If we are going to retrieve a new liberalism, however, my contention is that it must first be a *human* and not a *political* claim. We must hear the calls for a more "true humanism" and the critiques that liberal democracies prevent,[100] instead of facilitate, "the creation of man by himself."[101] To save liberal democracies, we must allow for the possibility of their demise at the hands of self-determining human beings. If there is to be a regenerated political sphere, it must rest on human beings who have regenerated themselves, having freely chosen to make themselves free in a world they share with others. I offer an account of how this can be done within the sphere of individual rights, but it does not preclude the attendant dangers of once again opening politics up to the question of what it means to be a self-determining human being. I do not, however, think that this danger can be avoided, even if we have managed to keep it at the gate for the time being. Human beings are self-regenerative creatures, and sooner or later the desire to make and remake the world, and ourselves, will win. There is nothing self-evident about the future success of the liberal democratic world or the free and equal human being. We must construct the evidence of these natural truths for ourselves, out of ourselves—making ourselves into what we believe we are.

I began the book claiming that there are no humans left, and this informs the content of everything that follows. This argument necessitates that I show that there is a way to think of the human being that is identifiable and defensible, and it also requires that I give an account of how and why there are no humans *left*—that is, that there once were humans in the kind of politics I am describing and advocating. In this respect, the first sentence of the book inspires both the normative and historical foci of the argument. The vision of the self-regenerative human being emerged in the Enlightenment period, particularly in the French Enlightenment, informing and inspiring the emergence of the Declaration of the Rights of Man and of the Citizen in the French Revolution. I will describe how this novel conception of human nature came about and why it was essential to the formation of the idea of universal right, and I will conclude with an analysis of the potential it offers for today's political world despite having been quickly abandoned following experience with the dangers (both real and perceived) of regenerative, revolutionary action.

Chapter 2, "The Palingenetic Consciousness," begins the historical argument, establishing the ground upon which a regenerative politics emerged in the French Enlightenment and French Revolutionary period. These politics emerged through a prior reimagining of human nature in which human beings were viewed as agents of their own self-transformation through the remaking of the world. In the French Enlightenment in particular, the idea of the human being underwent a vast reconfiguration, becoming enmeshed in a vitalist account of the transformative natural-historical movements of all living things. Seen not in a stagnant taxonomy but in a constantly de- and regenerating natural universe, human beings were liberated to become the agents of their own self-regeneration. I outline the turn toward vitalism in the work of two of the most prominent natural scientists of the period: Georges-Louis LeClerc, comte de Buffon, and Charles Bonnet. Bonnet believed humans possessed what he called a palingenetic, or regenerative, consciousness: the awareness that we are the only historical agents capable of giving ourselves a "second birth" and of changing our natural histories through renewal in political and moral improvement.[102]

For both Buffon and Bonnet, the human being was simultaneously a natural creature capable of regenerative perfection (and, likewise, subject to degeneration) and the site of his own regenerative power. What emerged in Buffon's natural science was a seemingly paradoxical account of human nature in which he asserted both that everything is malleable and subject to a particular historical construction *and* that there is a universal form, or an original prototype, for every species. In its dynamism between asserting both the historical malleability or regenerative capacity and the universal form behind historical change, Buffon provided the space into which it became possible to assert a right to change oneself through asserting rights themselves. Buffon's construction accommodated the fact that humans were irreparably defined by their historical moment—by their political context and world—but also maintained the position from which human beings could claim *not* to be defined by their historical moment: the position of the universal, which granted them the regenerative right to remake themselves.

Buffon provided what I call a distinctively modern telic account of human nature as self-regenerative, which opened the door to a foundational regeneration of the human being in the French Revolution through both the assertion of a universal nature and the claim that humans by nature have the right to change themselves by transforming their conditions. These were not the rights claims of a Hobbesian or a Lockean in which one would assert an inviolable natural right of the human being that any state therefore has the responsibility to acknowledge. The rights claims of the Revolution were regenerative, asserting that no right could be universally held until it was historically present, actively regenerated by self-making human beings. The unique modern telic conception of the human being was emancipatory because it facilitated a regenerative impulse, promising human beings that they could become what they are (universally) by changing what they are (in the world).

In chapter 3, "The Right to Renounce Dependence," I show that Jean-Jacques Rousseau's political philosophy was motivated by this self-regenerative conception of human nature and that it was through Rousseau's work that this vision truly took on its political power. Rousseau shared the modern telic idea of human nature with Buffon, positing both a universal natural prototype for the human being and acknowledging the capacity of human beings to change themselves and their political or worldly conditions. This was exemplified in Rousseau's presentation of the origin of human nature in a natural man who was free, independent, and entirely ahistorical, and in his simultaneous insistence that human beings were defined by their possession of a faculty called *perfectibility*— the ability to alter one's constitution and historical, social, and political context. This *duplex* of human nature was essential to Rousseau's political theory insofar as he wanted to maintain an openness for human beings to remake themselves and their rights entirely, while also affirming that there was a foundational universal quality of man that granted him the freedom to do so. For Rousseau, the human being was both completely constituted by the political world in which he lived—formed, transformed, or deformed by it—but could never be reducible to the political rights he was granted or through which he was made.

Employing an analysis of the *Second Discourse* and the *Social Contract*, I show that Rousseau established a distinction between the *first right* of the human being to remake the conditions of his own dependence, and the political rights established in the world. For Rousseau, in any condition of dependence, the human being never truly alienates his freedom, or first right, to call back and remake his rights and the political system on which those very rights depend for their legitimacy. The human being in this respect always maintains a claim against his own rights and always has the freedom to, in the words of Buffon, "alter, change, destroy, develop, renew, and produce" the conditions of his historical context.[103] Buffon and Rousseau therefore always leave human beings partly out of their given political system and historical epoch and allow them the right by nature to reconstitute and regenerate that system and themselves.

While many have seen only totalitarian conformity in Rousseau's work, I see instead an emancipatory, regenerative politics. The recognition that all political rights rest on the first right of the human being to refuse them is a genuinely transformative rights doctrine for the modern world—one that revolutionary actors recognized and seized for their political aims, regenerating themselves *by* themselves in the French Revolution and in its declaration of rights. It is the human being's fundamental irreducibility to political convention—even to that of his own making—that contains the universal and ever-present emancipatory potential of the human claim against the political order. What Rousseau shows most acutely is that rights can survive only so long as humans choose to remain actively dependent on them because there is always a universal claim that human beings can make *against* rights, and against the conventional world in which they find themselves.

The French Revolution was a microcosm of regenerative politics—exhibiting both how the regenerative human being could bring into being a universalizing Declaration of the Rights of Man and of the Citizen and justify abject terror. In chapter 4, "Regeneration and Revolution," I illuminate both the promise and the perils of a politics grounded in self-determination, or the first right identified by Rousseau to make, remake, or retreat from rights—even when these rights are declared inalienable. The most common association of regeneration with the French Revolution comes from Robespierre's Reign of Terror, during which the Jacobins declared their allegiance to Rousseau. Historians of the French Revolution such as Mona Ozouf and François Furet have tied the Jacobin vision of the self-remaking "New Man" to dangerous, and rights-eliminating, politics.[104] In this chapter, I lay out the regenerative vision of those involved in the Terror and discuss the historiography of the French Revolution that for a long time has been invested in connecting regenerative politics only with the excess and terror of the revolutionary period. My second goal in this chapter is to establish that the motivation of the first right of human beings also propelled the assertion of universal right. Employing a variety of historical sources (the archive of France's National Assembly, texts published about Rousseau in the French Revolutionary period, and pamphlets and speeches of the revolutionaries), I show that the Declaration was the result of a truly self-determinative conception of rights that kept the question of the human being open, and open to political (re)determinations, alive in the tension and relationship between what we believe we are by nature and what we make of ourselves in the world.

The modern telic vision of the human being was explicitly translated into a diversity of political programs in the French Revolution—it was itself the universal behind political transformation. The revolutionaries, drawing on and out of Rousseau's reimagining of human nature, saw that the foundational political motivation was not that humans have natural rights to claim but that human beings have the natural claim to make rights. It was also this self-regenerative conception of the ability to remake the world and remake oneself that propelled the rhetoric of the Haitian revolution, the interventions of women like Olympe de Gouges, and the further reformulations of the Declaration itself. While the Declaration of the Rights of Man and of the Citizen consecrated rights, it was always understood that the declared inalienable political rights were themselves subject to recall, revision, and regeneration by the universal subjects of their own definition: the human beings who were their originators. The "first rights" of nature served as the motivating force to make rights themselves, connecting self-regenerating human beings both to the efficient cause, and the institution and maintenance, of their own natural freedom and equality.[105]

Despite my rescue of regeneration's more positive instantiation in the Declaration, however, the risks of a truly regenerative politics are evidently present in the Terror. Rights won in the political space can always be lost, any shared conception of the human being can be changed, and every polity can degenerate and dissipate. Although, as I detail in chapter 5, these risks led swiftly to a condemnation of regenerative politics and of the vision of the human being to which it is tied, it is also the case that regenerative politics was the exercise of genuinely self-determining human beings—and our abandonment of its openness has foreclosed, I argue, its goods along with its possible evils.

Chapter 5, "After Enlightenment," offers a genealogical account of the fate of regenerative politics following the French Revolution. In the wake of the Terror came a widespread counterrevolutionary condemnation of regenerative politics coupled with a counter-Enlightenment position. Joseph de Maistre, Edmund Burke, Abbé Augustin Barruel, Jean-Thomas-Élisabeth Richer de Sérizy, and Antoine de Rivarol, for example, saw an irreparable link between the philosophy of eighteenth-century France and the horrors of the Terror, often naming an allegiance to the thought of Rousseau as one of the root causes of the descent of the French Revolution into violence. At the same time, a post-Thermidor movement arose among those Darrin McMahon calls "restoration liberals" to resuscitate and reinvigorate the original principles of the French Revolutionary project: the first commitments to universal rights and freedoms that were abandoned when political action transformed into the Terror.[106] This turn toward the liberal principles of the Revolution by thinkers such as Benjamin Constant and Madame de Staël was coupled in the early nineteenth century with a turn toward constitutionalism and what William Selinger has recently termed "parliamentarism."[107] Here the emerging liberals of the nineteenth century had to defend themselves against their own counter-Enlightenment opponents, who refused to believe that any values extracted from the French Revolution could be anesthetized from their attendant dangers. It was a commitment to structure and order, and to the basic preservation of minimalist rights and freedoms, that would undermine "the widespread belief (strengthened by the experience of the French Revolution) that liberal values and a vibrant political sphere were too dangerous."[108] Annelien de Dijn shares this perception of how liberalism emerged in response to counterrevolutionary fears, sapping nineteenth-century conceptions of freedom of their connections to democracy: "The French Revolution's descent into political violence—the Terror—turned many intellectuals and civic actors on both sides of the Atlantic Ocean against the effort to introduce bottom-up politics. The resulting counterrevolutionary movement propagated a new understanding of liberty, one that directly contested the democratic view by prioritizing the enjoyment of private independence."[109] The beginnings of what we now think of as the liberal commitments to individual rights and freedoms held *against* the state were a direct response to the regenerative politics of the eighteenth century—and designed to prevent it from returning.

At the same time, regenerative politics took on a new life in an alternative genealogical trajectory, one that now binds regeneration in retroactive perpetuity to terror, violence, and fascism. To tell this side of the story, I look to the appropriation of regenerative ideas in nineteenth-century Romanticism—rooted in not only the political regeneration of the Revolution but also the regenerative natural science of the eighteenth century. We see later regenerative thinking in the work of Percy Shelley and Friedrich Schelling and, more importantly, in the ideas of "social palingenesis" developed by Pierre-Simon Ballanche, continued by Charles Nodier and Pierre Leroux, and furthered in Henri Bergson's *Creative Evolution*. Bergson's post-Darwinian vitalism informed political actors like Georges Sorel, and, as Kevin Duong has recently argued, as a political movement socialism took on the regenerative thinking that the "abstract man" of the then liberalized 1789 Revolution was seen to be sorely lacking.[110] Also citing the regenerative thinking of Friedrich Nietzsche (an inheritor, like Bergson, of the vitalist Romanticism of the New Man), Sorel became connected to Mussolini—just as Rousseau was to Robespierre—when Mussolini proclaimed, "Who I am, I owe to Georges Sorel."[111]

Today, Nietzschean rhetoric in particular is invoked by the regenerative Far Right—a turn to which the political theorist Ronald Beiner has devoted much of his recent intellectual attention. A thinker who is, to Beiner, "forthrightly and bluntly antiegalitarian and antiliberal," Nietzsche stands directly opposed to liberal values and "self-consciously denounces the whole moral universe conjured up by the French Revolution."[112] Beiner joins the chorus of contemporary liberals who want to maintain a hard bifurcation of the proper, minimalist principles of the "true" French Revolutionary liberalism from regenerative political thinking. Isaiah Berlin separates negative from positive liberty. J. L. Talmon famously divides "the liberal type of democracy" from "the totalitarian type of democracy," the latter of which he sees as regenerative and messianic, tied to immanence, and foundationally grounded in "the Rousseauist idea of popular fulfillment and self-expression."[113] Regenerative politics is cast as the irrational evil twin of the rational and liberal recognition of the self-evident truth that we are, as individuals, all free and equal.

From the time of its inception in the French Revolution, then, regenerative politics has everywhere been seen as the antithesis of liberalism and the liberal commitment to rights and freedoms. As I will show, this is despite the fact that regenerative politics was *itself* the source of the universal claim to rights in practice in the French Revolutionary period. The almost immediate schism of rights from regeneration resulted in the coterminous detachment of our first right—that is, our right to determine ourselves—from our rights as they are conceived in liberal democratic regimes. Despite claiming to adhere to the principles of the French Revolution (in its most pacified iterations), today's liberals speak about the commitment to self-determination and freedom without allowing for the real motive power that would facilitate its activity: the self-regenerative practice of human beings truly empowered to make themselves. This failure has resulted in the hollowing out of rights themselves. They are signifiers of self-determining human beings that simply do not have a corresponding referent in the world.

Chapter 6, "Restoring Our First Right," is an argument for the restoration of the regenerative view of the human being and a return to the first right we possess to make the conditions of our own existence. I argue that we ought to embrace a truly regenerative politics in order to revive today's liberal democracies and to reconnect self-regenerating human beings with their rights. This is the only way that human beings can return to politics and to themselves. I conclude with what I imagine will be perceived as a conservative and antiprogressive, yet simultaneously deeply radical, argument: that we need to assert, rather than deny, a universal conception of human nature, which will mean giving up any claims to the self-evidence of rights and to the self-evident goodness of liberal democracy. This also means that we must open ourselves up to all self-determinative claims and therefore all possible determinations of the human. Regenerative politics is not about the restoration of rights but of our *first right*—and thus it is about reopening the question of human and political possibilities. Rights are always only one possible iteration of the human political experience in the world; they cannot be, in any way, self-evident if we are engaging in a genuinely self-determinative and regenerative politics. A regenerative politics entails the possibility of the loss of our rights altogether, but I also believe that it is the only way toward their reinvigoration and preservation. Liberal democracies and their attendant rights claims must constantly be regenerated in order to maintain their vitality—and they must be regenerated by human beings who see their natures expressed in determining themselves and thus determining the world in which they live.

The choice to engage in a regenerative politics may not be practical, and it may prove too risky to be considered by any of today's regimes. This argument will serve then, I hope, as a reminder or a warning—however theoretical—that when there are no humans left in a political world that ostensibly rests on the motive force of human self-determination, the life force of politics will remain perpetually outside, pressing further and further on the rights, laws, and norms we naively continue to presume are self-evident. If the growing extremism of today's politics foreshadows anything, it is the very real possibility that we will soon learn, against our wills, that nothing is self-evident unless it is also continually self-determined and actively regenerated.

2

THE PALINGENETIC CONSCIOUSNESS

A t the core of the contemporary critiques of today's liberal democracies is an attack on the legacy of the Enlightenment, on its supposed universalism and its hegemonic, "atomistic conception of the person."[1] Critics of the liberal democratic view of the human being on both the Left and the Right see only one Enlightenment: a period of history that wrought an exclusionary and vapid perspective of humanity founded on an unchangeable and nonregenerative set of principles about our rights and our nature. The contrary vision that I reconstruct in what follows—one that belongs especially to France and to the French Revolution—does not cohere with this reductive picture of the Enlightenment. I aim to restore a particular archaeology of the conception of universal right in the French Enlightenment period in order to demonstrate that a different way of thinking about rights was present in the French Revolution, one built on a novel reimagining of the human being and of human nature that was itself regenerative and open to continual reconstitution. In this, my intent is not to supply an account of *the* Enlightenment; I agree with the emergent scholarly consensus that there can be no one Enlightenment but only Enlightenments.[2] Rather, my goal is to show that a regenerative politics was not necessarily against the Enlightenment but in fact was integral to a dominant strain of this period's thinking—and was certainly connected to the development and assertion of universal rights in the Declaration of the Rights of

Man and of the Citizen. Contrary to the critics of the liberal democratic vision of the human being who see its error in the Enlightenment's lasting effects, I argue that our error is precisely in having left behind the regenerative and transformative vision of rights that we see in the French Enlightenment. It is because this regenerative vision is *not* the legacy of today's liberal democratic society that we have thus lost its attendant connection to self-determination in our own polities.

My reconstruction of the regenerative French Enlightenment shows that the call for universal rights emerged from a new vision of human nature and of natural right. With breaking scientific discoveries and tales from those who had traveled abroad, thinking about the human and its position in nature expanded rapidly, liberating human beings from the chains of thought in which they had previously been contained. The once-stagnant and unmoving Great Chain of Being became temporalized and changeable, and so, too, did scientific taxonomies. The once-unique human creature became entangled in identity with the great ape and with the animal kingdom more generally. Rousseau in particular took issue with social contract theory, which prefigured instead of allowing for the refiguration of the human being. And politically, the monarchical government of France fell in the French Revolution, liberating human beings for self-rule under the banner of rights and opening the door for the liberation of oppressed and enslaved classes and persons in France and across the world.

What facilitated the release of the human being from its chains in the French Enlightenment was a newly asserted vision of human nature that was foundationally regenerative, rooted in the belief that human beings were capable, by nature, of remaking themselves by remaking their political world. This dynamic opening-up of the understanding of the human being was premised on this new human identity remaining open, subject either to progress or degeneration over time or place and always reliant on the agency of human beings themselves to simultaneously maintain their proclaimed universality (in rights) and potential malleability (in transforming those rights). The human of eighteenth-century natural science was thus in constant formation, open to new forms of humanity, and dedicated to making the world a place where the self-regenerative human being could flourish. There was new territory to be mined and claimed by this self-making natural creature in the political sphere, but only if it could first shake off the yoke of its inauspicious enchainments.

THE GREAT CHAIN OF BEING

Natural science in the French Enlightenment was grounded in a plethora of new discoveries in the natural and animal kingdoms. With earlier scientific systems operating in fairly stable categorizations of living things, speculations about the place of creatures like the great apes or water polyps—the former seeming to straddle the line between human and animal, the latter between animal and vegetable—offered new possibilities of how to think about the world, and about the human's place in it. The Great Chain of Being, which Arthur O. Lovejoy identified as the dominant mode of thinking about the ordering of the world up to the nineteenth century, lost its explanatory power; its "sharp divisions, clear-cut differentiations, among natural objects, and especially among living beings,"[3] were no longer self-evident. Gone was the "conception of the plan and structure of the world which, through the Middle Ages and down to the late eighteenth century, many philosophers, most men of science, and, indeed, most educated men were to accept without question"; the "whole sensible universe," which was once "limited and boxed in" to a hierarchy of living things considered from the lowest to the highest points of intelligence or perfection, no longer held.[4]

The Great Chain of Being was not entirely abandoned in the eighteenth century, but it was transformed. Instead of purporting hard classificatory distinctions among living things, the Great Chain was now open to all of what the author of *Histoire naturelle*, Georges-Louis LeClerc, comte de Buffon, called the imperceptible degrees of nature's creations. When following the correct scientific method, according to Buffon, one would see that "these imperceptible nuances are the great work of Nature,"[5] and nature would defy attempts to define hard classificatory distinctions. According to Buffon, it was impossible to know anything definitively about the telos (the final cause) of any natural creature, given that the imperceptible degrees of nature were unknown and unknowable to the human intellect. To think that human beings could properly classify natural creatures was an act of hubris, especially when it came to human beings themselves. The "first truth that comes from [a] serious examination of nature," wrote Buffon, "is one which perhaps humbles man. This truth is that he ought to classify himself with the animals, which he resembles in all his material."⁶ The Great Chain of Being, which had previously supposed "a complete rational intelligibility of the world,"⁷ was no longer intelligible.

This claim may seem odd for a thinker such as Buffon, a man who wrote volume after volume of the *Histoire naturelle* describing animals, plants, and human beings in immense detail. What Buffon wanted to do, however, was to liberate the human mind from the presumption that nature could be known in its entirety. He believed his method respected nature's creative power. Nuances in the order of nature were always present, "not only in the sizes and forms, but in the movements, generations and successions of all species."⁸ That is, to think about nature properly, and about the Great Chain of Being, one had to remain sensitive not only to one's own lack of understanding of the purposes of things but also to the fact that one's perceptions of nature and oneself were obscured by temporal change. Any static system of classification—especially one concerning man himself—was inherently false, given that it could not accommodate shifts in appearance, behavior, or constitution that would take place over time.⁹

Buffon's "Initial Discourse" of the first volume of *Histoire* established his methodology and cast his fellow natural scientist Carl Linnaeus "as the villain" of his entire system.¹⁰ Phillip R. Sloan grounds Buffon's criticism of Linnaeus in a deep philosophical disagreement: "Rather than dealing with specific taxonomic issues, [Buffon] concentrated instead on a general philosophic critique of the root assumptions underlying all the taxonomic work of the time."¹¹ These were assumptions that discerned an order to the world that was intelligible and could therefore be logically systematized according to creatures' essential identities.¹² Lovejoy describes this clash of scientific method in his book *The Great Chain of Being* by outlining two opposing modes of thought: the first relying on categorical distinctions between living things, and the second presenting natural science as "a convenient but artificial setting-up of divisions having no counterpart in nature."¹³ While there were nuances in these positions, as Lovejoy acknowledges, this is the controversy that emerged between Linnaeus, the representative of the former camp, and Buffon, the representative of the latter.

The Linnaean method is often seen as rooted in the work of Aristotle¹⁴ and René Descartes—both thinkers who, Margaret J. Osler writes, embody "the view that the proper aim for science is certain knowledge of the real essences of things."[15] Aristotle saw scientific knowledge as "compris[ing] knowledge of the essential natures of things": their final causes.[16] As he writes in *Posterior Analytics*, "We suppose ourselves to possess unqualified scientific knowledge of a thing, as opposed to knowing it in an accidental way in which the sophist knows, when we think that we know the cause on which the fact depends, as the cause of that fact and no other, and further, that the fact could not be other than it is."[17] So, too, does Descartes claim in *Discourse on Method* that "there is only one truth concerning any matter [and] whoever discovers this truth knows as much about it as can be known."[18] Descartes writes, "As I practiced my method I felt my mind gradually accustomed to conceiving its objects more clearly and distinctly; and since I did not restrict the method to any particular subject matter, I hoped to apply it as usefully to the problems of the other sciences as I had to those of algebra."[19]

Buffon was not the first to question or refute the assertion of clear and distinct knowledge or the capacity of the inquiring mind to contemplate final causes. He was building on the work of the natural scientists and philosophers who immediately preceded him, the most impactful of whom were John Locke, Isaac Newton, and Gottfried Wilhelm Leibniz. While there are debates over the degree to which ideas were shared among these three,[20] for the purpose at hand they can be grouped together (controversies of authorship withstanding) as a representative collective of a new scientific method: one that turned away from certainty in final causes toward "an ordering of phenomenal experience which would enable them to predict nature's course, regardless of whether real essences exist or can be known."[21]

Isaac Newton's scientific method actively set aside causal explanations, restricting "itself to the mathematical principles of mechanics only."[22] Differentiating himself from Descartes, who relied upon causal hypotheses,[23] Newton rejected hypotheses, or conjectures about causes, as unscientific: "Hitherto I have not been able to deduce the cause of these properties of gravity from phenomena and I feign no hypotheses; for whatever is not deduced from the phenomena is to be called an *hypothesis*; and hypotheses, whether metaphysical or physical, whether of occult qualities or mechanical, have no place in experimental philosophy."[24] As Osler writes, "reacting to the aprioristic method of Descartes, Newton repeatedly insisted on the empirical nature of scientific statements; and he fully realized that the price for empirical grounds was the loss of meta-physical certainty."[25]

It is in this respect that Newton and Locke were united in their scientific methodology. In *An Essay Concerning Human Understanding*, John Locke distinguished between real and nominal essences. Because we "are directly acquainted only with the contents of our minds," human beings can only have knowledge, properly speaking, of nominal essences; real essences, the material essence and causal explanation of things, remain beyond our grasp.[26] For Locke, "the goal of natural philosophy is to learn about the properties and interactions of material substances. But our knowledge of substances is confined to nominal essences—to their phenomenal properties, that is to say, to the ideas they produce in our minds."[27] For reasons similar to Newton, Locke claimed that hypotheses "are a species of 'conjecture' or 'speculation' about empirical matters which attend the inevitable human propensity to 'penetrate into the Causes of Things.'"[28] Real essences, which Locke claimed relied on "small corpuscles," could not be known *in fact* by the human mind.[29]

Similarly inaccessible small corpuscles were at the center of Leibniz's philosophy. Leibniz held that these small units of nature were essentially unknowable to the human mind, but they also formed both the real and metaphysical grounds of his scientific theology, which saw God's essence in the monadic structure of the universe. By accounting for the creations of the natural world in terms of the monad, or the simple substance, Leibniz's *Monadology* sought to reconcile God as the source of essences (the eternal or teleological cause of things' existences) with organic beings viewed as kinds of "divine machine[s]" or "living automaton[s]."[30] Leibniz's philosophy accounted for the world in an atomistic manner and made it such that the material causes of things could be explained by the monadic structure while accounting for the harmony or order of the whole: "Because every monad is a mirror of the universe [and] is regulated with perfect order there must needs be order in what represents it."[31] The world of created things was composed of minute particles of matter—the soul of Nature—that reflected the divine purposes of God. As Virginia P. Dawson writes, Leibniz "believed that all of creation, both the organized and apparently unorganized, was connected by imperceptible degrees. . . . The idea of continuity supported his view of matter as dynamic and everywhere alive."[32] Leibniz's theory thus allowed for a consistent reconciliation of the fundamental unknowability of the purposes—or teloi—of compounds with the universal telos of the particles of matter, reflective of "the pre-established harmony, laid down by creation."[33] While we could not know with certainty what the order was, we could know that the world was ordered and that natural things were members of a Great Chain of Being.[34]

The Great Chain of Being as articulated by Leibniz and Locke postulates two things simultaneously: that there is a "hierarchy of beings" and that "between natural things the transitions are insensible and quasi-continuous."[35] There are imperceptible degrees in nature, unknowable to the human mind, that are yet part of the order and hierarchy of nature. Leibniz writes in a letter to Pierre Varignon in 1702,

> All the different classes of beings which taken together make up the universe are, in the ideas of God who knows distinctly their essential gradations, only so many ordinates of a single curve so closely united that it would be impossible to place others between any two of them, since that would imply disorder and imperfection. Thus men are linked with the animals, these with the plants and these with the fossils, which in turn merge with those bodies which our senses and our imagination represent to us as absolutely inanimate. And, since the law of continuity requires that when the essential attributes of one being approximate those of the other, it is necessary that all the orders of natural beings form but a single chain, in which the various classes, like so many rings, are so closely linked one to another that it is impossible for the sense or the imagination to determine precisely the point at which one ends and the next begins.[36]

Though the human mind cannot know, and human experience has not shown us, all of these imperceptible degrees of the natural order, we know that they are ordered by God, or a divine Reason. Leibniz's theory of possible worlds explains the order of the universe and the natural world. God, being infinite and good, must have had available to him all possible worlds of creation. Given that this is the world that was created, Leibniz claims, it can be only a perfectly ordered world: the best of all possible worlds. The Great Chain of Being is reasonable and ordered, though the human mind is finite and thus cannot know the reason for its order. What reveals this order to us is, in fact, the failure of nature to be classified: there are imperceptible degrees of living things, and thus classifications or taxonomies of living things are only human impositions on an order that itself defies taxonomic ordering.[37]

Locke also makes this argument in *An Essay Concerning Human Understanding*:

In all the visible corporeal world we see no chasms or gaps. All quite down from us the descent is by easy steps, and a continued series of things, that in each remove differ very little from one another. There are fishes that have wings. . . . There are some birds that are inhabitants of water. . . . There are animals so near of kin both to birds and beasts that they are in the middle between both. . . . And the animal and vegetable kingdom so nearly joined, that if you will take the lowest of one and the highest of the other, there will scarce be perceived any great difference between them; and so on, till we come to the lowest and the most inorganical parts of matter, we shall find everywhere that the several species are linked together, and differ but in almost insensible degrees. And when we consider the infinite power and wisdom of the Maker, we have reason to think, that it is suitable to the magnificent harmony of the universe, and the great design and infinite goodness of the architect, that the species of creatures should also, by gentle degrees, ascend upwards from us towards his infinite perfection, as we see they gradually descend from us downwards.[38]

It is the cosmology of the Great Chain of Being that holds together the tension at the heart of the chain: that nature is simultaneously divinely ordered yet degenerate (or less perfect) in comparison to divine order itself. The notion of infinite degrees of nature also implies degrees of perfection and imperfection; as Locke writes, the existence of natural degrees below human beings implies divine, and more perfect, degrees above. The Great Chain of Being can thus progress toward a greater perfection. As Leibniz writes in *Principles of Nature and of Grace*, although we cannot hope to attain divine happiness in knowing the order and

goodness of the world, our happiness can consist "in a perpetual progress to new pleasures and new perfections":[39]

> A perpetual and unrestricted progress of the universe as a whole must be
> recognized, such that it advances to a higher state of cultivation. . . . As
> for the objection which may be raised, that if this is true the world will
> at some time already have become paradise, the answer is not far to seek:
> even though many substances shall have attained to a great degree of
> perfection, there will always, on account of the infinite divisibility of the
> continuum, remain over in the abyss of things parts hitherto dormant,
> to be aroused and raised to a higher condition and, so to say, to a better
> cultivation. And for this reason progress will never come to an end.[40]

The gradual perfection about which Leibniz wrote was dramatically
transformed in the eighteenth century. Acknowledging the infinite
degrees of nature, Buffon made this progressive perfection the distinctive
capacity of human beings and thus evident in and through our natural
history. In Buffon's natural science we see a conflation of the work of all of
his predecessors: in the Great Chain of Being, the human being is embedded in an order of infinite degrees; as a human being, we can, as Locke
claims, thus order our thoughts and our science only around what we
know, which is ourselves; nature is, in comparison to the divine, degenerate, and thus subject to perfection and progress. But in Buffon's cosmology, the human being is the only animal capable of perfecting itself,
and thus humans as a species are uniquely capable of transforming both
themselves and the world, in and through time.

With this historicization and temporalization of the Great Chain of
Being, however, man became a creature "not in harmony with himself."[41]
The human being was now subject to what Lovejoy identifies as a
"tragi-comic inner discord."[42] This discord is beautifully expressed in
Alexander Pope's 1734 *Essay on Man*, one of the defining texts of the Great
Chain of Being in the eighteenth century:

> Know then thyself, presume not God to scan
> The proper study of Mankind is Man.
> Place on this isthmus of a middle state,
> A Being darkly wise, and rudely great:

With too much knowledge for the Skeptic side,
With too much weakness for the Stoic's pride,
He hangs between; in doubt to act, or rest;
In doubt to deem himself a God, or beast;
In doubt his mind or body to prefer;
Born to die, and reas'ning but to err.[43]

Along with the liberation from the static Chain of Being came deep anthropological doubt. What *was* man if he was also an animal? What could we know about ourselves, or the world, if it was not possible to know anything about essences or final causes with intelligible certainty? Everything, even the human being, was open to redetermination, not only in thought but also in the transformations of time—thus, Lovejoy claims, the "once immutable Chain of Being [transformed] into the program of an endless Becoming."[44]

Lovejoy believes that this shift in thinking demonstrates an "evolutionist tendency" in the Enlightenment,[45] predating Charles Darwin by more than a century. Certainly, there was vast speculation about the relationship of human beings to the great apes in this period. At the end of the seventeenth and the beginning of the eighteenth centuries, travelogues and reports described very human-like animals. The period's two initial and most formative scientific descriptions of the great apes came from Nicolaes Tulp, a Dutch anatomist, and Jacobus Bontius, an employee of the Dutch East India Company in Batavia. Tulp's *Observationes Medicae* was published in 1641 and Bontius's *De Medicina Indorum* in 1642. Tulp writes that because of the ape's "human appearance," it was called *Orang Outang* by the Indians, or "forest man."[46] Bontius writes of these creatures that "they sometimes walk on all fours, sometimes upright, [and] they have the appearance and posture of a human."[47] It was Carl Linnaeus who first linked human beings with the great apes taxonomically. In the many revisions of *Systema Naturae*, first published in 1735, Linnaeus's Table of the Animal Kingdom never diverged from including the genera *Homo* (including the species *Homo sapiens*) and *Simia* (i.e., apes) in the same taxon: *Anthropomorpha* (meaning "having human form"). In a 1747 letter to Johann Gmelin, Linnaeus expressed his discomfort with, but also his assurance in, his classifications: "It is not pleasing to me that I must place humans among the *Anthropomorpha*, but man is intimately familiar with himself. Let's not quibble over words."[48] Indeed, Linnaeus's explanation of the distinction of man from the rest of the animal kingdom and from his primate brethren in the Table of the Animal Kingdom was simply the words *nosce te ipsum* ("know thyself").

The problem was, however, that in the midst of great doubt and skepticism about what distinguished the human being from the animal kingdom, man did not know himself. He was not in harmony with himself, being enmeshed in the animal kingdom yet feeling apart from it. Linnaeus's contention that man could simply know himself intimately and taxonomically—self-evidently—was not satisfactory to Buffon. As Claude Blanckaert writes of Buffon's vision of the human being, man "is not an absolute given: it has to be maintained and can be retroceded" and is subject to manipulation,[49] shifting in the vicissitudes of time.[50]

POLYPS AND PERSONS

Buffon's dynamic and vital conception of nature and of the human being took its course from a transformative event: Abraham Trembley's 1740 discovery of the self-regenerating polyp (figure 2.1). The polyp was described by Trembley to a fellow biologist, Réaumur, as something that could attach itself to the sides of a beaker of water and to the stems of aquatic plants: " 'It is green, and seems at first glance to be a plant. Then one discovers several characteristics of an animal.' When touched or the beaker shaken, the body suddenly contracted . . . and [Trembley] described the polyp's ability to move about, its light-seeking tendencies, and finally its ability, after being cut in half, to form two separate living entities."[51] He repeated the cuttings numerous times—and numerous times on one body—each time with separate polyp fragments regenerating into whole organisms.

The discovery of the polyp was paradigm shifting for natural science and was hailed as a confirmation that nature resisted static classifications or taxonomies. As the philosopher Julien Offray de La Mettrie wrote, "Polyps do more than move themselves after being cut up; they regenerate in eight days into as many animals as there are cut portions. This makes me sorry for the system of generation held by the naturalists, or rather,

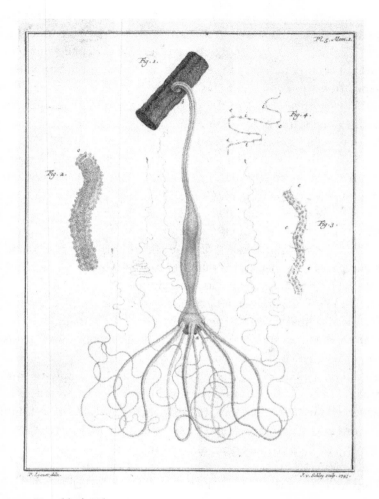

FIGURE 2.1 Trembley's Polyp.

Planche 5 from Abraham Trembley, *Mémoires, pour servir à l'histoire d'un genre de polypes d'eau douce, à bras en forme de cornes* (Leiden: Chez Jean and Herman Verbeek, 1744). Public domain.

it pleases me very much; for how well this discovery teaches us never to conclude anything general!"[52] La Mettrie wrote in a letter to Denis Diderot, "We do not understand Nature: causes concealed within herself . . . could have brought about everything. See . . . Trembley's polyp! Does it not contain within itself the causes which produce its regeneration?"[53]

The discovery of the polyp's self-regeneration entirely disrupted all ideas natural scientists and philosophers had about reproduction. As Dawson writes, the polyp "riveted the attention of men and women of the eighteenth century because they expected an animal cut in half to die. . . . Regeneration upset their notions of how animals reproduced."[54] And Keith R. Benson writes, " 'In the pieces of a cut-up polyp regenerating into new polyps, Trembley's contemporaries had the startling spectacle of Nature caught, as it were, *in flagrante* with the creation of life.' . . . More critically for the philosophers, if each part of an animal could regenerate the entire animal, where was the residence of the 'soul,' the recognized organizing principle of organic beings?"[55]

At the time of the polyp's discovery, there were two schools of understanding of animal reproduction: preformation and epigenesis. Preformationists argued that "since God placed extremely small germs in the progenitors of each species, the only real generation was consequently an act of Creation. What appeared as generation was merely the mechanical development of infinitely small germs, encased one within the other. . . . When the original supply of germs placed in the female (or male) of each individual pair at Creation was used up, life on earth would cease."[56] Nicolas Malebranche, for example, argued "that a single seed of an apple tree might contain an infinite number of seeds to supply an infinite number of centuries."[57] Because particulate matter was the source of the essence, or purpose, of Nature, then so, too, must souls—both human and animal—be preformed and indivisible, and the generation of a new living thing must be an actuality of the Creator through biological reproduction.

Epigenesists, on the other hand, argued via Aristotelian science that each living animal contained a germ that was "both the seed of the organism from which it came, of the horse, for instance, from which it was derived, and the seed of the organism that will eventually arise from it. . . . The seed is potentially that which will spring from it, and the relation of potentiality to actuality we know."[58] Aristotle claimed that "two modes of causality" were at play in reproduction: the reproduction of the telos in the offspring and the material reproduction of the living creature.[59] The seed that was passed from the male to the female passed along a teleological structure in which it could be assumed that the offspring would actualize itself according to the potentiality it was accorded at birth.

The epigenetic theory accounted for the manner in which the soul and form of the reproduced animal were modified by the particularities of the species and the body's sexual fluids—the reproductive process occurring between two sexes produces an offspring with hereditary characteristics of both the species and the individual parents.

The polyp threw both theories into chaos. The polyp's *parthenogenetic* (asexual) reproduction made it impossible to identify a seat of the soul in either the preformationist or epigenesist theory. For the preformationist, the soul of future creatures was contained in the seed passed from creature to creature in reproduction. But the polyp could be spliced into seemingly infinite pieces and still regenerate itself from each piece ad infinitum. For the epigenesist, reproduction relied on a teleological structure of potentiality being passed on through the interaction of two parents who gave particularity to the genetic structure of the offspring. But the polyp was its own parent, and it required no act of reproduction to regenerate itself. On all accounts of reproduction, the polyp was monstrous.

The polyp was not, however, called a monster by the scientists of the eighteenth century. It was proclaimed a miracle, and its miraculous nature earned the polyp an association in 1744 with "the chimerical ideas of the *palingenesis* or *regeneration* of plants and animals, which some alchemists have thought possible": "The serpent cut in two and said to join together again, only gave one and the same serpent; but here is nature going farther than our fancies."[60] Buffon embraced the polyp as a revelation, declaring its palingenetic regeneration the illumination of the mode of creation for all of nature.[61] The discovery of the polyp and of its regenerative mode of self-remaking inspired whole new conceptions of the operation of the natural world and of the temporal degeneration and regeneration of natural creatures. Not only did the polyp confirm the disruption of the taxonomic distinction of the vegetable and animal kingdoms but its regenerative reproduction also became, for Buffon, "the general principle of all production" in nature, grounded in motive organic particles.[62] As Jacques Roger writes, "It was from the model of the polyp's regeneration . . . that Buffon attempted to form a general theory. What had been an incomprehensible exception became with him the simplest cause of a universal phenomenon."[63] Buffon denied the preexistence of seeds or germs, insisting instead on the animated properties of organic molecules common to all living things. For Buffon, the polyp revealed the vitalism of nature.[64] This vitalism informed his scientific method, which affirmed the ever-present possibility of the discovery or reconstitution of forms in nature and across time, given that things were made up of motive molecular particles: "An infinity of nuances and even degrees will escape us, which nevertheless exist in the natural order of things."[65]

The discovery of the polyp also revealed new realms of understanding for Charles Bonnet, a contemporary of Buffon's. Bonnet, like Buffon, grounded his scientific method in an acknowledgment that matter was divisible to "an indeterminate degree":[66] "There are no sudden changes in nature; all is gradual, elegantly varied."[67] For Bonnet, "there is not one [living thing] which has no relation to the whole system," not only because all things are composed of the same particulate matter but also because "every being has an activity peculiar to it, whose sphere has been determined by the rank appointed for it in the universe. . . . The elements act reciprocally on each other according to certain laws which result from their relations, and these relations unite them into minerals, plants, animals and to men."[68] The polyp revealed to Bonnet a new view with which to examine nature: "Polypus's," Bonnet writes, "are placed at the frontiers of a new universe."[69] He continues, "We shall travel through a country, where we may be apt to imagine that nature is no longer like herself"; the discovery of a polyp is a "miracle" and "has astonished the world."[70] Describing the transformation that occurred in his thinking upon this discovery, Bonnet writes that "the polypus puts everything into motion in the brain of the naturalist."[71]

As Bonnet discusses in his *Contemplation of Nature*, the polyp was a miracle because it appeared to be an animal. Self-regenerative vine cuttings and graftings had long been observed and were found to be replicable with other vegetative matter. But, Bonnet asks, "before the different species of polypus's you have been contemplating were discovered, could any persons flatter themselves they were acquainted with animal nature?" He writes, "Polypus's have astonished us because on their first appearance there was no idea in our brains analogous to them."[72] Accepting that the polyp was an animal—because of its locomotion, sensitivity, and activity—meant that included in the understanding of "animal" was now the capacity to "regenerate anew in all its parts," to produce fully perfected forms of itself *from itself*, and, Bonnet writes, to be grafted to itself and manipulated: it may be "grafted by approximation or inoculation, turned inside outward like a glove, afterwards cut, turned back and cut again, without ceasing to live, devour, grow and multiply."[73] There is "scarce any miracle that may not be performed by means of the polypus."[74] The polyp's regenerative power, and its malleability, illuminated for Bonnet the foundations of the natural universe: "What light does not the polypus also throw on the first origin of organized beings?"[75]

The revelation of the polyp and the turn toward an understanding of nature as made up of motive particles would seem to lend itself immediately to a purely materialist interpretation of the natural world. If all organized beings were made up of the same primary stuff, and if nature moved in nonclassificatory degrees, what ground could there be for distinguishing the human from the animal or from plant matter? The materialist route was indeed taken by some philosophes in the eighteenth century, such as La Mettrie, Diderot, Claude Adrian Helvétius, and Baron d'Holbach.[76] D'Holbach, one of the eighteenth century's only open atheists, brazenly writes in *Système de la nature*, for example, "Man has no reason to believe himself a privileged being in nature, for he is subject to the same vicissitudes as all her other productions. . . . Let him but elevate himself, by his thoughts, above the globe he inhabits, and he will look upon his own species with the same eyes as he does all other beings."[77] A materialist nature, for d'Holbach, ought to be regarded as the standard for human life: "Man is the work of Nature: he exists in Nature: he is submitted to her laws: he cannot deliver himself from them; nor can he step beyond them even in thought. . . . Instead, therefore, of seeking out of the world he inhabits for beings who can procure him a happiness denied to him by Nature, let man study Nature, let him learn her laws, contemplate her energies."[78] While man has "gratuitously supposed himself composed of two distinct substances,"[79] he ought to see that he is subject to the same natural laws, the same necessities, and the same desires for happy and commodious living as the rest of nature's creations. Even when we suppose that we have an immaterial soul, d'Holbach writes, we must see that it "is continually modified conjointly with the body, is submitted to all its motion. . . . All the systems, all the affections, all the opinions, whether true or false, which man forms to himself, are to be attributed to his physical and material sense."[80] The spirituality of the human soul—the presumed marker of man's distinction from the rest of the animal and natural kingdom—was, according to d'Holbach, a destructive chimera: "It was upon the ruins of Nature that man erected the imaginary colossus of Divinity."[81]

But the materialist route was not the path taken by the most dominant and successful natural philosopher of the French Enlightenment, Buffon, nor was it Bonnet's vision. While the polyp was a miraculous discovery for them, it was one that reinforced rather than challenged the idea of a distinctive human nature. The regenerative principle of nature illuminated by the polyp most essentially unveiled the human being's capacity to regenerate itself and to give itself a second birth through moral education and politics. Although nature was now seen as universally regenerative, the human being was considered the only natural creature capable of consciously and actively regenerating itself in the world and across time. For Buffon and Bonnet, the vitality, vibrancy, and generativeness of nature revealed the vitality of the human being.

THE PALINGENETIC CONSCIOUSNESS

For Buffon, the polyp's evident capacity to repeatedly regenerate itself into identically perfected forms from degenerate pieces of its body was compelling not only because of the polyp's possession of its own regenerative motive power, or efficient cause, but also because of its repetitive perfectibility. As will become evident in the further explication of Buffon's natural science, the polyp was a natural instantiation of that which Buffon sought to recreate through human activity: the regeneration of species—particularly man—in view of their original form and through self-motivated, or self-imposed, mechanisms and powers. The evident power of one of God's natural creations to self-regenerate made it biologically, or naturally, permissible for man to do the same. It was only the human being that was conscious of its self-regenerative power and aware of the regenerative principle of nature herself; thus, it was distinctly human to have what I call a "palingenetic consciousness."

The primary principle of Buffon's scientific system was that the "first truth that comes from [a] serious examination of nature is one which perhaps humbles man . . . [which] is that he ought to classify himself with the animals, which he resembles in all his material."[82] However, moving beyond this seemingly reductive materialist position, he writes, "We have often said that Nature moves and proceeds in imperceptible degrees and nuances; this truth, which otherwise admits no exception, is here reversed: there is an infinite distance between the faculties of man and those of the most perfect animal, clear proof that man is of a different nature, that he himself constitutes a separate class, from which there are infinite degrees and nuances of descent before we arrive at the state of an animal."[83] Human beings are unique. Nevertheless, Buffon steered away from a dualism that would separate man and animal, or mind and matter, absolutely. He instead recast man as *Homo duplex*, an interior existence divided between sensory feeling ("which shines only in a tempest of obscurity" and consists of sensory impressions and passions[84]) and "the spiritual principle."[85] Though we are natural creatures and included in nature's infinite degrees of separation and association, we are also of a different kind: nonhuman "animals never invent, nor bring anything to perfection."[86] While animals distinguish what is agreeable to their present existence, Buffon claims, they lack the capacity—or the spirit (*esprit*, meaning both "mind" and "spirit")—to perfect themselves or change their conditions. The "spiritual principle" that is unique to man, Buffon writes, is "dependent on education":[87] while the "excellence of the senses is a gift of nature, art and habit may bestow on them a greater degree of perfection."[88]

Man is also, unlike the other animals, conscious of his own existence as a temporal being: animals are "conscious of their present existence," but in man, "consciousness of existence is composed of the perception of actual existence, as well as the remembrance of past existence."[89] The conclusion of Buffon's *Discourse on the Nature of Animals* in the fourth volume expands on the importance of man's temporal awareness:

> Let man, however, examine, analyze and contemplate himself, and he will soon discover the dignity of his being; he will perceive the existence of his soul; he will cease to degrade his nature; he will see, at one glance, the infinite distance placed by the Supreme Being between him and the brutes. God alone knows the past, the present and the future. Man, whose existence continues but a few moments, perceives only these movements: But a living and immortal power compares these moments, distinguishes and arranges them. It is by this power that man knows the

present, judges of the past and foresees the future. Deprive him of this divine light, and you deface and obscure his being; nothing will remain but an animal equally ignorant of the past and the future, and affectable only by present objects.[90]

As a temporal being, the human is endowed with the spiritual quality—the power—of being aware of time. The human being is also the only natural creature aware of the regenerative principles of nature. In that recognition, humans can also see that there are more and less perfect forms of things (in relation to the polyp, "spliced" and "perfect" instantiations of natural creatures) and that all things must be capable of a perfection they do not at present possess. Human beings as a species can strive toward a standard of perfection that does not exist in observable nature but must by nature be achievable. We are endowed with the capacity to regenerate ourselves through improvements. Both inside and outside of nature's imperceptible degrees, man is simultaneously a natural creature capable of regenerative perfection (and, likewise, degeneration) and the site of his own regenerative power. With the natural model of the polyp and the spiritually creative essence granted him by God, man could progressively change both his biology and his customs in view of a reborn and more perfect form.

This idea is carried forward into Buffon's natural history, which emerges in the later volumes of *Histoire naturelle* and rests on the reconciliation of biblical with natural time. Describing history as a sequence of epochs, Buffon claims that we are in the seventh epoch: only now does "the entire face of the earth bear the imprint of man's power. . . . It is with our hands that it has developed to its full extent, and came by degrees to the point of perfection and magnificence which we see today."[91] Yet we look back on "the sad spectacle" of revolutions and deaths of civilizations, "all produced by ignorance, [and] hope that the current and imperfect balance between the civilized nations will continue and may even become more stable."[92] Man cannot know in the present how his power may extend in time; his future power depends on his intelligence and the revelation of further truths; "the more he will observe, the more it will grow. . . . Who knows to what point man may perfect his moral and physical nature?"[93] It is not only a spiritual awareness that is born in this natural science but also a historical one, and man is an active participant in his own history. Buffon and Bonnet share this account of the human being's place in nature and claim that man has a palingenetic consciousness—a consciousness of himself that rests on the capacity to regenerate himself and the rest of nature and to make history.

Charles Bonnet brings this palingenetic natural history to its fullest expression in *La palingénésie philosophique* (*Philosophical Palingenesis*). Like the polyp, which as "the instrument of this future regeneration . . . will raise the polyp to a degree of perfection that does not much comport with the present state of things,"[94] so, too, will the passage of time raise human beings to a greater state of perfection. This is because of our distinctive capacity to change the world around us and change or regenerate ourselves through education: "The force of education," Bonnet writes, "modifies the force of the natural. *Education is a second birth* which imprints new determinations."[95] In *Contemplation of Nature*, Bonnet describes "less perfect" and "more perfect" species:[96] "In the assemblage of all the orders of *relative* perfections, consists the *absolute* perfection of th[e] whole."[97] While the whole of nature is—in its absolute—perfection itself, man stands apart from the rest of nature in being able to "combine and perfect without ceasing."[98] While the "brute is at its birth what it will remain its whole life,"[99] "man, the most *perfectible* of all the earth's species,"[100] is active in his own moral and social education: "The faculty of generalizing ideas, or abstracting from a subject what is common with others, and expressing it by arbitrary signs, constitutes the highest degree of spiritual perfection, and therein consists the difference between the human soul and the soul of brutes."[101]

Man's spiritual aspect—his capacity to generalize ideas—is reached at the pinnacle of comprehending nature's most comprehensive generality: that of the continuity and harmony of nature itself. Man's essence is not only reflective but also self-reflective insofar as he comes to understand his place in the ever-regenerating and ever-renewing complexity of nature. A soul deprived of speech, language, and reason, like the beast's, "does not reflect on its actions . . . does not generalize its ideas . . . [and] is incapable of morality."[102] Through the acquisition of knowledge, "man acquires of himself, becomes acquainted with the beings that surround him . . . [and] he is enabled to say, *Myself*, judge of his relations, conform himself to them, and thereby augment his happiness. By speech he becomes a truly sociable being; and those societies he forms, he governs by laws which he creates, changes, or modifies, as times, places and circumstances admit."[103]

The second birth of education is the result of and involves man's innovative capacity to modify his social and political circumstances and to rise from his habitual, or corrupted, state "incorruptible and glorious."[104] "The excellence of human reason shines likewise with new lustre, from the establishment of societies or bodies politic. In them, virtue, honour, fear, and interest, variously employ'd or combined, prove the source of peace, happiness and order. . . . From that the mechanical and liberal arts flourish. From thence are born poets, orators, historians, physicians, philosophers, lawyers, divines."[105] The human being is born again, or regenerated, in the presence of abstract ideas and the encouragement of the virtuous expansion of human knowledge, art, and innovation. For both Buffon and Bonnet, in a world where everything is striving toward a perfection that is both immediately and historically regenerative, man is the only true palingenetic agent in being capable of changing and perfecting himself. The palingenesis of the human being depends on morality, education, and politics, which are, in Buffon's words, the spiritualities of our soul, a distinctive vitality that we possess in a vital material universe.

While God is the source of all that is perfect, man is the manifestation of his own universal nature when he holds in himself both the history and the future progress of his species. We have the natural right, Buffon claims, to "alter, change, destroy, develop, renew, and produce."[106] Though we have seen dark periods of human history, and though it seems man is often "intent on destroying himself," the human species will nevertheless "germinate anew" through science, culture, innovation, and education.[107] Concern for the renewal, progress, and perfection of the species, as manifested in the moral and scientific education of individuals, is what makes us human. *Homo duplex* is a being suspended between natural and spiritual existences, between, as Buffon writes, the "laws of renovation" and the laws of "permanency."[108] The human being, however, has his futurity, renovation, and renewal in his own power. Buffon and his fellow natural philosopher Charles Bonnet thus share the assertion that the renewing and perfecting powers of man are the immanentized seat of a capacity to remake—or regenerate—themselves in a regenerative natural world.

THE MODERN TELIC

Buffon maintains both a confidence in a human essence and the capability of human beings to fundamentally change themselves by changing their conditions. The human being's suspension between what Buffon calls the laws of renovation and the laws of permanency forms a tension between the assertion of a universal nature and the awareness that natural creatures change, degenerate, and shift over time. All of Buffon's scientific observations and claims are generated from this tension. Describing in great detail the many animals, birds, fish, and plants found in nature, Buffon's *Histoire naturelle* is a treatise grounded in observations of the varieties of degenerate and less degenerate instantiations of the creatures of the earth. Buffon's capacity to observe these variations itself relies on the assertion of a universal nature for each thing—what he calls an original, or general, prototype:

> There is in Nature a general prototype of every species, upon which each individual is modeled, but which seems, in its actual production, to be depraved or improved by circumstances; so that, with regard to certain qualities, there appears to be an unaccountable variation in the succession of individuals, and, at the same time, an admirable uniformity in the entire species. The first animal, the first horse, for example, has been the external and internal model, upon which all the horses that have existed, or shall exist, have been formed. . . . The original impression is preserved in each individual. But, among millions of individuals, not one exactly resembles another, nor, of course, the model from which they sprung. This difference, which shows that Nature is not absolute, but knows how to vary her works by infinite shades, is equally conspicuous in the human species, in all animals, and in all vegetables. What is singular, this model of the beautiful and the excellent, seems to be dispersed over every region of the earth.[109]

This paradigmatic standard for each animal, the original prototype,[110] allows Buffon to account for the many variations or infinite degrees seen in individual members of a species while also explaining their fundamental biological similarities. Buffon's original prototypes also inform his most important philosophical contribution to eighteenth-century natural science: the assertion that only human beings have the capacity to be aware of original prototypes in nature and to bring themselves closer to their perceived prototypical form by changing the world around them, and thus changing themselves in the process.

The case of the mouflon (a wild sheep) is a good entry point into understanding the relationship between the unchanging natural prototype and the possibility for, and evidence of, man's capacity to reshape, or renew, natural beings.[111] Buffon begins his discourse on the mouflon by stating that it is certain that the domestic sheep as it exists today "might not exist on its own, that is to say, without the assistance of man"; however, "it is equally certain that Nature has not produced it as it is, but in our hands it has degenerated."[112] Climate, food, and human care have caused the variety now seen in sheep, but Buffon claims that the mouflon, which can still be found in "the mountains of Greece, the islands of Cyprus, Sardinia and Corsica, and in the deserts of Tartary," appears to be the "primitive stock of all sheep; it exists in the state of nature, it subsists and multiplies without the help of man," and it is "sharper" and "stronger" than all domesticated sheep.[113] Postulating about cross-breeding, Buffon writes, "There is every reason to believe that if we crossed a [she]goat with a mouflon instead of a domestic ram, she would produce goats approaching *nearer the species of goat*."[114]

It is undeniable that we have "altered, modified, and changed" these animals; thus, it is undeniable that they may be realtered by the hand of man.[115] Despite all of the species we have "handled" and "altered differently," there remains a "unique and common origin in Nature," which is properly called the species.[116] Buffon uses various phrases to differentiate the *species* (the unaltered natural prototype) and the "species" that have been differentiated by man. He calls the latter types, or varieties, of sheep variously "races," "genres," and "genera." Buffon's account of sheep serves—despite the various nomenclatures employed to describe their differentiation—as a microcosm of his broader perspective of man's relationship to the rest of nature: one in which the human being is able to alter natural creatures either away from or toward their *species* form. The degenerate sheep need not be degenerate given the power of man to change or modify its nature toward the fulfillment of its species, or its perfection.

Buffon's species scale of degeneration to perfection also informed his account of old-world versus new-world animal life, detailed primarily in "Animaux communs aux deux continents" ("Animals Common to Both Continents"). He begins by listing the animals that are found in both Europe and America: bears, roebuck, elk, reindeer or caribou, hares, squirrels, beavers, wolves, foxes, and so on. Despite appearing on both continents, however, "in the new continent, the animals of the southern provinces are very small in comparison with the animals of warm countries in the old continent."[117] Further still, "the animals that have been transported from Europe to America, such as horses, donkey, cattle, sheep, goats, pigs, dogs, etc.[,] all these, I say, became smaller; and those which have not been transported, but who went there themselves, those who are in a word common to both worlds, such as wolves, foxes, deer, [and] elk, are also considerably smaller in America than in Europe, without exception. There is therefore a combination of elements and other physical causes, something contrary to the aggrandizement of living [animated] Nature in the new world."[118] This accusation of the degenerative power of the New World in fact led to an amusing interaction between Buffon and Thomas Jefferson. As Justin E. H. Smith writes, "[Because] Buffon describes North American fauna as stunted and dwarf-like . . . in 1787, an indignant Thomas Jefferson sent him a counterexample in the form of a giant moose carcass."[119]

It was not, however, merely the climate of the Americas, or perhaps its varying climates of north and south, that caused the degeneration of these animals from their species prototype; for Buffon, it was the fault of the American man. In America, Buffon writes, man was "scattered in small numbers, wandering; where far from using this territory as his domain as a master, he had no empire; where having never had control over animals or the elements, nor having tamed the seas, directed the rivers, nor worked the land, he himself was only an animal of the first rank, and existed for Nature as a being without consequence, a kind of helpless automaton, incapable of reforming or seconding [the intentions] of Nature."[120] Not only, then, is the American man responsible for the degenerate nature of the continent's animal life because of his lack of control over, or manipulation of, nature, but man himself on this continent is degenerate—incapable of the truly human capacity for the propagation of artifice and civilizing progress. Men who do not change or regenerate nature are themselves degenerations of the natural human prototype, or species.

It is when Buffon begins to subject human populations to the same degenerative discourse as the rest of nature that his natural science enters difficult and historically problematic territory. As Andrew Curran has written in *The Anatomy of Blackness*, Buffon's *Histoire naturelle* is a kind of "flash-point" in Enlightenment studies, "a text where the reputation of the entire Enlightenment as either racist or non-racist seems to be at stake."[121] Interpreting, drawing on, or reading into "the Enlightenment" is always a fraught enterprise. Every scholar seems to have their own Enlightenment or Enlightenments: racist and oppressive or universalist and liberating, a negative legacy or a positive inheritance, secular or theological. In this book, I focus on two primary figures who sit at the center of these debates: Buffon and Rousseau. Buffon is both lauded as a transformative scientific figure, the founder of natural history and anthropology,[122] and criticized for having inaugurated "scientific racism."[123] Perceptions of Rousseau are similarly divided between those that condone his transformative vision of natural man in the *Second Discourse*—he is cited as the founder of ethnology by Claude Lévi-Strauss[124]—in which he anticipated Darwin by suggesting that the earliest humans were orangutans,[125] and those that condemn him for popularizing what Michel-Rolph Trouillot has called "the savage slot"[126] and the myth of the noble savage.[127] Beyond Buffon and Rousseau, the turn toward natural history in the eighteenth century in general is deeply embedded in debates about the relationship of the triumph of Enlightenment reason to the rise of colonialism and empire. The vision of the human being as a natural creature within a wider taxonomy is viewed as either the inception of grave historical injustices or a progressive development: the "animalization" of the human being allowed for and propagated the subjection of races and peoples, or it facilitated a new mode of thinking about human beings in naturalized terms, opening channels of understanding and more universalist modes of thinking about humans across the globe.

Buffon studies are thus divided between Buffon "apologists" and Buffon "critics."[128] E. C. Spary locates the critical mode most prominently in the work of Trouillot, and she concedes that the debates over skin color in the eighteenth century were framed within the "discussion of degeneration,"[129] which was developed in Buffon's *Histoire naturelle*:

"Degeneration and the means to correct it became politically prominent issues in France" because of Buffon's theory of "a departure of successive generations from the perfection of the original stock."[130] For the critics, Buffon's monogenesism was the origin of a racist natural history. Phillip R. Sloan argues that although it might offer some "glimmerings of egalitarianism,"[131] the postulation of an original prototype of the human being and the suggestion that all living things have degenerated from some prototypical form insert the human being into history, leading inevitably to an "invidious hierarchy of races and peoples."[132] Here, Sloan agrees with Claude-Olivier Doron, who argues that it is "by way of Buffon, and by way of his subordination of the logico-classificatory style of reasoning (which dominated natural history) to a genealogical reasoning (initially outside of natural history) that race and all the problems it referred to entered natural history's discourse."[133] Justin E. H. Smith similarly claims that the "insertion of the human being into the system of nature had profound implications,"[134] making possible the naturalized assertions of difference based on skin color and rendering differences of form or appearance as differences of kind.[135]

Others contend, however, that the Enlightenment, and the work of Buffon, "lacked any sustained discourse of race."[136] Scholars point to the variety of terms used in Buffon's natural history—he employs race but also genera, varieties, species, people, and so on. As Thierry Hoquet writes, "Buffon never speaks of irreversibly static or determined 'races.' On the contrary, he declares without ambiguity that everything converges to prove that human kind is not composed of essentially different species; that, on the contrary, there was originally but one single human species."[137] For Buffon's defenders, the monogenecist origin of humanity, when combined with an account of natural historical time that accommodates change, renders the Buffonian natural historical story revolutionary and transformative. It is exactly because of its genealogical focus that Buffon's theory of natural history resists racist thinking—it is only in the classificatory natural sciences, such as Linnaeus's, that we see ranked, and thus hierarchized and unchangeable, groupings of human beings according to appearance and race.

The vision of an original prototype of humanity committed Buffon to the position that time, climate, and circumstance cause things to vary throughout history. So, too, then, are species—including human beings—indefinitely subject to the possibility of reconstitution and regeneration.

Thus, E. C. Spary writes, race was only "discussed amid concerns about how social institutions and climate" affected persons and communities:[138] "Buffon's account of the mechanism of species degeneration or regeneration . . . made nature and society interpermeable. It weakened rather than constituted a 'modern' racism grounded in nature, by implying that even naturally originating racial differences were mostly reversible with the application of reason"[139] and by "altering living conditions, and changing government."[140]

This was an assertion of a radical mutability[141] at the center of an account of human nature and resulted from what William Max Nelson calls the "relational theory of time" that forms the core of Buffon's natural science.[142] Buffon writes, "Nature, I confess, is in a continual flux of movement; but it is sufficient for man to grasp the moment of his age, to throw glances backward and forward, and to try to glimpse what [Nature] was and *into what it could be made*."[143] The human being's unique capacity lies in its awareness of what nature *is* in the present and of its possible incongruence with what nature *is* according to its eternal prototypes. That is, human nature understood as the palingenetic consciousness of one's place in time adumbrates the competing demands of asserting a universal nature and acknowledging that everywhere natures are varied and diverse. The changeability of nature is what reveals to the human being that the renovation of living things always exists in relation to a natural permanency, whether or not nature is fully knowable:

> To Nature [man] is, at first, indebted for everything, without making her any return. No sooner, however, do his senses acquire strength and activity, and he can compare his sensations[;] then he reflects upon the universe; he forms ideas, which he retains, extends and combines. Man, after receiving instruction, is no longer a simple individual, for he then in large part represents the whole human species[;] he receives from his parents the knowledge which had been transmitted to them from their forefathers; and thus, by the divine arts of writing and printing, the present age, in some sort, becomes identified with those that are past. This accumulation of the experience of many centuries in one man, almost extends his being to infinity. He is born no more than a simple individual, like other animals, capable only of attending to present sensations; but afterwards he becomes nearly the being we supposed to represent the whole species[;] he reads

what is past, sees the present and judges the future; and in the torrent of time, which carries off and absorbs all the individuals of the universe, he perceives that the species are permanent, and Nature invariable.[144]

When it comes to the eighteenth-century discourse of the degeneracy of human beings, Sankar Muthu is correct to assert that even if one claims that human beings are historically malleable, when it comes to the representation of "savage" or foreign human communities or persons (for Buffon, this appears to include Thomas Jefferson), there is a standard of lesser and greater—despite the absence of a fully developed account of the permanently backward or underdeveloped versus the forwardly civilized that would emerge in the nineteenth century.[145] That is to say, it is still within the boundaries of Buffon's natural science to claim that some human beings are more in need of change and improvement than others. While this is certainly true of Buffon's meliorist position, it is also true that the world revealed by Buffon's construction of the unaltered prototype and his observations of the alterations of man is at root open to transformation and reconstitution. As Alyssa Sepinwall writes, the question of how "difference [could] be reconciled with equality" was solved through a Buffonian-inspired "revolutionary universalism [that] was made possible only through the mechanism of regeneration."[146]

In Buffon's revolutionary regeneration is thus a resistance to the kind of modern racism that emerged in the natural science of the nineteenth century,[147] which classed persons based on essences that were presumed to be permanent and also evident in the physicality of color or bodily constitution. For Buffon, there could be no such permanence, either in the present or across time—everything that had been, or could be, subject to degeneration was also open to renewal, or regeneration, through the improvement of conditions and the efforts of human beings. While Buffon remained committed to the position that nature was everywhere in flux, this was not a purely materialist ontology, nor was it what we would call in contemporary philosophy a simply contextualist argument. While all changes in animal and human populations are attributable to context—whether of climate, geography, society, or politics—the beings who are themselves subject to change are not defined only by their contextual constitution. The human being, like all other natural creatures, is not reducible to its historical environment. The original prototype maintained a position from which the human being could be reconstituted in time according to moral and political change—it served as a placeholder, a reminder, that if all things are in flux in natural history, a claim can always be made that the human being ought to be otherwise in the world.

Buffon's methodology has as its core principle the rejection of final causes, or, at least, the rejection of the notion that human beings can ever know the final causes of natural things, including the final cause of human beings themselves. The purpose of the unaltered original proto-type therefore cannot be telic in the Aristotelian sense, as an end toward which the human being is knowingly striving. What Buffon gives us instead is a distinctively *modern telic* account of human nature—one that posits a distinction for the human being in its capacity to change itself and its historical conditions while maintaining that the human being as a natural creature must have a universal, and thus unchanging, natural identity as a species. The openness to human reconstitution in the world holds both that there is a universal human nature that is irreducible to one's particular historical context and that one is therefore granted the right to fundamentally alter one's context—and, in the process, oneself—through regeneration.

All things for Buffon exist in this tension between the universal and the historical, but it is only the human being that is conscious of this simultaneously telic and unbounded existence, or the suspension between permanency and variability. The palingenetic consciousness—the mark of the human—opened the door to a foundational and revolutionary regeneration of the human being in the French Revolution through the assertion of both a universal nature and the right of humans by nature to change themselves by transforming their conditions. These were not the rights claims of a Hobbesian or a Lockean, in which one would assert an inviolable natural right of the human being that any state therefore has the responsibility to acknowledge and protect. The rights claims of the French Revolution were regenerative, asserting that no right could be universally held until it was historically or contextually present in the world, actively regenerated by self-making human beings. These were claims channeled through one of the eighteenth century's greatest admirers of Buffon, Jean-Jacques Rousseau.

In the next chapter, I will provide an account of Rousseau's political philosophy that places him with Buffon in constructing a modern telic account of human nature—one that asserts both an original natural prototype and a foundationally changeable and historical character. For Rousseau, as for Buffon, the question of the human being remains fundamentally open. Human beings are never entirely knowable and are always capable of degenerating or regenerating in time: the idea of "Man" is not an absolute given.[148] What Vincenzo Ferrone has called the "new humanism of rights" in Buffon and Rousseau became a "programme for the emancipation of man" in the Revolution that extended beyond France to calls for the abolition of slavery and the regeneration of human beings and states in colonies like Haiti.[149] This unique Enlightenment conception of the human being was emancipatory because it facilitated a regenerative impulse, or compulsion, promising human beings the ability to become what they are (universally) by changing what they are (in the world)—and this was enacted in the demand for a Declaration of the Rights of Man and of the Citizen in 1789.

A common reaction to Rousseau and to the French Revolutionary project is to claim that such an assertion of positive liberty breeds totalitarianism because it makes the state and the human being one entity, one closed unit of definition. Even Ernst Cassirer presents Rousseau's political argument in this light: "The idea of inalienable rights," which "was designed to draw a clear and precise line of demarcation between the sphere of the individual and that of the state and to preserve the independence of the former from the latter, is now asserted by Rousseau to belong to the sphere of the state."[150] A regenerative political movement is thus seen to collapse the human being into the political, to leave him nowhere to go once the state takes a potentially frightening turn. Once rights are seen not as inalienable possessions but as changeable constitutions of constitutions themselves, the human being has lost any claim against the state, against his context, against his fellows.

But this outcome is not at all what a regenerative political—and human— vision promises. In fact, it is the inverse. A state built on the assertion of inalienable and determined rights leaves human beings with nowhere to turn when they desire to truly determine themselves in relation to their historical or political context. There is no human that remains open, undetermined, or acontextual in what has now become the liberal democratic order—it is *this* vision, not the regenerative one, that collapses self and society. Buffon and Rousseau leave the human in part out of its given political system and historical epoch and allow human beings the right by nature to reconstitute and regenerate that system in itself. It is true that this naturally regenerative power and freedom makes the idea of "rights" subject to the state (for there can be no rights without the state), but it never fully subjects the human being. In this respect, human beings maintain a perpetual, much deeper, natural right always to change themselves and the rights and polities they might imagine and construct. It is to this human nature beyond the idea of rights that Rousseau directs his focus in *Discourse on the Origin and Foundations of Inequality Among Men*, and his image of the *first right* of natural man sets on course the regenerative claims of the revolutionary emancipation to come.

3

THE RIGHT TO RENOUNCE DEPENDENCE

Jean-Jacques Rousseau's *Discourse on the Origin and Foundations of Inequality Among Men* (or *Second Discourse*), published in 1755, is often integrated into what is broadly called the "social contract tradition." For obvious reasons, this is due to the fact that Rousseau wrote a companion piece to the *Second Discourse* entitled *Of the Social Contract* in 1762.[1] That Rousseau shares this tradition with Thomas Hobbes and John Locke is, on the surface, also subject to clear explanation.[2] Those who posit the need for a social contract and speculate about the foundations of political societies engage in speculation about the universal nature of human beings and the qualities or rights they possess by nature that either serve or detract from the political and social order.

For Hobbes, all human beings are governed by competing appetites and aversions and desire the "continual progress" and assurance of the future,[3] subject to a "perpetual and restless desire of power after power, that ceaseth only in death."[4] Hobbes presents the state of nature as consisting of the perpetual conflict (whether actual or potential) among human beings seeking to fulfill these powers and desires, causing quarrels of competition, diffidence, and glory.[5] Each man in the state of nature also possesses the right of nature—"the liberty each man hath to use his own power as he will himself"[6]—and is commanded by the laws of nature, or the "precept[s] or general rule[s], found out by reason, by which man is forbidden to do that which is destructive of his own life or taketh away the means of preserving the same."[7] Hobbes presents a solution to the inevitable state of war in the natural condition in the form of an absolute sovereign power, the Leviathan, which would end absolutely the conflicts between men and is necessitated by the logic of man's reasoning about what would best serve his preservation.[8] For Hobbes, then, the natural condition is in its explanatory role inextricably bound to the state he constructs: human nature is what dictates the content of the contract, or covenant, and the structure of the polity's power.

The same can be said of Locke's *Second Treatise of Government*. Locke conceives man's natural condition as one of perfect freedom and equality; however, he writes, "Though this be a state of liberty, yet it is not state of license. . . . The state of nature has a law of nature to govern it, which obliges every one: and reason, which is that law, teaches all mankind, who will but consult it, that being all equal and independent, no one ought to harm another in his life, health, liberty, or possessions."[9] Just as for Hobbes, the trouble in the state of nature comes from conflicts of power, or execution, for though the law of nature *ought* to govern all equally, the "execution of the law of nature is . . . put into every man's hands."[10] By exercising rights in the state of nature—the right to preserve oneself and the right to preserve all mankind by punishing offenders of the law—the human being is faced with all other human beings, each of whom is a judge in his own case. Thus, Locke writes, "Civil government is the proper remedy for the inconveniences of the state of nature, which must certainly be great, where men may be judges in their own case."[11] Locke objects to Hobbes's preferred solution of the absolute monarch, instead opting for a republican "body politic, wherein the majority have a right to act and conclude the rest."[12]

The presentations of Hobbes's and Locke's political arguments are here quite cursory and many distinctions separate their political theories of government. Nevertheless, their accounts are structurally identical: an explanation of some universal facets of human nature—tied to rights, law, and reasoning—leads logically and necessarily to the emergence of a social contract or covenant. It is this structural coherence to which Rousseau objects in the *Second Discourse*.[13] Rousseau writes his *Second Discourse* in response to a question posed by the Academy of Dijon: "What is the origin of inequality among men, and is it authorized by the natural law?" One of Rousseau's first moves is to reject the premise of the question altogether.[14] Without first knowing what nature and the nature of man are, Rousseau writes, "it would be quite difficult to concur about a good definition of natural law. Indeed, all those that are found in Books, besides not being uniform, suffer from the further defect of being derived from a range of Knowledge which men do not naturally have, and from advantages the idea of which they can conceive of only once they have left the state of nature."[15] Taking direct aim at social contract theorists, Rousseau continues, "One begins by looking for the rules about which it would be appropriate for men to agree among themselves for the sake of common utility; and then gives the name natural Law to the collection of these rules, with no further proof than the good which, in one's view, would result from universal compliance with them."[16] If we "do not know natural man," then, for Rousseau, we cannot know anything else, especially "the Law which he has received or that which best suits his constitution."[17]

Hobbes and Locke claimed to illuminate nature, Rousseau says, but they "succeeded [only] in stifling" it:[18]

> The Philosophers who have examined the foundations of society have all felt the necessity of going back as far as the state of Nature, but none of them has reached it. Some have not hesitated to ascribe to Man in that state the notion of the Just and the Unjust, without bothering to show that he had to have this notion, or even that it would have been useful to him; Others have spoken of everyone's Natural Right to keep what belongs to him, without explaining what they understood by belong; Others still, after first granting to the stronger authority over the weaker, had Government arise straightaway, without giving thought to the time that must have elapsed before the language of authority and of government could have meaning for men: Finally, all of them, continually speaking of need, greed, oppression, desires, and pride transferred to the state of Nature ideas they had taken from Society; They spoke of Savage Man and depicted Civil Man.[19]

Our continued "ignorance of natural man," according to Rousseau, also casts into "uncertainty and obscurity" "the idea of right."[20]

Instead, Rousseau goes further than his predecessors, describing the true natural man, who is detached from all civil, political, and social qualities:

"This same study of original man, of his true needs, and of the fundamental principles of his duties is also the only effective means available
to dispel the host of difficulties that arise regarding the origin of moral
inequality, the true foundations of the Body politic, the reciprocal rights
of its members, and a thousand similar questions, as important as they are
poorly elucidated."[21] Rousseau uses his *Second Discourse* to describe this
natural man and the course of his degeneration and corruption over time.[22]
Later, in *Of the Social Contract*, Rousseau offers the prospect of a legitimate political order that is not "incompatible with the nature of man" and
might turn human beings away from their corrupted condition.[23] Unlike
the theories of Thomas Hobbes and John Locke, however, Rousseau's
revolutionary imagination of the natural condition of human beings in
the *Second Discourse* does not entail as logical necessity the conclusion
or institution of the *Social Contract*—conversely, Rousseau's intention in
the *Second Discourse* is to establish that there is absolutely no connection
whatsoever between natural and political man. Further, Rousseau's claim
against philosophers like Hobbes and Locke is that they commit the fallacy of attributing to natural man qualities and abilities that belong only
to man's civilized identity, such as language, speech, reason, foresight, and
deliberative desire. Looking only to "the first and simplest operations of
the human Soul,"[24] Rousseau takes his reader back to the "pure state of
Nature,"[25] stripping the human being "of all the super-natural gifts he may
have received, and of all the artificial faculties he could have only acquired
by prolonged progress."[26]

Despite his distance from the civilized persons we are today, the
natural man of the *Second Discourse* serves as Rousseau's illumination of
"the life of [the] species," described "in terms of the qualities you received,
which your education and your habits could deprave, but which they
could not destroy."[27] For Rousseau, civilization provides no completion
for the human being, and the political sphere provides no solution to
human nature—instead, this presumed completion and solution are what
lead us further and further astray from understanding ourselves as we are
constituted by nature. While "self-preservation [is] almost [man's] only
care" in the natural condition, preservation of the self is in no way better
served by association with others in social or political arrangements.[28]
In the *Second Discourse*, Rousseau sees only poison in what Hobbes and
Locke imagined as a remedy for the human condition; for Rousseau,

"the bonds of servitude are formed solely by men's mutual dependence and the reciprocal needs that unite them."[29]

Rousseau imagines a human nature beyond civilization, beyond law, beyond reason, and even beyond the rights that Hobbes and Locke would naturally ascribe to human beings. In a fundamental sense, for Rousseau there can be no "rights" in the natural condition, whether they be understood as claims against or in relation to one another or as a consciousness of one's own liberty or will. The man of Rousseau's state of nature is described as entirely independent and "animal,"[30] "left by nature to bare instinct alone" and "deprived of every sort of Enlightenment. . . . His desires do not exceed his physical needs, the only goods he knows in the Universe are food, a female, and rest; the only evils he fears are pain and hunger";[31] "his soul, which nothing stirs, yields itself to the sole sentiment of its present existence, with no idea of the future, however near it may be, and his projects, as limited as his views, hardly extend to the end of the day."[32] Only by first imagining the human being in this way, Rousseau claims, is one "not obliged to make a Philosopher of a man before making a man of him."[33]

Rousseau's vision of human nature sets him on a distinct course from Hobbes and Locke, rethinking and reimagining the structural link (or, rather, lack thereof) between a state of nature and a social contract. For Rousseau, social contracts can bring human beings to ruin just as readily as they may regenerate some semblance of a less corrupted or degenerate existence when instituted correctly. For example, the social contract described in the *Second Discourse*—which Rousseau calls the "origin of Society and of the Laws"—only "gave new fetters to the weak and new forces to rich, irreversibly destroyed natural freedom, forever fixed the Law of property and inequality, [and] transformed a skillful usurpation into an irrevocable right."[34] In this contract, "all ran toward their chains in the belief that they were securing their freedom . . . [for] they did not have enough experience to foresee its dangers."[35] In the *Social Contract*, on the other hand, Rousseau sets his sights on the question of whether "in the civil order there can be some legitimate and sure rule of administration, taking men as they are, and the laws as they might be."[36] His task there is to "find a form of association that will defend and protect the person and goods of each associate with the full common force, and by means of which each, uniting with all, nevertheless obeys only himself and remain as free as before."[37]

The legitimacy of Rousseau's social contract is founded in his departure from, not his coherence with, the contract theorists who came before him. Rousseau sees rights as conventional and subject to the contract, not as the natural first premises of the contract's legitimacy or as the first possessions of human nature. He writes, "Since no man has natural authority over his fellow-man, and since force produces no right, conventions remain as the basis of all legitimate authority among men."[38] In nature, for Rousseau, there is no right that men possess over or even in relation to one another; but it is nevertheless the case that legitimate authority *is* grounded in right, and so all legitimate polities will be formed on a bedrock of conventional rights legislation. Directly refuting theorists such as Hugo Grotius who argue that men must alienate their right, Rousseau sees only absurdity in the premise that contract theorists before him held as foundational. There can be no renouncing or alienating of right in the social contract precisely because rights are not natural and in no way precede the contract itself. What is more fundamental to Rousseau is the deeper, more natural freedom to make and change rights themselves—to have and maintain power as a sovereign body over the constitution of the state. As he writes, "To renounce one's freedom is to renounce one's quality as man, [and] the rights of humanity."[39]

The remainder of this chapter provides a more thorough elucidation of how Rousseau's unique vision of human nature intersects with his political argument in the *Social Contract*, which lays the ground for the discussion in the next chapter of how truly emancipatory this vision is, for both Rousseau's time—as it translated into the French Revolution—and our own. My argument is that Rousseau drew his *modern telic* vision of human nature out of the work of Buffon, positing both a universal natural prototype for the human being and acknowledging the capacity that human beings have to change themselves and their political or worldly conditions. This *duplex* of human nature is essential to Rousseau's political theory insofar as he wants to maintain an openness for human beings to remake themselves and their rights entirely while also affirming that there is a foundational universal quality of man that grants him the freedom to do so. For Rousseau, the human being is both completely constituted by the political world in which he lives—formed, transformed, or deformed by it—and also always cannot be reducible to the political rights he is granted or through which he is made.

The human being is not by nature political and will never be natural in politics or solved or resolved by the correct political order.[40] But it is precisely this irreconcilability that contains the emancipatory potential of Rousseau's political philosophy: the human always has a claim against the world in which he finds himself, can always try to regenerate his degenerate or corrupt conditions, and can always remake himself by remaking politics and rights. By nature, the human being is never fully subjected to a political order, even if he is completely constituted by it. For Rousseau, becoming conscious of this irreducible nature is the first step toward forming a potentially legitimate political order, for man cannot see his chains until he is presented with an image of what it is like to be free. This is the founding work of the *Second Discourse*: the presentation of the original prototype, or universal nature, of humanity from which we have degenerated over time and through which we might regenerate our corrupt existence.[41]

ROUSSEAU'S MODERN TELIC

Rousseau's "study of original man"[42] in the *Second Discourse* is designed to go back to what Rousseau calls the "pure state of nature"[43]—a state that is imagined beyond and before any society, reason, language, or community. To understand what is natural for the human being, according to Rousseau, the human must be stripped of any quality that could have been acquired by artifice or convention, education or habits. In this, Rousseau sets himself, as he knows, a speculative task, for everywhere we look we see human beings only in societies, and with reason, language, and community. The story that Rousseau tells is a historical one, rooted in the transformations that have taken place across time from a pure and independent natural existence to a corrupt and civilized one. It is, however, a "hypothetical history,"[44] subject to "hypothetical and conditional reasonings; better suited to elucidate the Nature of things than to show their genuine origin, and comparable to those our Physicists daily make regarding the formation of the World."[45]

In the *Second Discourse*, Rousseau immediately aligns himself with natural scientists and their mode of historical speculation, and distances himself from political theories about social contracts and natural law. He writes in the Preface that "the most useful and the least advanced of all human knowledge seems to me to be that of man, and I dare say that the inscription on the Temple at Delphi alone contained a more important and more difficult precept than all the big Books of the moralists."[46] Rousseau's invocation of the famous Delphic inscription—"know thyself"— ties him to the natural-scientific mode of hypothetical historical thinking. Here, Rousseau includes a lengthy note, praising the "solid and sublime reason" of none other than George-Louis LeClerc, comte de Buffon, and approvingly citing *Histoire naturelle*: "However great may be our interest in knowing ourselves, I wonder whether we do not know better everything that is not ourselves."[47] In this note, Rousseau thus seems to ally himself with Buffon against the taxonomist Carl Linnaeus, who also invoked the Delphic inscription in his classification of Anthropomorpha. In his Table of the Animal Kingdom, Linnaeus classed the human being with simians, providing only a cryptic description of what might distinguish the human being: the scrawling of *nosce te ipsum* ("know thyself") next to *Homo sapiens* in the taxonomic chart. The foundational problem of philosophical inquiry for Rousseau, however, was precisely that man did *not* know himself—and in his attempt to provide a figurative answer to this problem, Rousseau was inspired by Buffon's historical and scientific method.[48]

When Rousseau was writing the *Second Discourse*, the first four volumes of Buffon's *Histoire naturelle* had been published, and I will restrict my comparison of their work here to these four initial volumes. From the outset of the *Second Discourse*, Rousseau's study of original man is marked by essential features of a Buffonian inquiry and anthropology. First, Rousseau adopts the mode of natural history. Like Buffon, Rousseau proffers a transformative conception of time for the human being and imagines the transformation of the species in terms of its temporal alteration from an original prototype. To even begin to see the human being in a state of nature, Rousseau claims that one is bound to the hypothetical historical method, for how else would "man ever succeed in seeing himself as Nature formed him, through all the changes which the succession of times and of things must have wrought in his original constitution" or disentangle "what he owes to his own stock from what circumstances and his progress have added to or changed in his primitive State?"[49] Rousseau writes of the "primitive" state of man, from which the "progress of the human species" continually moves away:[50] "Like the statue of Glaucus which time, sea, and storms had so disfigured that it resembled less a God than a ferocious Beast, the human soul adulterated in the lap of society by a thousand forever recurring causes, by the acquisition of a mass of knowledge and errors, by changes that have taken place in the constitution of Bodies, and by the continual impact of the passions, has, so to speak, changed in appearance to the point of being almost unrecognizable."[51] Seeking the "human constitution" in its "first origin" requires that one speculate about what might be underneath such a time-inflicted disfigurement or degeneration.[52] It requires that we posit an original prototype for the human species.

Second, Rousseau agrees with Buffon that the "first truth"[53] that comes from this natural-historical examination of the human being is that man "ought to classify himself with the animals, which he resembles in all his material."[54] Rousseau describes the "first Embryo of the species" from the physical, or material,[55] point of view as "an animal less strong than some, less agile than others, but, all things considered, the most advantageously organized of all: I see him sating his hunger beneath an oak, slaking his thirst at the first Stream, finding his bed at the foot of the same tree that provided his meal, and with that his needs are satisfied";[56] "his projects, as limited as his views, hardly extend to the end of the day."[57] The tranquility and simplicity of natural man's life, Rousseau claims, "are the fatal proofs that most of our ills are of our own making, and that we would have avoided all of them if we had retained the simple, uniform and solitary way of life prescribed to us by Nature. If it destined us to be healthy then, I almost dare assert, the state of reflection is a state against Nature, and the man who meditates is a depraved animal."[58]

The animal nature of Rousseau's natural man was the subject of much scholarly controversy in Rousseau's time and continues to be today. Because of Rousseau's further suggestion that the great apes seem to live like natural man, some see a groundbreaking pre-Darwinian evolutionism in Rousseau's *Second Discourse*. Based on accounts of travelers,[59] Rousseau depicts "pongos" (orangutans) as creatures that

> bear an exact resemblance to man, but they are much heavier and quite
> tall. They have a human face, with very deep-set eyes. . . . They live in the
> woods; They sleep in Trees where they build themselves a kind of roof

that shields them from the rain. . . . The Negroes who travel through the forests are in the habit of lighting fires at night. They notice that in the morning, when they have left, the Pongos take their place around the fire, and do not leave until it has died out: for although they are dexterous, they have not sense enough to keep the fire going by laying wood on it.[60]

"One finds in the description of these supposed monsters," Rousseau continues, "striking conformities with the human species. . . . It is not clear from these passages what the Authors' reasons are for refusing to call the Animals in question Savage men."[61] Scholars such as Robert Wokler thus claim that Rousseau was "the first to conceive that the last link in the natural chain—that is, the relation between apes and man—might be one of genetic continuity."[62] While Wokler sees Rousseau's animalization of natural man in progressive and positive terms, others were not so complimentary. In the year of the Second Discourse's publication, Hermann Samuel Reimarus wrote that Rousseau "has lately exerted his imagination, in representing to us, among other animals in a desert, an original man in his natural state, as a brute or something worse [plus bête que les bêtes]."[63] Rousseau's beastly man also provided fodder for the response of Voltaire, who, after reading the Second Discourse, wrote to Rousseau thanking him for his book "against the human species": "No one has ever been so witty as you are in trying to turn us into brutes: to read your book makes one long to go on all fours."[64]

Buffon also claims that human beings are, at root, animals. But for Buffon, this is not the last word on what it means to be human. While the first truth may be that human beings are animals, it is not the only truth. He writes: "We have often said that Nature moves and proceeds in imperceptible degrees and nuances; this truth, which otherwise admits no exception, is here reversed: there is an infinite distance between the faculties of man and those of the most perfect animal, clear proof that man is of a different nature, that he himself constitutes a separate class, from which there are infinite degrees and nuances of descent before we arrive at the state of an animal."[65] Man is possessed of a "spiritual substance" by which he is enabled to think and reflect.[66] Despite man's incapacity to know the causes of the objects of nature, he is still in possession of the consciousness of his own existence—what I have called the palingenetic consciousness.

Echoing Buffon's work, Rousseau also moves beyond thinking of man as simply animal because of the "spirituality of his soul."[67] In the first part of the *Second Discourse*, Rousseau provides a dually structured description of man from both the physical (animal) and metaphysical (or moral) points of view.[68] Considering natural man from the metaphysical perspective, Rousseau writes that, like all animals, man is "an ingenious machine," but in the "human machine" there are two additional qualities: free agency and perfectibility.[69] Where animals choose or reject "by instinct," man does so "by an act of freedom; as a result, the Beast cannot deviate from the Rule prescribed to it even when it would be to its advantage to do so, while man often deviates from it to his detriment."[70] Rousseau claims that "every animal has ideas, since it has senses; up to a point it even combines its ideas, and in this respect man differs from the Beast only as more does from less. . . . [But man] recognizes himself free to acquiesce or resist; and it is mainly in the consciousness of this freedom that the spirituality of his soul exhibits itself."[71]

Yet, because there is some ambiguity in what freedom is, Rousseau writes that he can identify only one "very specific property that distinguishes between [man and beast], and about which there can be no argument, namely the faculty of perfecting oneself," or *perfectibility*.[72] While "an animal is at the end of several months what it will be for the rest of its life, and its species is after a thousand years what it was in the first year of those thousand," man is, through his faculty of self-perfection, subject to enlightenment and error.[73] The faculty of perfectibility is thus a principle for Rousseau that contains the capacity for human beings to change themselves, whether for good or ill. Rousseau's identification of this faculty as the defining feature of the human being is perplexing to say the least. The unique capacity to change, as specified *against* the inability of animals to do the same,[74] seems to contradict entirely Rousseau's initial claim that the state of nature for the human being is tranquil, undisturbed, and always the same—that is, a nature that is in possession of "purely animal functions."[75] If perfectibility is for Rousseau the specific nature of the human being and the human species, how can it be antithetical to the description of the state of nature Rousseau himself provides?

This apparent contradiction may seem to provide ground for the interpretation of Rousseau as an evolutionist: supposing that Rousseau intended to subtly reveal that human beings, possessed of perfectibility, evolved from animal forebears who were possessed of no such quality would go some way toward accounting for the discrepancy.[76] Wokler, for example, sees a passage, or transformation, from the physical to the metaphysical over the course of the *Second Discourse*'s hypothetical history.[77] Other interpreters instead see Rousseau as constructing the physical side of the natural condition only to contrast it with the freedom that more truly defines human nature, establishing Rousseau as a metaphysical dualist. On this interpretation, the animalistic man in the state of nature serves as a kind of foil for what Timothy O'Hagan has called Rousseau's truly human "divided life."[78] On this reading, the separation of physical from metaphysical man in the *Second Discourse* is therefore also seen to divide the natural from the supernatural. Robin Douglass writes that "it is because freedom is part of man's metaphysical side that it cannot be illuminated by the natural sciences. . . . The proof for free will given [in Rousseau's other writings][79] suggested the spiritual depth to Rousseau's thought."[80] And Frederick Neuhouser: "Anything that counts as genuine freedom for Rousseau must incorporate an element of metaphysical independence from the causal laws of nature, and this aspect of human action can never emerge from a developmental story based solely on a theory of human nature that . . . is restricted to purely naturalistic explanations."[81]

In all of these interpretations there is an undeniable pull to separate, or detach, elements of Rousseau's work that, to my mind, he gave us no reason to suppose were separable. Interpreters imagine that there must be some rupture between the physical and the metaphysical, or between natural science and the spiritual. The human being must be explained by either of these modes—man must be *either* the animal of the pure state of nature (even in its evolutionary reading) *or* the perfectible and changeable creature—but never both. My argument is that the competing claims of a universal, unchanging nature and a nature defined by its transformative or changeable capacity seem irreconcilable only because the deep debt that Rousseau owes to Buffon's vision of human nature has not yet been attributed the importance it deserves.[82]

According to Buffon, man is *Homo duplex*,[83] an interior existence divided between sensory feeling ("which shines only in a tempest of obscurity" and consists of sensory impressions and passions) and "the spiritual principle."[84] Buffon claims that "animals never invent, nor bring anything to perfection."[85] While animals distinguish better what is agreeable to their present existence, they lack the capacity to change their conditions. Man is also conscious of his existence as a temporal being: animals are "conscious of their present existence" (through a sentiment of present existence), but in man "consciousness of existence is composed of the perception of actual existence, as well as the remembrance of past existence."[86] Buffon's distinctions are echoed almost verbatim in Rousseau's accounts of physical and metaphysical man. Physical man is governed only by a "sentiment of present existence" (a phrase borrowed from Buffon): his "soul, which nothing stirs, yields itself to the sole sentiment of its present existence, with no idea of the future."[87] Metaphysical man, however, possesses the spiritual principle of self-perfection and a consciousness or awareness of time—and thus the capacity for both foresight and curiosity. This is precisely the temporal, historical, and transformative awareness of the self and of nature that defines the palingenetic consciousness that we see in the work of Buffon and Bonnet.

There are, in this sense, two first truths about human beings for Rousseau, just as there are for Buffon. The first is that we are animals. We belong to nature as natural creatures—we live and die, we procreate, we exist in concert with all other things that degenerate and regenerate over time. The second first truth, however, is that we are conscious of our life and aware of our death, we make choices about whom we procreate and spend time with, and we change the circumstances, spaces, and persons with whom we exist in concert. We degenerate and regenerate ourselves because we have the ability to do so. This ability is something that defines our nature as a species: it is human nature to change our conditions and to change ourselves. Without this ability, we would not be human but some other thing entirely. Rousseau wants to resist, however, what will become the defining feature of the modern self: the presumption that there is an unlimited freedom to create the self and the world in the human consciousness, or an unbounded nature to the human being.[88] For Rousseau, we must suppose that there is a nature for the human being, a pure state, and a desire to see ourselves as Nature formed us. If we are to transform our degenerate and corrupted civilization, we must "disentangle what is original from what is artificial" in man's nature.[89]

Like Buffon, then, Rousseau sees a need to posit an original prototype for humanity as a counterpoint to the degenerate men he sees in society.[90]

He concludes the *Second Discourse* as follows: "Savage man and civilized man differ so much in their innermost heart and inclinations that what constitutes the supreme happiness of the one would reduce the other to despair. The first breathes nothing but repose and freedom. . . . By contrast, the Citizen, forever active, sweats, scurries, constantly agonizes. . . . The Savage lives within himself; sociable man, always outside himself, is capable of living only in the opinion of others and, so to speak, derives the sentiment of his own existence solely from their judgment."[91] The original prototype of the human being is one in which man truly lives only in the sentiment of his own existence, derived only from nature and never from others—not from conventions, from habits, from education, from politics, or from society. It would be, according to Rousseau, a life of independence, "the simple, uniform and solitary way of life prescribed to us by Nature."[92]

A point of frustration for all students of Rousseau, he insists that this origin story is hypothetical and conjectural, and is descriptive of a "state which no longer exists, which perhaps never did exist, which probably never will exist, and about which it is nevertheless necessary to have exact notions in order to judge our present state adequately."[93] This is because the only things that do exist in the world are human beings: real, living, and changeable human beings. Every person is born into a world in which he is subject to the choices of others, and every person is raised in a condition that is not of his own choosing, whether concerning his economic place in society, the political climate, his education, and so on. But if all there was to the human being—to human nature—was our capacity for transformation and change, there could be no claim against a society that we judge to be corrupt. Without an acontextual prototype of the human being, there would be no ground upon which to fight the inequality of our given contextual world and its artificial presentation of how we ought to be, derived solely from the opinions and decisions of others.[94]

For Rousseau, there can thus be only one genuine claim against the world in which you find yourself: the claim of being human by nature. This means that you have the capacity to change your conditions. More importantly, however, this also—and always equally—means that when those conditions change, you do not lose your liberty and independence, as these are not subject to your context but belong to nature and to all human natures universally. The original prototype of the human being is the figure on which all degenerative and regenerative transformation depends and provides the permanent and unchanging claim that human beings maintain against their given circumstances to transform their existence. It is a defining nature: an origin that inspires a purpose and facilitates its own transformation.[95] This is a distinctively modern telic conception of the human being that can serve as the foundation for a transformative politics.

A NEW NATURAL RIGHT

It is useful here to be reminded of the related and transformative power of Buffon's regenerative vision of nature in which he also posits a universal prototype for each species and details how each degenerated from its original form. The unaltered prototype serves as the ultimately unknowable model of all the alterations of a given natural creature that exist in the world. For Buffon, this is evident in the physical variations of species across space and in the variations that occur according to climatic and geographic conditions. Because he is a natural scientist committed to observational knowledge, Buffon suggests that one can know and speculate only based upon what one sees, and in this case the evidence is of alterations and of physical or character traits that make individual animals more or less conformable to what one might posit as a universal (that is, shared) form of their species.

This kind of comparative observational knowledge is possible only for human beings, and it facilitates the formation of judgments about the degrees of degeneration of the stock of a particular animal. Human beings also possess the power to alter the course of events, regenerating natural things away from their degenerate instantiations. Most importantly, human beings have the capacity for self-regeneration by altering their conditions through political and educational transformations. Because a regeneration of this kind would transform the human beings themselves who are effecting this change, Buffon's vision of the human being's place in nature is one that affirms a universal human nature while also facilitating its historical change over time. The natural right to "alter, change, destroy, develop, renew, and produce" is a constantly regenerative force that human beings maintain and can activate in and against their historical or political context and their contextual self-understanding.[96]

Buffon's regenerative natural right is thus seemingly set against any particular adumbration of the distribution of political power in a given historical epoch. While human beings can harness this ability to alter, change, and renew, it is not unique to the human being in Nature to be part of this natural right; what is unique to the human being is that this ability can be directed and actively engaged. What is regenerative in nature universally, for Buffon, becomes actively *self*-regenerative in the human being; likewise, the right to alter and renew, which belongs to nature universally, becomes a *human* right only in its active engagement, or in the claiming of the right through self-transformation or the regeneration of worldly conditions. Buffon's *Homo duplex* thus maps onto a dual conception of right(s): that there is (1) a foundational or first right of regeneration that subjects (2) all political right(s) to the possibility of perpetual alteration. The human being is itself the only mediator of this regenerative activity by using its natural right to change its own nature and rights.

This conception of right is implied in Buffon's theory. It is Rousseau, I argue, who gives it a fuller expression and thus provides the modern telic human being with an explicitly political avenue for self-transformation and regeneration in the *Social Contract*. I also argue that the *Social Contract* does not work without Rousseau's *Second Discourse*, a text written to persuade readers that the world around them is degenerate—and to show them that it does not have to be that way. The *Social Contract* thus becomes a particular vision for the regeneration of the corruption of human beings in the world, but it is one that rests on human beings first having been persuaded that they are not living according to nature—a nature given life only in the *Second Discourse*.

At its foundation, the vision of natural man in the beginning of the *Second Discourse* is a kind of anticivilizational paradigm or archetype of acontextual independence. It is a state that is prior to all states or societies, in which the human being lives solitary, free, and as untroubled by its own existence as any other animal. Once human beings become conscious of themselves and of one another, and thus begin to form relational aversions and attachments, this pure state of nature is lost, as is the independence from subjugation: "Since the bonds of servitude are formed solely by men's mutual dependence and the reciprocal needs that unite them, it is impossible to subjugate a man without first having placed him in the position of being unable to do without another; a situation which, since it does not obtain in the state of nature, leaves everyone in it free of the yoke."[97] Whereas human beings in the state of nature "had not the slightest idea of thine and mine,"[98] Rousseau writes that the state of nature concludes finally when "the first person who, having enclosed a plot of ground, bethought himself to say *this is mine*" and thus founded civil society.[99]

The passage from natural man to this state of "thine and mine" was a long one, however, and depended on what Rousseau calls many "difficulties" and "fortuitous concatenations of circumstances . . . that might very well never have occurred."[100] In part 2 of the *Second Discourse*, Rousseau follows Buffon in first placing these historical happenings in the realm of geography and climate:[101] "In proportion as man spread, difficulties multiplied together with men. Differences of soil, Climate, seasons, may have forced them to introduce differences into their way of life. . . . [The] repeated interaction of the various beings with himself as well as with one another must naturally have engendered perceptions of certain relations in man's mind . . . that we express by the words great, small, strong, weak, fast, slow, fearful, bold, and other such ideas."[102] This was a "new enlightenment" that produced in man "some sort of reflection."[103] Gradually, human beings made advances in industry and collective living, establishing families and crude properties—conveniences that Rousseau identifies as things that sadly "degenerated into true needs."[104] "The first yoke" that men imposed on themselves, spurred on by habitual dependence on others in society, was thus the first degeneration of the original state of man.[105]

As human beings became accustomed to making comparisons among things, so, too, did they begin to make comparisons among themselves, developing feelings of their own self-worth and the worth of others in relational assessments.[106] Despite the dependency of this primitive condition and its distance from "the first state of nature,"[107] Rousseau claims it was nevertheless the "happiest and the most lasting epoch" for man as it was a condition "at equal distance from the stupidity of the brute and the fatal enlightenment of civil man."[108] But "the moment one man needed the help of another; as soon as it was found to be useful for one to have provisions for two, equality disappeared, property appeared, work became necessary, and vast forests changed into smiling Fields that had to be watered with the sweat of men, and where slavery and misery were soon seen to sprout and grow together with the harvests."[109] From this point forward, "man, who had been previously free and independent, is now so to speak subjugated by a multitude of new needs to the whole of Nature, and especially to those of his kind whose slave he in a sense becomes by becoming their master; rich, he needs their services; poor, he needs their help. . . . In a word, competition and rivalry on the one hand, conflict of interests on the other, and always the hidden desire to profit at the expense of others."[110]

At this point, Rousseau claims, the rich concocted a plan. They would present this degenerate condition of horrors and war as man's natural state. Only the "specious reasons" supplied by the rich man would then be able to save human beings from such a wretched situation.[111] This specious reasoning was that of the social contract. " 'Let us unite,' " the rich man proclaims in Rousseau's hypothetical history, " 'to protect the weak from oppression, restrain the ambitious, and secure for everyone the possession of what belongs to him: Let us institute rules of Justice and peace to which all are obliged to conform, which make no exception for anyone. . . . In a word, instead of turning our forces against one another, let us gather them into a supreme power that might govern us according to wise Laws, protect and defend all the members of the association, repulse common enemies, and preserve us in everlasting concord.' "[112] The men were persuaded, and "all ran toward their chains in the belief that they were securing their freedom; for while they had enough reason to sense the advantages of a political establishment, they did not have enough experience to foresee its dangers."[113]

This was, Rousseau writes, "or must have been, the origin of Society and the Laws, which gave new fetters to the weak and new forces to the rich, irrevocably destroyed natural freedom, forever fixed the Law of property and inequality, transformed a skillful usurpation into an irrevocable right, and for the profit of a few ambitious men henceforth subjugated the whole of mankind to labor, servitude, and misery."[114] From this point forward in the Second Discourse, Rousseau invokes a comparison between savage and civilized man, contrasting the misery of the latter with the freedom of the former. "Barbarous man," he writes, "will not bend his head to the yoke which civilized man bears without a murmur, and he prefers the most tempestuous freedom to a tranquil subjection";[115] the civilized "do nothing but incessantly boast of the peace and quiet they enjoy in their chains,"[116] whereas savages want nothing but to "preserve their independence."[117] He concludes his conjectural story with a striking image of comparison, contrasting the men of history with the man of nature:

> In thus discovering and retracing the forgotten and lost paths that must have led men from the Natural state to the Civil state . . . every attentive reader cannot but be struck by the immense distance that separates these two states. It is in the slow succession of things that he will see the solution to an infinite number of problems of ethics and of Politics which Philosophers are unable to solve. He will sense that, since the Mankind of one age is not the Mankind of another age, the reason why Diogenes did not find a man is that he was looking among his contemporaries for the man of a time that was no more. . . . In the long run the objects of our needs and our pleasures change . . . [and] as original man gradually vanishes, Society no longer offers to the eyes of the wise man anything but an assemblage of artificial men and factitious passions that are the product of all these new relations, and have no true foundation in Nature.[118]

The concluding image is unmistakable. We are meant to see, if Rousseau has persuaded us, that all the things we consider to be enlightening or ennobling in civilization are in fact artificial and corrupt and are themselves consequences of the degeneration of the human race from a more natural, or original, condition. It is also not meant to be the case that only at present are things so degenerate, but in all times and places of history—in all conditions of dependence, and certainly in all political conditions, the human being is in chains. The very social contracts that have been presented to us as protecting our freedoms and independence—and our rights—are themselves the source of the greatest injustice and the most severe subjugation. This is the case not only because of the malicious intent of the founders of our civilization but also because, according to Rousseau, social contracts (of the likes of Hobbes and Locke) enshrined forever the very mistaken perception of the human being as a creature in need of dependence, which laid the ground for the inevitable perpetuation of unequal conditions and the permanent erasure of human freedom.

The natural man invoked at the conclusion of the *Second Discourse* appears in relief to the miserable, civilized man as a beacon of freedom, an imagistic representation of the vast preference one ought to have for living according to nature as opposed to civilizational servitude:

> Savage man and civilized man differ so much in their innermost heart and inclinations that what constitutes the supreme happiness of the one would reduce the other to despair. . . . The Savage lives within himself; sociable man, always outside himself, is capable of living only in the opinion of others. . . . [And so] in the midst of so much Philosophy, humanity, politeness, and Sublime maxims, we have nothing more than a deceiving and frivolous exterior, honor without virtue, reason without wisdom, and pleasure without happiness. It is enough for me to have proved that this is not man's original state, and that it is solely the spirit of Society, together with the inequality it engenders that changes and corrupts all our natural inclinations in this way.[119]

The anticivilized man—the man of nature—resists contextual dependence and definition. He stands for the claim that every person has against the social or political order and serves as an image of what one ought to desire: to be free of the present oppressive conditions, described by Rousseau with such poetic condemnation. There is, however, a more substantive philosophic argument undergirding Rousseau's project here, and a deeper claim about what it means to be a human being in the world. It is not just that one ought to desire freedom from one's current historical form of oppression. *All dependence* of any kind is itself already a degeneration from the desirable state of independence and freedom.

For Rousseau, there is no human who has ever lived this way in fact. The original state remains hypothetical and conditional—and *animal*—because it is fundamentally an inhuman condition when conceived in its purest form. To be human is always to be a product of both the sentiment of one's existence and the consciousness of one's existence—to be both animal and the creature of perfectibility, both independent of one's context and entirely dependent on it.[120] What this *duplex* of identity preserves is the universal claim the human being has to reshape the conditions of his own existence, and to remake himself in the process. Because there is nothing natural in the present world, saturated as it is with artifice and corruption, and because there is no necessary relation between the nature of the human being and the degenerate world in which he finds himself, there is always potential for the world's regeneration. The *Second Discourse* is a text designed to instigate a regenerative transformation of the world, if it proves to be persuasive. Providing an easily digestible image of the independent natural condition and demonstrating that the present world could not be further from this picture of freedom, Rousseau initiates a self-transformation in his reader. The reader sees his own natural condition in himself—that of the free, independent, and equal human being— and simultaneously recognizes in himself that he possesses no such nature.

The conclusion of the *Second Discourse* is meant to make us see most of all that we are not free, independent, or equal. Yet I think it is clear that it is also meant to inspire a self-transformation into this nature that we lack by changing the conditions of the world around us. For this transformation, the seemingly contradictory accounts of human nature in Rousseau's work must work in tandem. Human beings must harness their perfectibility (their capacity to change the world around them and thus build their contextual artifice) in the service of making real a nature (that of the free and independent person) that does not exist but is nevertheless posited as the universal, permanent, and unchanging essence of the human species. This modern telic vision of the human being serves as the foundation for Rousseau's political work in the *Social Contract*, which opens with the declaration that "man is born free, and everywhere he is in chains."[121] The human being is both universally free and at the same time evidently unfree in the world.

In the *Social Contract*, Rousseau makes no claim to free the human being from these chains absolutely; he seeks only a way to make those chains legitimate. Dependence is inevitable for human beings, but because that dependence is fashioned only on convention and never on a condition that is natural for man, those conventions can always be remade. Rousseau writes, "The social order is a sacred right, which provides the basis for all the others. Yet this right does not come from nature; it is therefore founded on conventions. The problem is to know what these conventions are."[122] The illegitimate social contract in the story of Rousseau's *Second Discourse* did establish the social order and the basis for all rights shared or protected among human beings in political society. But, for Rousseau, this social contract is also a convention, subject to judgments about whether it serves for good or ill in relation to the human beings who are determined by and dependent on it. Rousseau's own judgment is a harsh one, presenting this social contract as a condition of subjugation, injustice, and grossly degenerative dependence. These conventions of politics make the human beings who are subject to them subject to them absolutely: once one thinks that one's rights and freedoms are protected only in a given condition of social or political order, one has renounced all freedom or right to remake that order itself.

Instead, Rousseau writes, people should always have "the right to renounce Dependence."[123] This right is the foundational right of human beings by nature—the universal claim they maintain against their context, their conventional circumstance, and against any artifice or dependence on any other person. This is the only form of right that Rousseau will concede is a purely natural (that is, nonconventional) "right." Thus, it is, like the human being in the state of nature, a condition shared with the animals: "The ancient disputes about whether animals participate in the natural Law are [here] brought to an end: For it is clear that, since they are deprived of enlightenment and freedom, they cannot recognize that Law; but since they in some measure partake in our nature through sentience, with which they are endowed, it will be concluded that they also partici-pate in natural right."[124] For human beings, the natural right to renounce dependence remains universally hypothetical; for it to be realized, human beings would need to take it upon themselves to *make themselves* free and independent by remaking, or regenerating, the context and conditions in which they find themselves. Because the human being is the only natural creature that possesses perfectibility, it is only the human being that can take this natural right and have its image of freedom and independence serve as the inspiration for the refashioning of conventional rights and protections—the remaking of dependence—in the body politic. This is the project of Rousseau's *Social Contract*.

A DIFFERENT SOCIAL CONTRACT

Where the *Second Discourse* accounts for the problem of "what we have become, abandoned to ourselves," Rousseau's *Social Contract* is an answer concerning the means of "correcting our institutions and grounding them unshakably [which will forestall] the disorders that would have resulted from them."[125] In the *Social Contract*, Rousseau establishes a contrast between what he variously calls "natural freedom"[126] or "first rights"[127] and all things belonging to convention, which include "conventional freedom" and "rights."[128] The latter form of right is the focus of Rousseau's *Social Contract*, the full title of which is *Of the Social Contract, or Principles of Political Right*. To make my argument consistently intelligible, I will adopt the language of contrasting "first rights" with "political rights," where "first rights" pertains to the natural right discussed in the previous section of this chapter; that is, the universal freedom human beings possess by nature to remake the conditions of their dependence—and especially to remake conventional "political rights."

For Rousseau, all political rights belong to the state and to the conventional establishment and protection of their legitimacy. Rousseau's critique of previous accounts or systems of political right revolves around the conflation of first rights with political rights. If a social contract involves renouncing one's freedom, then the contract is illegitimate and absurd: "To renounce one's freedom is to renounce one's quality as a man, [and] the rights of humanity."[129] In the theories of Thomas Hobbes and John Locke, natural freedom is the content of natural right, and the contract depends on its renunciation or alienation. For Locke, human beings provide their consent, whether expressly or tacitly, to resign their natural freedom and right in the contract.[130] For Hobbes, it is a foundational premise of the natural law, and thus of the conditions of the social covenant, that a man be content "to lay down his right to all things."[131]

Much of the reductive conflation of Rousseau with these other contract theorists arises from Rousseau's own claim that the clauses of his legitimate contract can all be boiled down "to just one, namely, the total alienation of each associate with all of his rights to the whole community: For, in the first place, since each gives himself entirely, the condition is equal for all."[132] Rousseau claims that this total alienation would result in a "perfect" union in "which no associate has anything further to claim: For if individuals were left some rights, then, since there would be no common superior who might adjudicate between them and the public, each, being judge in his own case on some issue, would soon claim to be so on all."[133] The community becomes the arbiter of political rights for all equally, against which the individual cannot have a political claim because rights are conventionally established. For Rousseau, all rights therefore seem to be political rights, belonging to the political community.

This aspect of Rousseau's thought—the "total alienation" of each to the general will of the whole[134]—has led many to associate Rousseau's political theory with totalitarianism, or with what J. L. Talmon calls a "totalitarian democracy,"[135] setting Rousseau against thinkers like Hobbes and Locke who have comparatively liberal understandings of individual rights. Rousseau seems to advocate the complete sacrifice of the individual to the collective and the total and permanent collapse of the human being to the political will:

> If, then, one sets aside everything that is not of the essence of the social compact, one finds that it can be reduced to the following terms: *Each of us puts his person and his full power in common under the supreme direction of the general will; and in a body we receive each member as an indivisible part of the whole.* At once, in place of the private person of each contracting party, this act of association produces a moral and collective body made up of as many members as the assembly has voices, and which receives by this same act of unity, its common *self*, its life, and its will.[136]

This totalitarian reading, however, ignores completely Rousseau's explicit claim that he is doing the opposite. *Against* thinkers like Hobbes and Locke, Rousseau sees himself protecting the very human freedoms they collapse into the state in their social contracts. For Rousseau, there is absolutely no condition in which the alienation of one's *political* rights (or shared, conventional rights) would entail the sacrifice, as he writes in the *Second Discourse*, of "the right to renounce Dependence."[137] The human being is always two things at once for Rousseau: a product of his conditions, subject entirely to convention, and by nature a creature that can never be reducible to artifice, remaining outside and prior to any dependence on others. The social compact, once instituted, is totalizing in its conventional and political power. It will define the laws and rights that will be respected equally, and will thus shape the way of life for those who participate in its general will and administration. But for Rousseau, "there is no fundamental law which could not be revoked, not even the social pact."[138] This is the very foundation of the social contract's legitimacy: the fact that at any time it could be declared illegitimate and all laws and rights, being conventional, could fall. Individuals, when considered from the perspective of the political, have indeed renounced or alienated all of their rights to the power of the whole, or of convention, so that it may establish equality and freedom, but the human being has never, in this process, truly alienated its freedom, or *first right*, to call back and remake rights and the political system on which those rights depend for their legitimacy. The human being in this respect always maintains a claim against his own rights and always has the freedom to alter the conditions of his historical context and dependence.

Together, Rousseau's *Second Discourse* and *Social Contract* provide a radically emancipatory political argument. In the light of Rousseau, the social contract theories of Hobbes and Locke appear comparatively comforting: Hobbes and Locke assert some universal facets of human nature (passions, rights, laws) that lead inevitably and reasonably to a stable political conclusion. But these political theories are closed loops. While the state may also fall apart according to Hobbes and Locke, human beings in this case return to the same state of nature, and the same rights and laws, that they possessed before the institution of the social contract. Ostensibly, the same state ought to result from the collapse if human beings are thinking reasonably about their rights and desires. In claiming to go further than Hobbes and Locke, Rousseau sets his state of nature, and thus his natural condition for man, beyond this closed loop. There is nothing inevitable or even reasonable about the establishment of rights and law for Rousseau, even in one's own nature. The human being can recall or remake the conditions of his dependence, and his rights and laws, only because they depend entirely on the rupture between nature and convention. No particular political right for Rousseau will ever be a satisfaction of nature and thus human beings always have the first right, by nature, to remake and redefine themselves in the world. This pertains as much to a totalitarian state as it does to a liberal democratic one. They are equally self-transformations. As Rousseau claims, the "transition from the state of nature to the civil state produces a most remarkable change in man" from an animal to an intelligent being—that is, according to the story of the *Second Discourse*, from nature to convention.[139]

Rousseau's modern telic vision of the human being concedes that we are inevitably embedded in a condition of conventional dependence.

There is no doubting that we exist in a given historical and political context, and according to Rousseau we have been born into a condition of gross inequality, artifice, and corruption. The vision of natural life in the *Second Discourse* is meant to serve as an image of what it would be like to exist outside of these circumstances and thus is meant to make readers desire a refashioning of the world and of themselves. The freedom and independence of natural man in the *Second Discourse* is the model of both what political life is *not* for modern civilized man and the inspiration for the principles of a legitimate form of conventional sovereignty, which would require remaking the social and political order entirely. The purpose of the *Social Contract* is to leverage this image for political reconstitution. Rousseau writes in the *Social Contract*, "If one inquires into precisely what the greatest good of all consists in, which ought to be the end of every system of legislation, one will find that it comes down to these two principal objects, *freedom* and *equality*."[140] To make men pursue and feel passionate about these objects, they must be reminded, as he writes in the *Second Discourse*, that by nature man "breathes nothing but repose and freedom,"[141] that the "essential Gifts of Nature" are "life and freedom,"[142] and that the state of nature was one in which inequality did not exist: "The equality nature established among men [has been destroyed by] the inequality they have instituted."[143] Men in the state of nature were "naturally as equal among themselves as were the animals of every species."[144] This is the "first origin" of man[145]—an origin that has, according to the narrative of the *Second Discourse*, been forgotten.[146]

If "man is born free, and everywhere he is in chains," the principal goal of political change ought to be man's "recovering its freedom."[147] The human being must be persuaded to use his perfectibility—his unique capacity to remake and change the world around him—to refashion his political circumstance. In seeing his freedom, the human being thus becomes conscious of his ability to recall the conditions of his subjugation and to regenerate them into a legitimate form. The *Second Discourse* is the attempt to make human beings conscious of themselves; the *Social Contract* provides the means for a conscious and determined shift toward a more free and independent existence. Because the source of liberty always remains outside of the compact or convention itself, however, there is no closed loop for Rousseau. No polity will ever satisfy the desire for freedom and independence, and human beings will always maintain a claim against the rights and freedoms they establish for themselves in the state.[148] Convention and dependence—in both legitimate and illegitimate forms—are subject to perpetual alteration by the creatures who create and maintain the conditions of their own existence.

The artifice, or conventional definition, of the freedom and equality that could be achieved in the *Social Contract* is essential to the legitimacy of the state. Chapter 1 of book 1 establishes immediately that the "social order is a sacred right, which provides the basis for all the others. Yet this right does not come from nature; it is therefore founded on conventions."[149] Because "conventions remain as the basis of all legitimate authority among men,"[150] the act of association creates a "moral and collective body" that is meant to supplant the natural and "produces a most remarkable change in man."[151] In the state, "what man acquires is civil freedom," whereas what he "loses by the social contract is his natural freedom."[152] When the social contract is renounced, it is thus our "conventional freedom" that goes with it, along with all of its attendant inalienable rights.[153]

While Rousseau is not as attentive to parsing out distinctions concerning equality, the same could be said of the transformation of equality in the institution of the social contract. A moral equality is gained in the state that supplants our natural condition, which Rousseau (very infrequently) associates with a kind of equality of independence. Had inequalities not been socially revered and dependence engendered by communal need, he writes in the *Second Discourse*, things "could have remained equal":[154] "As long as [men] applied themselves only to tasks a single individual could perform and to arts that did not require the collaboration of several hands, they lived free, healthy, good, and happy as far as they could by their Nature be, and continued to enjoy the gentleness of independent dealings with one another; as soon as it was found to be useful for one to have provisions for two, equality disappeared."[155] Rousseau's equality is itself premised on a natural *in*equality: on the different skills that individuals possess by nature and the happiness accorded by the independence of their exercise. Once human beings become socially dependent, this equality of inequalities dissipates immediately through the recognition and imposition of value—through the elimination of the independence from and the indifference we have toward one another in nature.

The move toward dependence on others is therefore irrevocably coupled, for Rousseau, with the first step toward the vices of inequality, just as it is with the loss of our natural liberty and independence. The illegitimate contract of the *Second Discourse* is also meant to demonstrate that the men who rushed toward their chains thinking they were securing their freedom also believed that this act was uniting them under an equality designed to "protect and defend all the members of the association."[156] The promise of equality in the *Social Contract*, on the other hand, depends entirely on the awareness of its conventional establishment; in finding themselves unequal, men must substitute this inequality for "a moral and legitimate equality . . . [so that] while [men] may be unequal in force or genius, they all become equal by convention and by right."[157]

But for Rousseau, doing so would not truly eliminate the problem of equality, which is that it is possible to be equal while also being unfree. The conclusion of the political story of the *Second Discourse* provides a grim picture of the consequences of the course of human dependence, ending in a condition in which we are ruled by a despot. "Here is the last stage of inequality," Rousseau writes, "and the ultimate point which closes the Circle and touches the point from which we set out: This is where all private individuals again become equal because they are nothing. . . . [This is] a new State of Nature, different from that with which we began in that the first was the state of Nature in its purity, whereas this last is the fruit of an excess of corruption."[158] The men that were "naturally as equal among themselves as were the animals of every species" are here returned to a condition of equality—against their wills, and contrary to their freedom and independence.[159] "Under bad governments," Rousseau writes, "equality is only apparent and illusory."[160]

The legitimate rule of the *Social Contract* bears an eerie resemblance, however, to the despotic equality that concludes the *Second Discourse*. The rule of the general will would entail "the total alienation of each associate with all of his rights" through which "each, by giving himself to all, gives himself to no one."[161] This is a kind of mirror image of the form of rule in which all are equal because they are nothing, and it is an image that has led those like Talmon to identify Rousseau with a form of totalitarian democracy. This reading of Rousseau presumes, however, that the *Social Contract* presents us with a system that is supposed to be permanent, rather than foundationally permeable and regenerative. Rousseau acknowledges that the coming together of this alienation with the preservation of our freedom is so fragile, and that "the clauses of this contract are so completely determined by the nature of the act that the slightest modification would render them null and void; so that although they may never have been formally stated, they are everywhere the same, everywhere tacitly admitted and recognized; until, the social compact having been violated, everyone is thereupon restored to his first rights and resumes his natural freedom while losing the conventional freedom for which he renounced it."[162] Rousseau insists on the priority of the first right to call back the very conditions of our rights and equality—the right that is prior even to that which we consider inalienable.

Whatever equality we are capable of achieving in a legitimate social contract is thus both unnatural and, like our inalienable rights, fundamentally impermanent: equality, like political right, is revocable and contingent, never guaranteed even when it appears to be so. Like the image of our freedom in the *Second Discourse*, the fleeting image of equality that Rousseau provides of our naturally independent existence is designed for a regenerative purpose. Together, the *Second Discourse* and *Social Contract* are meant to inspire people to become what they believe they are (naturally free and independent) by changing what they are (human beings in the world, unfree and dependent). But for Rousseau, a confluence or compatibility of "what we believe we are" and "what we are" is, at root, impossible: there can be no natural polity, no genuinely independent dependence, no conventionally natural person.

So too will there never be a condition of perfect political equality. While Rousseau claims in the *Second Discourse* that the form of government closest to nature is a democracy, formed by those "whose fortunes or talents were less uneven, and had moved least far from the State of Nature," he writes in the *Social Contract* that "a genuine democracy never existed, and never will exist. . . . If there were a people of Gods, they would govern themselves democratically. So perfect a government is not suited to men."[163] A genuine political equality, like a truly independent natural freedom, is unachievable. But it is precisely this impossibility of the resolution of nature with convention that makes Rousseau's politics emancipatory and regenerative. The human being is never going to be perfectly one with the political order, and so the political order always remains subject to the human claim to determine its contours. The question of the human in the world is never settled, always open, and always subject to regeneration. Our rights and equality are not incontrovertible facts upon which to build a state, and they are not facts of human nature seen to be properly achieved by our conventional regimes. The self-regenerating human being cannot be solved by its political order—it makes it and makes itself by changing the world.

When Rousseau is translated into the rhetoric of the French Revolutionaries, his vision of human nature and of the potential for political reconstitution renders itself into a transformative and powerful rights discourse. The overturning and remaking of the state in the French Revolution and the universalizing Declaration of the Rights of Man and of the Citizen were propelled by a distinctively regenerative mode of conceptualizing the rights of human beings. The revolutionaries, drawing on and out of Rousseau's reimagining of human nature, saw that the foundational political motivation was not that humans have natural rights to claim but that human beings have the natural claim to make rights. When Pierre-Toussaint Durand de Maillane declared at the National Convention in 1789, "A people that has lost its rights, and that demands them, must know the principles of its regeneration,"[164] he was calling on this regenerative and self-making vision of the human person, affirming the essential mutability of convention and its reliance on the human claim to always recall and remake its own political definition and constitution. The *act*, rather than the object, of the Declaration was the formative and regenerative activity of the human being at liberty to reconstitute itself in and against the world. As François Furet has argued, it is thus "by virtue of the project of regeneration that the Revolution belongs to Rousseau."[165]

A FIRST RIGHT AGAINST RIGHTS

Rousseau's theory of the state of nature was an intentional rupture from that of his predecessors. In going further back to nature and to the nature of the human being, Rousseau also discovered and established what he saw as a truly universal and primordial first right: the right to make rights themselves.[166] The apolitical and anticivilizational image of the natural human being facilitated the sequence of the historical story told in the *Second Discourse*, which established that no political or social order could be seen as natural to the human being and thus that all social and political orders were, as conventions, subject to reconstitution and alteration. It is precisely because the human being possesses *no* inalienable rights that he is, by nature, capable of exercising his freedom—as Rousseau shows, this is a freedom that must be exercisable against the very concept of inalienable rights presented in illegitimate social contract theories. No political right is inalienable, and all polities, all societies, all historical epochs are just as capable of degenerating as they are of being regenerated.[167] So, too, is it the case that any condition of equality established by convention is not the last word on what human beings are by nature; if it were, we would have no resource, no claim, to make against the kind of equality achieved under a despot in which we are all equally nothing.

Rousseau is by no means a progressive thinker. In fact, his pessimism[168] about the prospect of a positive human reconstitution or regeneration in politics extends to his claim that degeneration begins immediately upon the inception of a newly formed state: "The body politic, just like the body of man, begins to die as soon as it is born."[169] This pessimistic outlook is also where Rousseau fundamentally departs from his natural-scientific interlocutors who maintained a kind of progressive optimism about the passage of time. Politics is for Rousseau a regenerative enterprise—but it is not linearly progressive. It lives and dies continually throughout history: "If Sparta and Rome perished, what State can hope to last forever? If we want to form a lasting establishment, let us therefore not dream of making it eternal."[170] Instead, for a lasting polity, Rousseau focuses on the "principle of political life," the sovereign authority of the state, which is the active power of a legitimately legislating government.[171] This political life rests first on the life it is granted by the human beings who constitute its motive power as the sovereign body—a life force that is renewable across generations and over many lifetimes but only if it is actively and vigilantly regenerated. This requires that the human beings making up the body politic, who always and universally have the right to renounce their dependence entirely, maintain their affirmation of its rights and principles.

In "Considerations on the Government of Poland"— written as a set of practical principles for the rejuvenation of the country—Rousseau put this theory into more particular terms of advice. He details the means by which the Poles could come to love liberty and to give themselves a "second birth."[172] Just as Bonnet claims in "Essai de psychologie" that education is a "*second birth* which imprints new determinations" and is a force that "modifies the force of the natural,"[173] Rousseau claims in "Poland" that this "second birth" depends on an education that will teach the men of the country to "make and keep it happy and free."[174] He writes that the educational program for Poland is one in which we must "infuse, so to speak, the soul of the confederates into the entire nation, to establish the Republic in the hearts of the [citizens]."[175] Continually drawing his readers back to the *Social Contract*, Rousseau claims that the Poles must learn most of all to "love freedom."[176] Replicating exactly the palingenetic language of Buffon and Bonnet, Rousseau writes that learning to love freedom will facilitate the act of Poland *"renewing itself so to speak by itself."*[177]

While many have seen only totalitarian conformity in Rousseau's work, I see instead an emancipatory, regenerative politics. It is the human being's fundamental irreducibility to political convention—even to that of his own making—that contains the universal and ever-present potential of the human claim against the political order. What Rousseau shows most acutely is that rights can survive only so long as humans choose to remain actively dependent on them because humans can always make a universal claim *against* rights, and against the conventional world in which they find themselves. The recognition that all political rights rest on the first right of the human being to refuse them is a genuinely transformative rights doctrine for the modern world—one that the revolutionary actors recognized and seized for their own political aims, regenerating themselves by themselves in the French Revolution and its Declaration of rights.

4

REGENERATION AND REVOLUTION

The French Revolution was saturated with the language of regeneration, and the political use of this term was entirely new to this historical epoch. Alyssa Sepinwall traces the swift transformation and political appropriation of *régénération* across the century in the definitions of the *Dictionary of the French Academy*.[1] In 1762, the following two meanings of *regeneration* are provided:

1) the regeneration of the flesh/ it is said in chemistry *la régénération des métaux*; and
2) speaking of baptism/ it is said figuratively for Renaissance, *There is no salvation without regeneration in Jesus Christ*.[2]

In the sixth edition of the dictionary published in 1835 (following the Revolution), however, a new figurative sense is added:

1) Reproduction cf. the regeneration of flesh/ it is used figuratively and means Reformation, improvement, renewal. *The regeneration of morals. The regeneration of a people*; and
2) is also said figuratively in speaking of Baptism and means Renaissance/ *The regeneration in Jesus Christ*.

As early as 1798, when the fifth edition was published, the Academy also wrote that *regeneration* "symbolically signifies correcting, reforming, extirpating the root of abuses and vices 'to regenerate morality' or to 'regenerate an Empire.'"[3]

Contemporary scholars have addressed the revolutionary appropriation of *regeneration* in relation to the politicization of its Greek root, *palingenesis*, deriving, Roger Griffin writes, "from *palin* (again, anew) and *genesis* (creation, birth)."[4] Griffin contends in *The Nature of Fascism* that regenerative, or palingenetic, politics in the modern world is almost exclusively a form of "populist ultra-nationalism," which invokes "the myth of renewal, of rebirth."[5] This regenerative thinking is tied to the French Revolution's culmination in the violent and bloody Reign of Terror under the rule of Maximilien Robespierre and was cast forward to the fascistic regimes of the twentieth century. While Griffin concedes that all political ideologies "assume a palingenetic dimension when they operate as a revolutionary force to overthrow an existing order," he claims that it is distinctively characteristic of a fascistic regime to remain committed to a "continuing palingenesis": "fascism's mythic power" can sustain itself only through the "momentum and cohesion [of] continually precipitating events which [seem] to fulfill the promise of permanent revolution."[6] Fascism is committed, as were the Jacobins, to a community *"yet to be realized"*; thus, society and the human being require a kind of rebirth instigated by political reconstitution.[7]

Drawing a line from the palingenetic Jacobins to modern fascism is not uncommon, and most often this association passes through a condemnation of Rousseau. Waller Newell claims that we can trace a line from "Rousseau's Legislator, who 're-creates' human nature with a godlike determination, and from there to the incorruptible Robespierre, a prime example of the 'secular saint' who destroys thousands, without personal malice, for the sake of the collective. It leads finally to ascetic police state mass murderers including Dzerzhinsky and Himmler."[8] Bertrand Russell sees in Rousseau "the complete abrogation of liberty and the complete rejection of the doctrine of the rights of man."[9] Of Rousseau's philosophy he writes, "Its first-fruits in practice was the reign of Robespierre; the dictatorships of Russia and Germany (especially the latter) are in part an outcome of Rousseau's teaching."[10] If it is "by virtue of the project of regeneration that the Revolution belongs to Rousseau,"[11] the regenerative project stands condemned with him.

The radical Jacobins who perpetuated the Terror were undeniably committed to regeneration. Sean Quinlan writes, for example, that "much has been made, quite correctly, of the Reign of Terror as a force of regeneration. During the radical revolution, regeneration assumed its most disturbing guises, drawing upon images of heroic sublimation, self-sacrifice, redemption through violence and purification by blood. J. L. David's violent works such as *The Triumph of the French People* (1793–4) demonstrate this point; similar images of masculine rebirth can be found in J.-L. Parée's popularized engraving, *L'homme régénéré* (1795)."[12] The Jacobins famously installed the Fountain of Regeneration in 1793 at the site of the Bastille (figure 4.1). It was to be used as part of the celebration of the Cult of the Supreme Being, and the "milk spouting from a female statue's breasts [was meant to] spark the nation's regeneration."[13]

FIGURE 4.1 The Fountain of Regeneration.

La fontaine de la régénération sur les débris de la Bastille, le 10 août 1793.

Drawing by Charles Monnet, engraving by Stanislas Helman (Paris: Musée de l'Armée, 1798). Public domain.

At the inaugural Festival of the Supreme Being, Marie-Jean Hérault de Séchelles proclaimed, "Sovereign of the savage and enlightened nations, O Nature! This immense people gathered together, at the first rays of day, before your image, is worthy of you: it is free. It is in your womb, it is in your sacred springs that it has regained its rights, that it has regenerated itself. . . . Those fruitful waters which spring from your breasts, and that pure drink which nourished the first humans, consecrate in this cup of fraternity and equality the oaths which France makes to you on this day."[14] So too did Séchelles state to the "French People," "Nature had made you free; Slavery then degraded you; You have regained your liberty. By this return to the rights of nature, you have regenerated yourself."[15]

For Mona Ozouf, these regenerative Jacobins represented the new sense of regeneration as "a limitless program," which was "at once physical, political, moral and social" and "aimed for nothing less than the creation of a new people."[16] The historian Lynn Hunt also writes that the Terror sprouted from the effort "to reconstitute human nature" as swiftly and completely as possible.[17] As the culmination of the revolutionary commitment to remaking the human being, the Jacobin project associates regeneration with the presumed limitlessness of modernity and of the modern self. A humanity that now "had to construct itself out of itself" was seen to be released from any natural limitation, set forever on a course in which history and its progressive human self-reconstitutions were boundless.[18] Rousseau is also looped into this associative interpretation when he is seen as the "father of progressive history"[19] and the thinker who took the "crucial first step toward the concept of the self-defining, self-grounding subject" by presenting a "radically historical understanding of human nature."[20]

The link between Rousseau and the Jacobins is claimed by the leader of the Jacobin Club, Maximilien Robespierre, who declared Rousseau "worthy of the ministry as preceptor of humankind."[21] Robespierre adopted Rousseau's regenerative philosophy, believing that men could recreate themselves and give themselves a "second birth" by reconstituting the state in the name of nature. The Jacobins desired to "return France to 'nature' and to a *seconde naissance* ["second birth"]. 'If nature created man good,' declared Robespierre, 'he must be brought back to nature.'"[22] In his *Mémoires* of 1778, Robespierre promised Rousseau that he would "remain constantly faithful to the inspiration I have drawn from your writings."[23]

The association of Robespierre with Rousseau seems to have forever sealed Rousseau's political fate, perpetually binding him to the despotic extreme of the end of the French Revolution. So, too, has the regenerative thrust of the Terror inextricably tied the idea of political regeneration itself only to totalizing violent upheaval, in what Kevin Duong has recently termed "redemptive violence."[24]

One of the core concerns of French Revolutionary historiography is to sort out the place of the Terror in relation to the rest of the revolutionary project. The Terror is seen as either the necessary conclusion of French Revolutionary principles or a corruption of them. As Darrin McMahon states, the Terror was either "a perversion, an aberration, in no way related to the glorious achievements of the first, moderate revolution of 1789–1792," or "the revolutionary project was a unified undertaking, [and] the Terror inscribed the dynamics of *philosophie*."[25] Marcel Gauchet has recently written, too, that in all of this Robespierre can "be either the saint or the demon," a defender of the "rights of man" or a "precursor of Lenin."[26] In the battle over the causes and legacy of the French Revolution, the push for regeneration is assigned to the root of the Terror and is linked to future fascistic regimes. There is an inevitable relation, Mona Ozouf claims, "between the French Revolution and totalitarianism, both of which seek to create a new man."[27] "Only Rousseau," writes Ozouf, "abandoned all consideration of what was possible, and that abandonment is one of the reasons why the Revolution was all his from the beginning. It was the sudden, unprecedented character of the revolutionary rupture that blazed a trail for the idea of regeneration and made it irresistibly attractive."[28] According to Ozouf, the Revolution converged on the idea of regeneration and resulted in competing liberal and nonliberal interpretations of the regenerative project. It was, however, the "coercive regeneration" that triumphed, containing within itself "the seeds of a totalitarian adventure."[29]

In *Interpreting the French Revolution*, François Furet presents the Terror as "an integral part of revolutionary ideology."[30] For Furet, "Robespierre is an immortal figure not because he reigned supreme over the Revolution for a few months, but because he was the mouthpiece of its purest and most tragic discourse."[31] While he does not wish to call Robespierre a necessary result of Rousseau's political philosophy, he nevertheless believes that Robespierre is the most crystallized expression of "the democratic principle" that was "explored by Rousseau": a coming together of self- and political reconstitution "fused in the discourse of the people's will."[32] Furet sees the Terror as the logical outcome of the revolutionary project:

> The truth is that the Terror was an integral part of revolutionary ideology, which, just as it shaped action and political endeavor during that period, gave its own meaning to "circumstances" that were largely of its own making. There were no revolutionary circumstances; there was a Revolution that fed on circumstances. The mechanism of interpretation, action and power I have attempted to describe . . . was fully operative from 1789. There is no difference in kind between Marat in 1789 and Marat in 1793. Nor were the murders of Foulon and Berthier fundamentally different from the massacres of September 1792, any more than Mirabeau's aborted trial after the October Days of 1789 was different from the sentencing of the Dantoninsts in the spring of 1793.[33]

While Dan Edelstein does not want to suggest that the logic of the beginning inevitably led to the end of the Revolution in the Terror, he also draws attention to the continuity between 1789 and 1793: "The Declaration of the Rights of Man and of the Citizen is generally viewed as antithetical to the political violence that reached a climax in France in 1793–1794. And yet, at the very height of this repression, its agents repeatedly and enthusiastically proclaimed their adherence to the Declaration and to human rights."[34]

Isaiah Berlin tries to save the liberal principles of the French Revolution—human rights, equality, freedom of speech—from their affiliation with the Terror and sees the end of the French Revolution as a failure to preserve its Enlightenment principles. The counter-Enlightenment position of the Terror, characterized by its "future-directed dynamism"— that is, its regenerative vision of transformation—fundamentally unbound the "set of universal and unalterable principles" that defined the French Enlightenment and the early phases of the Revolution.[35] The "bloodstained monster Robespierre," "together with the notion of Romantic heroism and the sharp contrast between creative and uncreative, historic and unhistoric individuals and nations, duly inspired nationalism, imperialism, and finally, in their most pathological form, fascist and totalitarian doctrines in the twentieth century. The failure of the French

Revolution to bring about the greater portion of its declared ends marks the end of the French Enlightenment."[36] Berlin's vision seeks to detach the "true" principles of liberalism, born of the early phases of the French Revolution, from what he perceives to be the dangerous dynamism of the regenerative Terror.

The affiliation of regenerative politics with totalizing violence and with the radical stream of the Jacobin Terror in the French Revolution is undeniable. The interpretive questions thus revolve around whether the regenerative thrust of the Terror and its attendant violence were already contained in the first phases of the Revolution and whether one could thus abstract the first principles of the Revolution away from their regenerative culmination. The categories in and through which these historiographical debates have occurred, however, obscure the vast influence of the idea of self-regeneration and its deep connection to the development of universal right. As I have argued, the use of regeneration in relation to political and moral reconstitution is indebted to the overall transformation of this idea in the natural science and political philosophy of the French Enlightenment. The emergence of what I have called the palingenetic consciousness of the human being entailed the reimagining of what it means to have a human nature and to have a *first right* to change the conditions of the world and to change oneself in the process.[37]

In the French Revolutionary period, it was not only the Jacobins who invoked these themes. The regenerative spirit called for throughout the Revolution was echoed by both moderate and radical political actors. The Parliamentary Archives reveal 463 results for a search of "regeneration" in 1793 (the year of the Terror) and a similar number, 408, in 1789 (the year of the beginning of the Revolution and the institution of the first Declaration). In 1789, we have calls to "regenerate the nation," to "restore to man his first rights,"[38] and to "regenerate *moeurs* and put an end to corruption";[39] "France can only be regenerated, and in some manner, have a new life, by reconstructing it on those principles as ancient as the world, which are engraved in all hearts and whose nature is to exist, though often forgotten."[40] In 1790, Armand-Gaston Camus makes a speech to the National Assembly: the "Frenchman again becomes a man" when he exercises "his love for liberty, his perfect enthusiasm for gentle enjoyments and the principles of nature. . . . [When] our primitive rights [are] recovered, [and] all servitude annihilated, the most perfect equality [will be] established."[41]

Into 1791 (still a moderate phase of the revolution), we see speeches against material inequality, which, if corrected, would "regenerate *les moeurs* and make men simpler and better."[42] Adrien Duport counsels the National Assembly, "May your views . . . be directed toward the means of inspiring the people with generality . . . and a profound humanity; [cultivate the] virtues . . . so natural, which form the most beautiful character that man can receive from nature and society. To do this, make man respectable to man; increase, reinforce with all the power of the laws, the idea that he must have of his own dignity, [and] you will have done everything by inspiring in him the principle of all the virtues[;] I mean the respect for himself and the pride which is founded not on vain distinctions, but on the full enjoyment of all the rights which belong to man."[43] In 1792, Pierre-Antoine Antonelle reports: "When all the ferments of our old depravities will be destroyed, austere morals will then have regenerated the species. . . . When servitude [has] disappeared, [and there is] a truly new posterity, [there will be] a generation of men created by the constitution and worthy of perfecting it because they will be better. . . . [Then will we] open or renew to the human race the true age of glory and bliss."[44] On August 10, 1792, M. Lavigne states in the National Legislative Assembly that "the decrees of the legislative body . . . had regenerated [the people] to liberty and equality";[45] this year, Pierre Victurnien Vergniaud declares on January 7, 1792, "a nation at last broke its chains, it regenerated itself."[46] At the beginning of the revolution, Louis XVI was even associated with the regenerative promise of a political reconstitution, as was written in the *Memorandum on the Regeneration of the Public Order* (1789): "The king developing the intensity of his thought, imperiously affixing it to the perfect seal of justice, will ordain, will command, that at the instant peace is born, Man [will] be regenerated."[47]

The echoes of Rousseau are unmistakable in the parliamentary materials, with emphases on breaking chains and the invocation of first or primitive rights. Louis-Sébastien Mercier, a moderate of the French Revolution and a member of the National Convention, sang the praises of Rousseau as the regenerator of the human spirit in his *De J.-J. Rousseau considéré comme l'un des premiers auteurs de la Révolution* (1791): "Rousseau was never weary of repeating—Man is at once creator, inventor, builder, and reformer. But the last name is the noblest of all, proclaiming as it does a yet higher degree of intelligence. When, in virtue of these faculties, man

REGENERATION AND REVOLUTION   103

strikes a blow for the regeneration of the world, he will not all at once attain perfection, but he will be able to reduce the sum of his miseries. Every reform is a step towards greater happiness. Meditate carefully the writing of Rousseau—He never ceased to say to Man: use the noblest privilege thou hast! Be a reformer!"[48] As C. E. Vaughan writes of Mercier's pronouncement, "This is not the letter of Rousseau's teaching, as recorded in his books. But Mercier was not wrong in believing it was the spirit."[49]

In this chapter, I provide some more evidence that Rousseau and his natural-scientific interlocutors, Buffon and Bonnet, resonated throughout the regenerative impulse of the Revolution and in many instances were cited and employed explicitly. While these details are important, it is still the case that much of the regenerative motivation for political reconstitution in this period came in the form of what Vaughn calls the "spirit" of the time, or a kind of idée-force: something difficult to substantiate but nevertheless evident everywhere. In the preceding chapters, I established that a regeneration of human nature occurred in eighteenth-century France, reimagining the human being in *modern telic* terms. It is this human being that is everywhere evident in the genesis of the Declaration of the Rights of Man and of the Citizen: one with the right to regenerate itself by making its own political world, thereby transforming the way humans exist. The revolution was not simply an effect of the desire for political reconstitution, but an activated awareness—or palingenetic consciousness—on the part of the revolutionary actors, motivating them to transform their world, and themselves, and binding them to the process of making their rights through affirming a universal nature in their particular historical context.

Employing the language of Rousseau in the États généraux and National Legislative Assembly, the restoration of man to his "first rights" was a demand for a regenerative political life;[50] it was a human claim *against* the political or conventional order calling for human beings to be put back into that political and conventional order as regenerative actors instead of suffering recipients. In the swift degeneration into the Terror, however, this human claim against rights and convention illuminated the risk of a regenerative politics, which is that it can always turn against political rights. This turn against rights is precisely what has sealed the association of regeneration with the Terror and with what became contemporary totalitarianism—an association that is not incorrect. What I wish to debunk here is the presumption that regeneration belongs exclusively to these political outcomes. The regenerative vision of the human being was equally essential to the inception of universal right in the French Revolution, and the revolutionary actors understood and harnessed the power of self-regeneration—the creation of a "New Man"—to make and claim their rights. Universal rights and regeneration were not a contradiction in terms; they were bound together.

While I do not believe that the link between rights and regeneration in the French Revolution means that any regenerative project will inevitably descend into terror, I also do not think that the establishment, maintenance, and protection of rights can be assured by rejecting the regenerative political mode. The assumption that rights can survive only if they are detached from the kind of regenerative politics that characterized the Terror is incorrect, and it is a mistake to think that we can extract the abstractions of rights and their attendant universalism from the regenerative self-understanding of our first right that is required for their maintenance and preservation. The rights of the French Revolution depended on the openness of the humans involved in political remaking to the prospect of their own reconstitution. The risk of the Terror may always be present in the modern telic conception of the human being, but with this risk the regenerative conception of rights also offers a corresponding openness to all human claims. While the self-regenerating human being may give itself rights through political reconstitution, however, no political right is assured unless it has what Rousseau called a political life: the desire for its maintenance by those human beings who made it, and the palingenetic consciousness that the self-as-free-and-equal exists universally only if—or once, or so long as—it exists contingently. Our first, regenerative right was the motivating force of the French Revolutionary Declaration's political life, and it was in this spirit that change was effected so magnificently.

THE REVOLUTIONARY MODERN TELIC

Though Rousseau did not explicitly use the language of regeneration, in the French Revolutionary period his name became synonymous with it. Joan McDonald writes that second only to Emmanuel Joseph Sièyes's

Qu'est-ce que le tiers-état ? (*What Is the Third Estate?*), the most widely read pamphlet on the convocation of the États généraux was *Mémoire sur les États généraux* by Louis-Alexandre de Launay, comte d'Antraigues, which appeared in three reprintings from 1788 to 1789. In the first part of the pamphlet, which reads like a summary of the first three books of the *Social Contract*, d'Antraigues employs Rousseau's work as the "basis for the regeneration of the state."[51] While McDonald acknowledges d'Antraigues's detailed invocation of Rousseau for the purposes of regeneration, she objects to the association of regeneration with Rousseau, claiming that he does not in fact have a theory of regeneration but rather that the concept was simply " 'in the air' ":[52] "The word 'regeneration' was on the lips of many orators and writers from 1788 onward, [and so] d'Antraigues may be regarded as writing in the language of his times rather than as spreading a new idea culled from the pages of the *Social Contract*."[53]

McDonald's analysis is grounded in the presumption that what Rousseau wrote was of no import to the association of his work with the idea of regeneration and that the revolutionaries were not careful readers of Rousseau.[54] But, in fact, as James Swenson demonstrates, the revolutionaries read both his moral and political works as regenerative texts. Swenson links the interest in Rousseau's sentimental works and his political treatise explicitly through the idea of regeneration. *Emile* and *La nouvelle Héloïse* are individual, subjective accounts of regeneration that were appropriated for the political context: "The experience of subjective regeneration and renewal . . . must have at the very least suggested a powerful analogy to the demands made for a regeneration of the nation."[55] As Judith Shklar has written, too, while one of Rousseau's favorite activities was to complain that he was misunderstood, in fact "those who read him understood him very well . . . [and] he was understood by [a] highly intelligent and knowledgeable audience."[56] While Shklar argues that Rousseau is assuredly writing to an audience much wider than that of his Enlightenment contemporaries—in speaking of the great and perennial subject of human nature—if one is going to discuss the import of Rousseau's thought, attention must be paid to those with whom he was engaged and those who read and engaged with him.

Ample evidence demonstrates that the revolutionary actors were quite sophisticated readers of Rousseau and that they did read a theory of regeneration into his work, informing how they conceived their first right and their capacity to change their own natures in the world. D'Antraigues is merely one example of many who invoke Rousseau in the name of regeneration. Gary Kates writes that at the 1790 opening address of the Cercle social (a French Revolutionary organization, also known as The Society of the Friends of Truth), "the participants pushed and shoved though the door. . . . Included among the well dressed people were deputies of the National Assembly, local politicians, and members of other patriotic societies."[57] They had all come to hear the opening address of Claude Fauchet: "'A magnificent idea brings us together,' Fauchet began. 'It concerns the beginning of the confederation of men, the coming together of useful truths; tying them into a universal system, getting them accepted into national government; and working in general harmony with the human spirit to compose world happiness.' The French revolution had inaugurated an 'epoch of regeneration,' wherein all states would recognize the essential goodness of men and exploit potential love among them. France was the vanguard of a 'regeneration of the social order.'"[58] Fauchet grounded this regeneration in the philosophes, "all of the profound political writers," which included Montesquieu, Mably, and Raynal. But "there was one book that itself had revolutionized political language and summarized all of the important political themes of the new epoch: Jean-Jacques Rousseau's *Social Contract*."[59] Fauchet in fact announced that each subsequent meeting of the group "would be devoted to a particular section of the *Social Contract*."[60] He founded a revolutionary book club, which ran from October 1790 to April 1791, to usher in this new epoch of regeneration. Restif de la Bretonne's literary series, published from 1769 to 1789, also contained a volume entitled *The New Émile*, which examined and paid homage to Rousseau's *Émile*. Bretonne's text, Antoine de Baecque writes, "located the foundations of the dreams of total regeneration of society, its morals, and thus of the subtlest forms of society, in a utopian space."[61]

The most stunning example I have located, however, is François d'Escherny's "Éloge de J. J. Rousseau," written and published in 1790.[62] D'Escherny begins by proclaiming Rousseau the man who "brought the lost titles of the nobility of our origins back to the human race" and "who recalled men to the simplicity of nature."[63] It is by Rousseau's works, d'Escherny claims, that France is able to "regenerate its empire."[64] While this sounds like the work of a general sentimentalist, d'Escherny acknowledges that Rousseau thought deeply about paradoxes, and d'Escherny spends much of his work explicating Rousseau's philosophy. He discusses Rousseau's relationships to Descartes, Fontenelles, and Montesquieu and claims that Rousseau approaches philosophic paradoxes with the "timid march of a skeptic."[65] The most foundational paradox, according to d'Escherny, is that of nature, which he analyzes through Rousseau's *Emile* and *Second Discourse*.[66] To understand Rousseau's work, it is "necessary to find out what nature is."[67]

D'Escherny writes that there are in fact two models of nature in Rousseau's work: one the simplistic origin and the other, to which it is bound, the "ideal model." This is what d'Escherny calls the Archimedean point of Rousseau's work: "Archimedes demanded one point to support the globe, to raise the world. What Rousseau said, what Rousseau did, executed it. . . . He seized upon a state that never existed, a state at odds with everything that exists; This is the state of nature, in which he finds his support. By making this metaphysical lever move, it raises and renews the whole system of our moral knowledge, [and] disrupts all of our ideas."[68] It is by using and applying this model that we can regenerate the state. The word *nature* for Rousseau involves goodness and a kind of perfection, but nature in its second sense is truly an "ideal model of perfection."[69] It is from this model, d'Escherny writes, that "all his writings breathe humanity, the taste of virtue, and the love of equality and liberty. It is on this model that we base the principles of natural and political law."[70] This is the model employed in *Emile*, in which the paradox of the human condition is expressed: "Everything is natural in man, and he alone is the source of art, and in this sense art belongs to nature."[71] The "art of forming men is the first of all the arts [and] is the foundation of the social order,"[72] and so, d'Escherny claims, we must use our natural art to make ourselves natural through regeneration.

D'Escherny thus asserts that Rousseau is himself the Archimedean point of the revolutionary spirit with precisely the regenerative structure I outlined in the previous chapter. It is Rousseau's image of the first state of nature—or the first right—that informs and motivates the transformation of political rights; but only because we can harness our human nature (that is, in Rousseau's terms, our perfectibility) to make ourselves natural (free and equal). Rights insofar as they are to be proclaimed in the Declaration are transformations to be achieved by human beings in the world through a co-constitutive process of political and self-regeneration.

For human beings to *be* free and equal, according to nature and according to natural right, they must make themselves so through political regeneration. As Mona Ozouf has written, the "New Man" of the French Revolution was thus both "the beginning and the end of the enterprise," and this is precisely what d'Escherny recognized in Rousseau's philosophy and natural man.[73]

This is the modern telic vision of the human being, asserted most comprehensively by Rousseau and Buffon and translated into the political program of the French Revolution. The postulation of an original prototype of the human being—a universal and unchanging nature—is met in equal terms of importance with the assertion that human beings and their environments are subject to transformation and change and can be changed at the hands of human beings. Seemingly paradoxical but entirely coherent, the self-regenerative vision of humanity holds that human beings must use what they are by nature (creatures of perfectibility, change, and historical context) to become what they are by nature (universally free and equal). The 1789 Declaration of the Rights of Man and of the Citizen relied on men asserting rights by nature through regenerating the morals and institutions of the state—and in regenerating the state, the revolutionaries were, as they knew, regenerating themselves. The act of instituting the Declaration provided documentary evidence of and for the regenerative project, beginning with the statement, "The representatives of the French People, formed into a National Assembly, considering ignorance, forgetfulness or contempt of the rights of man to be the only causes of public misfortunes and the corruption of Governments, have resolved to set forth, in a solemn Declaration, the natural, unalienable and sacred rights of man, to the end that this Declaration, constantly present to the members of the body politic, may remind them unceasingly of their rights and their duties."[74]

The revolutionaries poetically expressed their palingenetic consciousness of making history through remaking themselves in their 1789 pamphlet *Political Painter, or The Rate of Present Operations*:

> The epoch of a new revolution is moving on the wings of time. . . . The earth opens up, entire regions disappear; the sea takes their place; the universe seems to reach its dissolution. But no, on the contrary, another world has arisen from its waters, under which it has been fertilized and made fruitful, in order to feed thousands of generations, who will disappear one

day along with it, when the need for a renewal has returned. The course of events is the same on the surface of the earth. All that exists, all that crawls on the earth, disappears only to provoke a new procreation. Thus everything is destroyed and re-created alternately: everything masters and yields in its turn. This variation stems from nature. It makes itself felt morally, physically, politically.[75]

This is the regenerative universe of Buffon and Bonnet, and in it man is seen as the regenerative agent: capable of effecting epochal change by regenerating himself in the world and in time.[76] This vision was conflated with Rousseau's by Fauchet, who declared an "epoch of regeneration" with the institution of the Declaration. Mercier also declared the beginning of a new epoch of human history in his "Farewell to the Year 1789": "Great year! You will be the regenerating year, and you will be known by that name. History will extol your great deeds."[77]

McDonald's dismissal of the influence of Rousseau on the regenerative politics of the eighteenth century is grounded in the presumption that for something to be "in the air" or to have informed the "spirit" of a transformative age, it must have been achieved in a nonspecific and unparticularized way. On the contrary, I believe that it is because of the specifics of Buffon's, Bonnet's, and Rousseau's image crafting of the self-regenerating human being that we see the language of regeneration permeating the French Revolution, and witness the idea of the self-regenerative human being propelling political change and the reconstitution of rights.[78] Regeneration was employed in the Revolution to the end of making rights and involved the invocation of the first right that belongs to all human beings to freely constitute their own nature in the world. In this respect, many rights of the Declaration were inspired by the work of a wide variety of philosophes or scholars[79]—but the *act* of making those rights, inspired by the vision of the self-regenerative human being, was as an idée-force the first origin of them all.

REGENERATING RIGHTS

The materials from the Parliamentary Archives spanning the period of the French Revolution show that regeneration was understood as a transformative force belonging to human beings through which they could activate their "first rights"—often identified with "principles as ancient as the world" and a "primitive" condition—in making themselves human beings with political rights. With a successful Declaration and revolution, there would be a "generation of men created by the constitution," and a world would "open or renew to the human race."[80] The regenerative project of the French Revolution was thus not solely totalitarian, belonging only to the Terror; rather, as Sean Quinlan has written, "the evidence suggests that revolutionaries experienced physical and moral rebirth as profoundly authentic and associated it with individual emancipation. . . . Individuals saw revolution as a positive force in personal transformation."[81]

The emancipatory side of regeneration in the French Revolution is most commonly tied to one figure: the revolutionary leader and abolitionist Henri Grégoire (also referred to as the Abbé Grégoire). Grégoire is "depicted at the forefront of Jacques-Louis David's famous painting, *The Tennis Court Oath*, [and he] also presided over the Assembly during the storming of the Bastille, led the efforts to justify the Revolution's nationalization of the Catholic Church, and authored many of the most famous reports on revolutionary cultural policy. One of the most radical members of the National Convention, he was the deputy who introduced the resolution abolishing the monarchy."[82] He also brought forward a motion to the Convention for racial equality in the midst of the Revolution and in 1808 wrote *De la littérature des Nègres*, a text that was widely read and respected in Haiti following from Grégoire's involvement in and commitment to the cause of the Haitian Revolution. Sepinwall writes, too, that "according to Jean Price-Mars, [Grégoire was] the statesman and 'dean of the Haitian intellectuals,' who has been called the father of *négritude*, [and] Haitians 'always devoted a fervent cult to his memory.' Even now, the main shopping street in Pétionville (a wealthy suburb of Port-au-Prince) is called Rue Grégoire."[83]

Sepinwall grounds Grégoire's political advocacy in his "idea of 'regeneration' (making people anew, chiefly through political action)."[84] William Max Nelson also calls Grégoire "one of the central theorists of regeneration" in the French Revolutionary period.[85] Grégoire's regenerative project was rooted in his confidence that human beings could be reconstituted by reconstituting their conditions—and this idea applied to the political circumstances of both France and the colonies. Grégoire's regenerative theory was also tied explicitly to Buffon and to Rousseau: in his famous "Essai sur la régénération physique, morale et politique des juifs" (1788), Grégoire cites Buffon the first time he employs "a *re-* or a *de-* form of generation,"[86] and he drew heavily from Rousseau when speaking at the Convention.[87] A defender of universal suffrage, Grégoire is most well known for his advocacy of the rights of the Jews and peasants of France. He supported extending immediate political rights to all people living in France, including women, and saw this as necessary for the regeneration of human beings. Grégoire stated to the legislature that the degenerate, corrupt, and unequal conditions of France required that the "enormous gap" be filled "between what we are and what we could be. . . . Let us reconstitute human nature by giving it a new stamp."[88]

He also extended this call to the Haitian colony. As Sepinwall writes, "Grégoire's involvement with Haiti during the Restoration has much to teach us about his vision of regeneration for the world during these years since Haiti was the beacon (*phare*) that would spread light to all other nations, including France. 'Free Haiti,' Grégoire noted, 'is a beacon elevated from the Antilles toward which slaves and their masters, oppressed and oppressors, turn their gaze.'"[89] Grégoire brought the regenerative successes of Haiti and France into dialogue with each other, writing, for example, in his Lettre aux citoyens de couleur et nègres libres Paris 1791, 1, 12: "You were men, now you are citizens. . . . One day the sun will shine down among you only on free men; its rays will no longer fall on chains and slaves."[90]

Supporting the extension of political rights to other groups in France and to the colonies following 1789, Grégoire continued the project of determining how to "apply the universalism of [the] Declaration to the realities of French society" and solving the problem of how "difference [could] be reconciled with equality."[91] For Grégoire, as for the other revolutionaries, the solution was a faith in the symbiotic process of political regeneration and self-regeneration. This Enlightenment and revolutionary vision, grounded in the natural-scientific view of Buffon and the political philosophy of Rousseau, saw the universal and the particular—or the natural and the historical—working in tandem in a regenerative conception of human nature, premised on the assertion that human beings are always both universally the same and fundamentally different in the world and in time. Human beings would continue to change, reconstitute, and remake their particular political rights by (re)making themselves into the bearers of those rights in a regenerative self-transformation founded in a universalist claim.

When it came to the Haitian Revolution, the universalism of the French Revolution's demands was harnessed explicitly for its regenerative force in the particular circumstance of the colony.[92] The revolutionary leader Vincent Ogé, who led the 1790 rebellion in Saint-Domingue, saw that liberty was a universal human claim that must be achieved through a regenerative reconstitution of the world. Addressing the Club Massiac in Paris in 1789, he said, "This word liberty that can only be uttered with enthusiasm, this word which embodies the idea of happiness, if only because it seems to want to make us forget the harm we have suffered for centuries, this Liberty, the greatest of possessions, the primary one: is it made for all men? I believe so. Should it be given to all men? Again, I believe so. But how should it be given? This, gentlemen, is for us the greatest and most important of all questions."[93] When the National Assembly in France convened to address Ogé's 1790 revolt, they spoke of both the dangers and triumphs of the Declaration having been received and harnessed in Haiti, using the language of "consecration" to describe the successful institution of rights in France.[94] Toussaint Louverture later adapted this language of self-consecration (or "self-givenness") to describe his revolutionary mission in Haiti: "You are aware, brother[s], that I have undertaken this vengeance, and that I want freedom and equality to reign in Saint Domingue. I have been working since the beginning to bring it into existence to establish the happiness of all of us."[95] Equality and liberty were not rights that were presumed to exist for human beings universally in Haiti except for when they were brought into existence through the regeneration of the state. As Louverture stated, "Brothers and Friends . . . Who is it who laid the foundation for this general liberty, the cause for which you are fighting against your friends? Are we not its originators? . . . Join me and you will enjoy your rights sooner."[96]

The Declaration of the Rights of Man and of the Citizen did not inspire a claim for universal rights in the Haitian Revolution grounded in the equality of possession of those rights by nature.[97] Rather, the Haitian revolutionaries saw and appropriated the truly revolutionary, regenerative motive force of the transformation of rights in the first right of human beings to change and determine the conditions of their world. The human being was the originator of liberty: asserting it as a natural origin while originating it through bringing it into existence in the act of self-determination. The regeneration of the state entailed the regeneration of the self into a rights-bearer from having been—and maintaining the nature of being—a rights-maker. The regenerative politics of rights-making in the French Revolution became a potential source of emancipatory power for other groups in France and in the colonies precisely because people could make *human* claims against established political rights and conventions.

Within France, this regenerative politics also persisted throughout the revolutionary period. While the 1789 Declaration was the first and founding documentary claim of rights, it was subject to much redrafting throughout the Revolution. It was rewritten in 1791 and again in 1793 when Robespierre proposed a revised Declaration to be instituted as part of his refashioning of the state. While the Declaration of the Rights of Man and of the Citizen consecrated rights, it was always understood that the declared inalienable political rights were themselves subject to recall, revision, and regeneration by the universal subjects of their own definition: the human beings who were their originators. The first right of nature served as the motivating force to make rights, connecting the self-regenerating human being to both the efficient cause and the institution and maintenance of his own natural freedom and equality. It was the universal liberty and equality of all persons by nature that made it possible to remake and reconstitute the universal liberty and equality proclaimed in a declaration of rights.[98]

This was precisely the claim that the feminist activist Olympe de Gouges made against the French Declaration, for example, in her Declaration of the Rights of Woman and of the Female Citizen of 1791, in which she compelled her female compatriots to make real for themselves the same freedom and equality now enjoyed by the men: "Women, wake up; the tocsin of reason sounds through the universe; recognize your rights. . . . Enslaved man has multiplied his force and needs yours to break his chains. Having become free, he has become unjust toward his companion."[99] Jacques Rancière offers a compelling analysis of de Gouges's claim for rights in highly regenerative terms, positioning her appeal for political right in the liminal space between the claim of a universal and the demand for historically contingent recognition: "'Women's and citizen's rights' are the rights of those who have not the rights they have and the rights they have not. They are arbitrarily deprived of the rights that the Declaration attributes to the members of the French nation and the human species without discrimination. But they also exercise, by their action, the citizen's rights that the law refuses them."[100] For Rancière, this is the defining action of politics: "the action of subjects who, by working in the interval between identities, reconfigure the distributions of the public and the private, the universal and the particular."[101]

Far from being solely the totalitarian Terror of the Jacobins, regenerative politics in the French Revolutionary period was also the source of emancipatory human claims in both Europe and the colonies. The conception of the self-regenerating human being was integral to the structure of declaring and maintaining universal rights. Only by making real in a particular historical and political circumstance the universal nature that one was presumed to have by virtue of being human was it possible to proclaim a universal right at all. This was also seen as a regenerative process, opening itself up to human claims against the limitations of the political declaration of universality and subjecting itself to the constant potential for recreation and reconstitution. Regenerative politics compelled human beings to be active in the assertion of their universal nature while also forcing the recreation of that nature through conflicts and claims in the world. In this vision, politics is the site of human emancipation, but it is not the final or first source of human freedom. The freedom to regenerate oneself and the world always maintains the place of a first right—outside of the political convention that it has in fact constituted for itself. The tension between this first right and conventional rights is, as Rousseau knew, the principle of political life, and it turns on a perpetual dynamism and openness to regenerative reconstitution. Roger Griffin sees this dynamism—the "continuing palingenesis" of a future "*yet to be realized*" as distinctively fascist mysticism, unique to movements like Jacobinism and Nazism.[102] What the French Revolutionary period reveals, however, is that a continuing palingenesis is also the source of hope for future human emancipation that can be exercised in and through rights.

RISKS AND REWARDS

While my goal here has been to show that a regenerative politics contains the potential for future emancipation, I do not mean to diminish
its significant risks. The regenerative vision of the human being, founded
as it is in the human claim to reconstitute the world—and thus reconstitute the self—by nature, entails both the establishment and the rejection
of political or conventional rights. The positive picture of regenerative
rights is not without its dark sides. Olympe de Gouges was ostracized
and guillotined. While many in France belonged to the *Société des amis
des Noirs* (Society of the Friends of the Blacks), many also opposed the
freedom of Black people living in France and the liberation of slaves in the
colonies. There is also no denying that the open-ended nature of regenerative dynamism facilitated the emergence of Robespierre just as much as
it allowed for the expansion of rights and freedoms.

Marcel Gauchet sees Robespierre as "the man of the Rights of Man
and of the Citizen,"[103] no less committed than Olympe de Gouges to
the refashioning of the human being through political reconstitution:
"The task he set himself had always been to clarify the nature of the
revolutionary movement, to make the chaotic unfolding of events
comprehensible, to point the way forward amidst the fog of circumstances, to illuminate the purposes of the Revolution."[104] You can see this
desire to clarify the principles of the remaking of the human being in
Robespierre's proposed redrafting of the Declaration and Constitution
on June 24, 1793, beginning with a rewritten preamble that emphasized
the Declaration's iterative function for the preservation and consecration of the inalienability of rights:

> The French people, convinced that forgetfulness of and contempt for
> the natural rights of man are the sole causes of the misfortunes of the
> world, have resolved to set forth these sacred and inalienable rights in
> a solemn declaration, in order that all citizens, being able constantly
> to compare the acts of government with the aim of every social insti-
> tution, may never permit themselves to be oppressed and degraded by
> tyranny, in order that the people may always have before their eyes the

bases of their liberty and their happiness, the magistrate the guide to his duties, the legislator the object of his mission. Accordingly, in the presence of the Supreme Being, they proclaim the following declaration of the rights of man and citizen.

1. The aim of society is the general welfare
   Government is instituted to guarantee man the enjoyment of his natural and inalienable rights
2. These rights are equality, liberty, security and property
3. All men are equal by nature and before the law
4. Law is the free and solemn expression of the general will; it is the same
   for all, whether it protects or punishes; it may order only what is just
   and useful to society; it may prohibit only what is injurious thereto.[105]

What Ruth Scurr has called the "fatal purity" of Robespierre's commitment to the rights of man became tied irreparably to his totalizing Terror,
and his allegiance to the enforceability of the general will—a concept that
he drew from Rousseau—led him to his violent reign.[106]

With the postrevolutionary Thermidorian period, following the defeat
and execution of Robespierre, came a swift condemnation and eradication
of regenerative politics. The Constitution of the Year III of August 22,
1795—once again rewritten—eliminated not only the preamble of the
Declaration but also all language of nature and of the co-constitutive link
of nature and the law through political institutions:

Declaration of the Rights and Duties of Man and Citizen:
[no preamble]
The French people proclaim, in the presence of the Supreme Being, the
    following declaration of the rights and duties of man and citizen.
Rights
1. The rights of man in society are liberty, equality, security and prosperity
2. Liberty consists of being able to do whatever is not injurious to the
   rights of others
3. Equality is a circumstance in which the law is the same for all, whether
   it protects or punishes
Equality does not admit any distinction of birth, or any inheritance of
    powers

4. Security is a consequence of the concurrence of all to assure the rights of each individual

. . . .

6. Law is the general will, expressed by the majority of citizens or their representatives.

After the Revolution, rights were stated as facts, not put before people's eyes as objects of their nature to be achieved and preserved through self-reconstitution. In response to the extremes of the Terror, and in fear of future upheavals and revolutions, all natural and regenerative language was removed.

In the next chapter, I provide a postrevolutionary genealogy that replicates this pattern of the Thermidorian Reaction. In the nineteenth and twentieth centuries, efforts continued to extract regenerative dynamism from rights claims and turn instead toward a liberal minimalism for the protection of basic rights and the establishment of negative freedoms. This is what Bernard Harcourt has recently called "liberal legalism": "the idea that we should conform to the rule of law as a way to avoid political strife."[107] At the same time that it has been removed from the liberal conception of rights, the idea of regenerative politics has been reduced to solely a mode of *illiberalism*, associated only with the Jacobin Terror or with violence and carried forward in time into an association with contemporary fascistic regimes and palingenetic ultranationalism. Rights and regeneration in the postrevolutionary period are seen as warring political worldviews.

The nineteenth-century establishment of liberal rights and freedoms as protections from dangerous forms of regenerative politics has obscured the fact that regenerative politics was at the center of establishing the very principle of universal rights. In now seeing regeneration and rights as mutually exclusive forms of politics, it is thus not only that history has been misrepresented. We have in fact lost the dynamism at the core of the conception of universal rights in the modern world. The regenerative conception of rights holds, as I have shown, that no persons are free and equal by nature unless they also make themselves free and equal. Human beings have universal rights by nature only insofar as they make and regenerate their universal rights in the world. In the eighteenth century, this palingenetic consciousness was founded in a modern telic vision of human nature that held that there was a human claim to be made against any particular context. It would seem that a theory of human nature grounded in the fundamental irreconcilability of humans and the conventions they create would facilitate a divide of human beings from their politics—but in fact the inverse is true. A political world that presumes that human rights and human nature are and can be met in the establishment of the correct political order—even if that nature is assumed to be minimally demanding and thus met in a maximally pluralist liberal sphere—by default forecloses the regenerative potential of human beings. Only a political world that holds that its existence is subject to conventional constitution and reconstitution by human beings who are never reducible to or completed by it keeps humans involved and engaged in what Rousseau called "the principle of political life."[108]

The risk of regenerative politics is evident in the French Revolution: that rights won in the political space can always be lost, any shared conception of the human being can be changed, and every polity can degenerate and dissipate. But so, too, can we see the rewards of a regenerative politics: the potential for all human beings to make claims against their political order, the possibility of keeping the question of the human being open, and the maintenance of the dynamism of the political space we make and occupy. Isaiah Berlin wants us to think that the Terror undid the "universal and unalterable principles" that ought to characterize a properly liberal conception of human beings.[109] I do not agree. We did not lose the principles of right through the Terror; rather, the Terror made clear how impermanent the claims are for inalienable rights. The postrevolutionary response of extracting the liberal principles from the Revolution while abandoning any possibility of regenerative reconstitution had the effect of stabilizing certain aspects of our political world. But this outcome was achieved at the cost of the real self-determinative agency of the human beings who constitute those political worlds—who, in the end, always have the right to refuse or reconstitute the political principles they have made.

Gauchet identifies Robespierre as, above all, a reminder of the "destabilizing potential" contained in the modern rights regime.[110] While the liberal rights of 1789 "have enjoyed a magnificent resurgence" and the "year 1793 has unmistakably receded into the realm of the unspeakable," Gauchet worries that although "the original experiment is behind us as a tragedy, more than ever it looms in front of us as a problem."[111]

This, I believe, is what we are witnessing in today's calls for regeneration: a desire for political destabilization against a calcified conception of the human being and its political constitution and, with this desire, the potential for the degeneration or reconstitution of our rights altogether. For liberals, there is a strong temptation to repeat history and to dig into the conception of the self-evident inalienability of rights, insisting that these sorts of regenerative claims are foundationally illiberal and unreasonable. To counteract this temptation, in the concluding chapter of this book I offer an alternative vision of the restoration of our first right: an affirmation of the self-regenerating nature of human beings and their fundamental right to make and remake their political world, even if that means undoing rights. I propose the reunification of rights and regeneration: the two ways of thinking about politics that in the wake of the French Revolution have—as I show in the next chapter—been seen as irrevocably antithetical.

5

AFTER ENLIGHTENMENT

The historian Paul Huot relates a captivating story about the radical Jacobins of the French Revolution in *Les prisonniers d'Orléans: Épisode révolutionnaire* (1868). Huot claims that "after the tenth of August [1792][1] the Jacobins of Versailles (Society of the Friends of the Constitution) marched to the [king's] ménagerie—drum beating, leading with the flag—and the leader declared to the director that they had come in the name of the people and in the name of nature to liberate the beings that had emerged free from the hands of the Creator and had been unduly held by the pomp and the arrogance of tyrants."[2] This image of freeing animals from their prison is saturated with revolutionary symbolism. The slogan "*Vive la liberté*" was often accompanied on posters with birds freed from their cages, and the same image appears in the title illustration of Rousseau's *Social Contract*. Huot's tale suggests, however, that beyond the Rousseauian revolutionary ephemera, the Jacobins were committed to the actual liberation of beasts and that the release of the animals contained in the menagerie at Versailles was an extension of "*liberté et égalité*" to all the creatures of France.[3]

Despite the story's charm and historical perpetuation, however, it is likely "an anti-revolutionary tall tale."[4] While it is unclear when and how this fable about the Jacobins was invented, it is possible to construct a theory as to the purpose of its fabrication. The story is part of a long-standing tradition of associating the Jacobin revolutionaries with a radical commitment to natural equality, grounded in the leveling of man and animal in the work of the eighteenth-century philosophes. The revolutionaries, so the argument goes, were committed to anarchic "social leveling,"[5] spurring on the "light which Philosophy ha[d] spread" in the Enlightenment and undoing social order in the name of unbounded freedom and equality.[6] The Jacobins were described by counterrevolutionary scholars as the denigrators of man, and they were often depicted in reactionary propaganda as beasts themselves.

When Maximilien Robespierre was defeated on 9 Thermidor II (July 27, 1794), the Thermidorian period of French history transformed the radical Jacobin political order into the more conservative republic of the Directory. The Jacobin clubs of Paris were closed, and the Constitution of 1793 was suspended because of its threat of anarchy. François Antoine de Boissy d'Anglas, once an ally of Robespierre, rejected the 1793 document for its seeds of tyranny and for its growth into the beastly Terror. Counterrevolutionary reactionaries condemned not only the Jacobins but also eighteenth-century philosophy and the project of the Enlightenment altogether. Joseph de Maistre wrote that "Rousseau's seductive eloquence deluded the mob, which is controlled more by imagination than reason. Everywhere he disseminated distrust of authority and the spirit of revolt. It was he who systematized ideas of anarchy."[7] At bottom, however, de Maistre claims that "the glory of the revolution belongs exclusively to neither Voltaire nor Rousseau. The entire philosophical sect claims its part."[8] He cites Richer de Sérizy, who reproached the philosophes in his journal *L'accusateur public*: "You, mad philosophes, who in your presumptuous wisdom claim to guide the universe; apostles of tolerance and humanity, you who prepared our GLORIOUS revolution and extol the progress of intelligence and reason: leave your tombs. . . . Your writings are in the pockets of the tyrants; your maxims on their lips; your pages shine forth in their testimony in court. . . . There is not one of your works that is not on the desk of our forty thousand revolutionary committees. They left you only a moment, Diderot, to sign the order for mass drownings!"[9]

The Abbé Barruel's 1797–1798 *Memoirs, Illustrating the History of Jacobinism* is the most lengthy and well-known critique of the Jacobins (its four volumes span approximately three thousand pages). Barruel claims that the French Revolution and all the egregious harms and injustices that were its result derive from the Jacobins, all of whom were philosophic atheists, Illuminati, and Freemasons. He begins the first volume, "At an early period of the French Revolution, there appeared a sect calling itself Jacobin, and teaching that *all men were equal and free!* In the name of their equality and disorganizing liberty, they trampled under foot the altar and the throne; they stimulated all nations to rebellion, and aimed at plunging them ultimately into the horrors of anarchy."[10] Barruel claims that all have been "obstinately blind to the causes of the French Revolution,"[11] which consist primarily in Enlightenment philosophy: Rousseau, Montesquieu, and Voltaire are cited as the most directly responsible, with d'Alembert, Diderot, Condorcet, d'Holbach, and many others also listed as the initiators of the atheistic and terrorizing spirit that would come to haunt the Revolution. In volume 2, Barruel writes that the philosophes "perceived that by means of these two systems, the same ideas of Equality and Liberty, which had proved such powerful agents against Christianity, might prevail also against all political governments. Till this period, the hatred which the school of Voltaire, or the brethren of D'Alembert, had conceived against kings was vague and without any plan. In general, it was a mere thirst after equality and liberty, or a hatred of all coercive authority."[12] The Jacobins propelled the philosophy of the Enlightenment into the political sphere: "What are these great events which the learned atheist claims in the name of philosophy? They are those of a Revolution which discovers man breaking the shackles of slavery, and shaking off the yoke with which audacious Despots had burdened them. It is the people recovering their inalienable right, of making alone the laws, of despising Princes, of changing or continuing them according to their will and pleasure."[13]

In 1755, Hermann Samuel Reimarus identifies Rousseau as a seditious, beastly thinker: "It is well known that M. Rousseau, of Geneva, has lately exerted his imagination, in representing to us, among other animals in a desert, an original man in his natural state, as a brute or something worse (*plus bête que les bêtes*). This is not done, with the view of other writers of the Law of Nature, to shew . . . that such a state is rather unnatural and extremely miserable . . . but to maintain that nature has formed man only for a brutal state, and that he would be most happy in such a state."[14] In the nineteenth century, Hippolyte Taine phrases his aversion to the political anarchy caused by this corruption as "a return to nature, meaning by this the abolition of society. . . . [It] is the war-cry of the whole Encyclopedic battalion. The same shout is heard in another quarter, coming from the Rousseau battalion."[15] The return to nature in eighteenth-century France is cast by the counterrevolutionaries as the destructive triumph of an animalized picture of humanity. The nature of man, tied by Rousseau to the nature of animals, released human beings from all forms of order and all previous conceptions of what was required for human flourishing.

The story of the Jacobins releasing the animals of Versailles resonates throughout counterrevolutionary accounts because it was the perfect example of the kinds of excess to which philosophy might lead: a commitment on the part of the revolutionaries to "changing or continuing [things] according to their will and pleasure," founded in the unlimited right and freedom granted by nature. As Darrin McMahon writes, "Polemicists writing after the Terror picked up, sharpened, and restated long-standing anti-*philosophe* charges, altering them only to accentuate *philosophie*'s inherent trajectory toward the revolutionary telos";[16] "an abstract system, intolerant, fanatical, atheistic, and radical—responsible at once for the moral corruption of the Old Regime and the bloody excesses of the Revolution—these were the charges for which *philosophie* stood condemned and convicted. Whereas anti-*philosophes* during the Old Regime and the early Revolution had looked for signs of the apocalypse on the horizon of the future, their counterparts in the 1790s believed they had witnessed it first hand."[17] De Maistre, Barruel, de Sérizy, and Rivarol forged in their minds an "unbreakable link between *philosophie* and the Terror" that "severed the great chain of being."[18] The openness of the definition of the human being that they had seen in the French Revolutionary period and the corresponding opening up of political possibility were dangers rather than liberations.

Edmund Burke famously condemned the excesses of the French Revolution. Burke cast the position of the revolutionaries and of the philosophes who inspired them as an "insult upon the Rights of Man."[19] The reduction of the human being to its natural definition, according to Burke, degraded humanity: "These philosophers, consider men in their experiments, no more than they do mice in an air pump, or in a recipient of mephitic gas. Whatever his Grace may think of himself, they look upon him, and every thing that belongs to him, with no more regard than they do upon the whiskers of that little long-tailed animal, that has long been the game of the grave, demure, insidious, spring-nailed, velvet-pawed, green-eyed philosophers, whether going upon two legs or four."[20] The philosophes and revolutionaries "betrayed the most sacred of all truths, and by breaking to pieces the great links of society . . . brought eternal confusion and desolation on their country."[21] "The revolution harpies of France," Burke writes, who sprang from "chaotic anarchy, which generates equivocally 'all monstrous, all prodigious things,' cuckoo-like, adulterously lay their eggs, and brood over and hatch them in the nest of every neighbouring state. These obscene harpies, who deck themselves, in I know not what divine attributes, but who in reality are foul and ravenous birds of prey . . . flutter over our heads and souse down upon our tables, and leave nothing unrent, unrifled, unravaged, or unpolluted with the slime of their filthy offal."[22]

The Terror of the French Revolution is thus ascribed to the anarchic animalism of the revolutionaries and to philosophes who disastrously failed to understand the difference between humanity and the rest of nature. In the response of Edmund Burke, in particular, we can see the beginnings of the political categories that would come to define discussions of rights and political reconstitution after the Enlightenment. Against the perceived dangers of the revolutionary project, Burke declares in his *Reflections on the Revolution in France*, "We are not the converts of Rousseau."[23] Following the Revolution, proper human rights are explicitly anti-Rousseauian—they are not Jacobin, they are not revolutionary or unlimited, and they are certainly not subject to regeneration or political reconstitution. A Manichean view of the Enlightenment and its relationship to the Revolution begins to take hold, in which regenerative politics is to be feared and rights are seen as a protection against the reemergence of its foul extremes. Out of this isolation of rights from regeneration, we gain liberalism; when regeneration appears in the world, we experience Romanticism, vitalism, and future fascistic and totalitarian regimes.

The remainder of this chapter is a twinned genealogical account of the emergence of liberalism in response to the French Revolution, which was coupled with a sequestering of regeneration within the realms of antiliberal and rights-denying politics. While there were some nuances in how this dueling Revolutionary inheritance emerged historically, in the contemporary political landscape this nuance is all but nonexistent.

In the wake of the Second World War, rights and regeneration have become entirely antithetical, as have liberalism and regenerative politics.

While many are to blame for this severance in the twentieth century—which crystallized in the Cold War, as Samuel Moyn has recently and convincingly argued[24]—it is Isaiah Berlin who most forcefully propagated it. Berlin not only placed Rousseau in what Moyn has termed the "anti-canon" of liberalism, calling Rousseau "one of the most sinister and formidable enemies of liberty in the whole history of modern thought";[25] more importantly, Berlin clearly and intentionally divided positive from negative freedom as well as regenerative politics from liberal, Enlightenment universalism. The "one set of universal and unalterable principles" that were "the central dogma of the entire Enlightenment"[26] were betrayed and abandoned by postrevolutionary Romanticism, a movement Berlin saw as defined by "perpetual self-creation" and "the notion of the indomitable will: not knowledge of values, but their creation, is what men achieve. You create values, you create goals, you create ends, and in the end you create your own vision of the universe."[27]

Good liberals, according to Berlin, are not regenerative revolutionaries. He writes, "For Constant, Mill, Tocqueville, and the liberal tradition to which they belong, no society is free unless it is governed by at any rate two interrelated principles: first, that no power, but only rights, can be regarded as absolute, so that all men, whatever power governs them, have an absolute right to refuse to behave inhumanely; and, second, that there are frontiers, not artificially drawn, within which men should be inviolable, these frontiers being defined in terms of rules so long and widely accepted that their observance has entered into the very conception of what it is to be a normal human being."[28] This is "almost at the opposite pole," Berlin continues, "from the purposes of those who believe in liberty in the 'positive'—self-directive—sense."[29] The culmination of the French Revolution in the Jacobin Terror was "an eruption of the desire for the 'positive' freedom of collective self-direction on the part of a large body of Frenchmen . . . [and] the result was, for a good many of them, a severe restriction of individual freedoms."[30] For Berlin, the contrast is stark: liberals defend inalienable, unalterable rights and inviolable frontiers; regenerative, tyrannical Romantic thinkers destroy these protections for the human being.

Berlin gives forceful clarity to the lasting effect of the French Revolution: a schism in the heart of what I have called the *modern telic* human being, detaching the self-making, regenerative and historicist side of the *duplex* of human identity from its universalist partner. Both sides of this schism accept some part of the vision of the human being that was born in the Enlightenment. Each side accepts that the human being is universal *or* historically contingent, rights-bearing *or* self-creating, but never both terms together, never the whole. When liberalism came to define itself as more dependent on the conception of the self-evidence and rationalism of rights, so, too, did the idea of regenerative politics and the regenerative human being become a position of reprehensibility, unreason, and inhumanity. Yet because the modern telic human being is the shared root of this schism, the self-conception that informs both liberalism and its enemies in the modern world remains incomplete and at odds with itself. Having spliced this one modern, founding conception of the human being into two, we are currently in a condition in which there are no humans left in the contemporary political world—we have only partial and competing divided beings, and partial and competing political worlds.

COUNTERREVOLUTIONARY LIBERALISM

The descent of the French Revolution into the Terror swiftly brought about a counterrevolutionary and counter-Enlightenment movement. Darrin McMahon describes the core elements of this "emergent right-wing vison": "the fundamental importance of religion in maintaining political order, a preoccupation with the perils of intellectual and social license, the valorization of family and history, the critique of abstract rights, the dangers of dividing sovereignty, and the need for a strategic alliance between throne and altar."[31] "Even more fundamental" to the counter-Enlightenment position, he writes, "was a Manichean readiness to divide the world in two: between good and evil, right and wrong, Right and Left."[32] Predominantly conservative and Catholic, the anti-philosophes saw in the revolutionaries a severance of the connection of "all humans to God. Their abstract individual was thus cut off from the past, their abstract society cut off from all that came before it."[33] This was not a new critique coming from the postrevolutionary Right; rather, the Revolution had confirmed the dangers of leveling human and animal and of the denigration of the human spirit that they had seen in the philosophy of the French Enlightenment: "Their apparent foresight gave to enemies of the *philosophes* a credibility far greater than they had previously enjoyed, and the excesses of the Revolution itself imbued the anti-*philosophe* discourse with renewed explanatory power. Providing a ready means to comprehend the otherwise incomprehensible, the anti-*philosophe* discourse was now directed at the past, indicting the *siècle des lumières* and its leading lights in sweeping, historical judgment."[34]

What was new to this critique was the affiliation of the *siècle des lumières* (Age of Enlightenment) with inevitable political violence. As Graeme Garrard writes, "In the minds of many, the violent excesses of the Revolution tainted the Enlightenment and spawned a new generation of enemies."[35] In what Garrard calls the continuity thesis of the French Revolution, critics like Burke, Barruel, and de Maistre lamented the Revolution's betrayal of humanity, rooted in the abhorrent philosophy of the Enlightenment. For these critics, no distinction was to be made between the Declaration's principles of universalism and the resulting Terror of Robespierre: they were inextricable and one and the same. De Maistre's critique was rooted in the Enlightenment's abandonment of all structures of authority and correspondingly all commitment to order. Jean-Yves Pranchère writes, " 'Think for yourself' is the formula of what Maistre at the end of his life will name individualism. . . . It is, in a certain sense, the very formula of Satanism to the extent that thinking for oneself means: thinking without God, thinking from the self rather than from God. This can also be expressed as thinking without authority, without the authority of a rule of universal truth. . . . Luther, Calvin, Locke, Voltaire, and Rousseau thus appear as the diverse heads of a single hydra, which Maistre summarily describes as 'haine de l'autorité.' "[36] Philosophy's repugnance to authoritative ordering thus led inevitably to the anarchic and disordered violence of the Terror.

In constructing her history of liberalism, Helena Rosenblatt sees Benjamin Constant and Madame de Staël as thinkers committed to rescuing the liberal principles from the Terror in the immediate aftermath of the Revolution, defying the continuity thesis of the counter-Enlightenment critics. Rosenblatt writes that, in contrast to counter-Enlightenment critics, more liberal historians wanted to interpret the Terror as a "derailment of the revolution: a relatively moderate and peaceful first phase [that] gave way to a second, more radical, and more violent one."[37] Constant's *Principles of Politics Applicable to All Governments* (1815) shows that he "had learned the lessons of the Terror and Napoleon's authoritarian rule. He had seen how easily popular sovereignty could ally itself with dictatorship."[38] Liberalism, for Rosenblatt, was thus "forged in an effort to safeguard the achievements of the French Revolution and to protect them from the forces of extremism, whether from the right or the left, above or below."[39] Both Constant and de Staël "wanted to consolidate and protect the main achievements of the revolution by preventing both a counterrevolution and a return of the Terror. . . . Thus began the thinking that would lead to the invention of liberalism."[40]

McMahon sees the same pattern in the postrevolutionary period:

> It was precisely at this moment, in the wake of the Thermidor, that repentant republicans and constitutional monarchists began to elaborate a view of the Revolution that would characterize the liberal position until well into the twentieth century. In this view, the Terror, admittedly, was an abomination. But it was also a perversion, an aberration, in no way related to the glorious achievements of the first, moderate revolution of 1789–1792. If the monster Robespierre and a few bloodthirsty cohorts had succeeded in subverting the laudable principles of 1789, this did not cast aspersion on the revolutionary project itself but rather underlined the pressing need to strengthen these same principles. The search for viable means to ensure them—through the balance of power, constitutional guarantees, and the rule of law—constituted one of the central problems of French politics in the aftermath of the Terror, exercising the faculties of liberal theorists from Madame de Staël and Benjamin Constant to those of important critics in our own day. To these observers, the principles of the Enlightenment—human rights, religious tolerance, freedom of speech, and civil equality—produced the most noble aspects of the Revolution. Under no circumstances could they be held accountable for its excesses.[41]

Those whom McMahon calls "restoration liberals" sought to redeem the Enlightenment philosophes along with the earlier phases of the

Revolution:[42] "Just as they argued that the [moderate Revolution] was necessary and advantageous, betrayed by the Terror but bearing no relationship to it, so did they defend the *philosophes* from charges of extremism, arguing that their humanitarian ideals had also been betrayed by subsequent misinterpretation. The *philosophes* did not cause the Revolution, which was the product of myriad other forces."[43]

The emergence of liberalism in the nineteenth century was thus primarily characterized by its effort to define itself against the perceived causes of the extremes of the Terror. This attempt to save certain aspects of the Enlightenment along with its moderate revolutionary principles—such as human rights, tolerance, and equality—also resulted in a bifurcation of Enlightenment and counter-Enlightenment, or liberal and antiliberal, philosophes. Favored were those like Kant who could be cited in favor of the claim that the Enlightenment was inherently antirevolutionary: "A public can achieve enlightenment only slowly. A revolution may bring about the end of a personal despotism or of avaricious tyrannical oppression, but never a true reform of modes of thought."[44] Slipping into disrepute were thinkers like Rousseau, whose association with the Jacobins was impossible to shake.

But the nineteenth-century reinvigoration of the philosophic roots of the more moderate or liberal phase of the Revolution was met with a renewed and more forceful counter-Enlightenment critique. This time, McMahon writes, the critics directed their ire toward *liberalism*: "In conflating eighteenth-century *philosophie* with nineteenth-century liberalism, critics transposed the principal categories of the anti-*philosophe* discourse onto the modern adversary. Thus, whereas anti-*philosophes* had repeatedly decried *philosophie* as a system—one made up of heterogeneous parts but tending, nonetheless, toward common ends—so did their modern counterparts condemn the *système liberal*."[45] The disorder of the revolutionary spirit was translated into the disorder of the liberal worldview. McMahon shows that in 1821, for example, *La France chrétienne* stated, "The Liberals are in permanent conspiracy against legitimate governments,"[46] and the *Ami de la religion et du roi*, "Do not the Liberals seek without end to advocate or excuse our Revolution and those who took part in it? Do they not constantly praise the revolutions and revolutionaries of other countries? Do they not constantly rally together all seditious persons and all those who are enemies of established governments?"[47]

Barruel's book on Jacobinism was abridged and reprinted in 1829 as an antiliberal screed. Moreover, as Rosenblatt writes, "a series of politically motivated assassination attempts" served as a transformative moment for the denigration of liberalism: "On March 23, 1819, in Mannheim, Germany, a student activist murdered the conservative poet and journalist August von Kotzebue. A few weeks later, an attempt was made on the life of Nassau president Karl von Ibell. Conservatives now intensified their defamation campaign, accusing liberals of instigating assassinations as a prelude to revolution. 'Liberalism is progressing,' [Klemens von] Metternich fumed, 'it's raining murderers.'"[48]

The affiliation of liberalism with Enlightenment philosophy was ground enough for critics to fear that the Terror was inevitably going to repeat itself. The reinvigorated counterrevolutionary reaction compelled liberals to solidify their position against the extremes of the French Revolution by even more explicitly extracting the earlier principles of 1789 from their conclusion in 1793. The accusations of Jacobinism, Rosenblatt writes, "forced liberals to defend themselves, and in so doing, they honed their principles and disseminated them to an ever growing public. Liberals, they insisted, were fighting for the good of everyone. They stood for equality before the law, and constitutional and representative government. Their adversaries, on the other hand, favored despotism."[49] Aurelian Crăiuțu also paints the French liberals as confronting

> the daunting task of finding the best ways of defending and legitimizing the Revolution in the face of its conservative opponents and left-wing critics. On the one hand, liberals such as Constant, de Staël, Guizot, and Royer-Collard stressed again and again that there was no way back into the past and warned that any attempt to restore the Old Regime would be futile and dangerous. On the other hand, the liberals believed that their task was to bring the Revolution to an end by building various representative institutions. "Let us confess without hesitation," claimed Guizot, "As a destructive [phenomenon], the Revolution is done and there is no question of returning to it; as a founding moment, it only commences now."[50]

The Doctrinaires (French liberal Royalists) saw that their task was to "demonstrate that the principles of 1789 could create stable and free government after being 'purged' of any anarchic elements,"[51] many of which were associated with Rousseau.

Whether explicitly or implicitly, the Terror of the French Revolution began to carry with it the associative dangers of democratic sovereignty, anarchy, and regenerative politics. It was in battles over the inheritance of the French Revolution that the Manichean split of rights and regenerative politics began to emerge. Liberals, who believed that rights and freedoms could be protected only through properly instituted government, fashioned themselves as symbols of the good, fighting against the despotism of their critics. The same schismatic framework lay at the base of the accusations of the counterrevolutionaries; for them, it was the liberals who were the Jacobins, and only a more conservatively ordered government and society could properly respect and protect the rights and dignity of human beings. Regenerative political change and the reconstitution of the human being through popular sovereignty were to be feared; rights were the antithesis of this kind of politics, providing stability and order.

To counter the accusations of Jacobinism and distance themselves from the regenerative politics of 1793, liberals therefore transformed themselves into committed defenders of constitutionalism, or what William Selinger has recently called parliamentarism.[52] Selinger writes, "It was the spread and durability of parliamentary regimes that undermined the widespread belief (strengthened by the experience of the French Revolution) that liberal values and a vibrant political sphere were too dangerous to contemplate in most of Europe. By the end of the nineteenth century, insofar as it had seemed increasingly obvious that European nations were capable of free government, this was the achievement of parliamentarism."[53] Selinger sees the turn toward the stability of parliamentarism as already implicit in the French Revolutionary constitutional debates—a phase of the Revolution turned to for support by later liberals such as Jacques Necker, Germaine de Staël, Jean Charles Leonard Simonde de Sismondi, Benjamin Constant, and François Guizot. In their eyes, Selinger writes, "to live in a state ruled by a parliament was to be *free*."[54] Annelien de Dijn sees a similar transformation occurring in the nineteenth century, when liberals "began to propagate a different way of thinking about liberty. Freedom, many came to argue, was not a matter of who governed. Instead, what determined freedom was the extent to which one was governed."[55] De Dijn also sees this change occurring primarily in response to the French Revolution and its "descent into political violence," which "turned many intellectual and civic actors on both sides of the Atlantic Ocean against the effort to introduce bottom-up politics. The resulting counterrevolutionary movement propagated a new understanding of liberty, one that directly contested the democratic view by prioritizing private independence."[56]

As anyone who works on liberalism knows, it is next to impossible to find a set of principles that can define it universally,[57] and much of the recent historical work that I have been discussing here has been done to add some nuance to the origins and commitments of liberal politics. But I do think that in the response to the counterrevolutionaries we can see the shared origin point of liberalisms: classical liberalism, modern liberalism, libertarianism, and what Moyn has termed Cold War liberalism. Liberalism as we know it originates in a doubled movement away from regenerative politics and toward the presumed protection of individual rights and freedoms.

Raymond Geuss defines classical liberalism explicitly as a rejection of the French Revolution, citing Constant as one of its founders: "For the early liberal Constant, Robespierre's *'republique de la vertu et de la terreur'* is a natural outcome of taking Rousseau's central conceptions at face value."[58] For Geuss, there are "four chief components of the classical liberalism of Constant, Mill, and de Tocqueville": a commitment to toleration, the ascription of normative importance to human freedom, the primary good of individualism, and the fear of "unlimited, concentrated, or arbitrary power."[59] Similarly, Alan Ryan associates classical liberalism with John Locke, Adam Smith, Alexis de Tocqueville, and Friedrich Hayek, those he calls cautious liberals. Here, Ryan sees a focus "on the idea of limited government, the maintenance of the rule of law, the avoidance of arbitrary and discretionary power, the sanctity of private property and freely made contracts, and the responsibility of individuals for their own fates."[60]

This presentation of classical liberalism is opposed to what Ryan calls modern liberalism, or the progressivist strand of the nineteenth-century liberalism of John Stuart Mill, extended into the liberalism of Leonard Trelawney Hobhouse. Mill was committed to the idea of moral and cultural progress and to individualism and is an interesting figure in the history of liberalism. Mill can be viewed as either a liberal or a socialist, and his appropriation into the canon of liberalism as a protolibertarian is certainly misplaced. As Rosenblatt writes, Mill was living in a time when it was possible "for a liberal to be a socialist,"[61] and as such he was dedicated to social reform through the defense of individual freedom. It remains the case, however, that Mill's "one very simple principle" of *On Liberty* prioritizes the sovereignty of the individual. This principle is "that the sole end for which mankind are warranted, individually or collectively, in interfering with the liberty of action of any of their number, is self-protection. That the only purpose for which power can rightfully be exercised over any member of a civilized community, against his will, is to prevent harm to others. . . . Over himself, over his own body and mind, the individual is sovereign."[62] It is easy to see how Mill intends this principle to prevent precisely the kinds of collective, regenerative politics that would, on his view, overstep the boundaries of individual freedom.

Duncan Bell argues that the conflation of so-called canonical liberals—such as Locke, Kant, Mill, and Rawls—is a product of historical change; for Bell, "the liberal tradition is constituted by the sum of arguments that have been classified as liberal, and recognized as such by other self-proclaimed liberals, across time and space."[63] Thus, in the twentieth century when liberalism becomes an explicit defense of negative freedom and individual rights against totalitarianism, Mill's priority of the sovereign individual comes to be seen as one and the same with Locke's defense of natural rights: "the Lockean narrative," in particular, "was consolidated in Britain and the United States between the 1930s and the 1950s, as liberalism was reconfigured as the ideological other of 'totalitarian' ideologies, left and right."[64] Having had to define itself against socialism in the nineteenth century, liberalism now had to become the "other" of both communism and fascism. This story, Bell writes, "began to coalesce during the 1930s, in a context of radical anxiety about the fate of liberalism. This was an era where, as Mussolini proclaimed, 'all the political experiments of our day are anti-liberal' ";[65] "liberalism came to be viewed through a wide-angle lens, as a politico-intellectual tradition centred on individual freedom in the context of constitutional government."[66] Alan Ryan writes, too, that "the history of liberalism is a history of opposition to assorted tyrannies"; what makes the liberal defense of constitutionalism distinctly *liberal* in its battle against collectivist politics is the claim "that absolute rule violates the personality or rights of those over whom it is exercised"[67]—a position whose roots Ryan finds in Locke.

Most recently, Samuel Moyn has shown that this solidification of liberalism as a politics of negative freedoms took place just as much through the development of an "anti-canon" as through the retroactive establishment of the canon of rights-protecting liberals. "Cold War liberals," Moyn writes, "relegated not only the Enlightenment but their sources to their anti-canon. No longer were they the wellspring of a credible liberalism; now they were the profoundest threat to its survival."[68] Drawing on the work of Judith Shklar, Moyn presents this relegation as an explicit turn away from the French Revolution, Rousseau, and Jacobinism: "Liberals 'abandoned' the Enlightenment because it came to seem plausible to defend limits to governmental authority and commitment to personal liberty in a fatalistic spirit born of hatred of Jacobin radicalism. Conservatism was originally given unity as a strategy 'to resist Jacobinism' but this did not define it distinctively since 'soon liberalism came to join conservatism in this preoccupation.'"[69] The Cold War liberalism of the thinkers addressed by Moyn—Judith Shklar, Isaiah Berlin, Karl Popper, Gertrude Himmelfarb, Hannah Arendt, and Lionel Trilling, among many others—abandoned the hope of politics facilitating emancipation, instead "casting its truths as an embattled but noble creed that the free world had to preserve in a struggle against a totalitarian empire."[70] Moyn writes, "The brand of theory that Cold War liberals invented in the 1940s and 1950s, far from being emancipatory, insisted on strict limits to human possibility. Belief in an emancipated life was proto-totalitarian in effect if not in intent. . . . It was most important to preserve existing liberty in a vale of tears; it was brittle and fragile and always on the verge of assault or collapse."[71]

Moyn's characterization of the general trend of twentieth-century liberalism goes along with a general attempt by twentieth-century liberals to disown Rousseau entirely, to throw him and everything he stood for over to the side of "the enemy." Isaiah Berlin, Bertrand Russell, and Irving Babbitt all castigated Rousseau's Romanticism, seeing it as a precursor of modern totalitarianism; Russell writes in his *History of Western Philosophy* (1945) that "'Hitler is an outcome of Rousseau.'"[72] Moyn calls J. L. Talmon's *The Origins of Totalitarian Democracy* "the archetypal Cold War liberal text" owing to "Talmon's conviction that the democratic ideal itself paved the way to tyranny, unless it was subjected to the English tradition's pragmatic constraints on reform and limits to political aspiration."[73]

As Talmon writes in *Origins*, it is "the extreme form of popular sovereignty" that was born in the French Revolution that leads to totalitarian democracy. Rooted in a form of "political Messianism," "the totalitarian democratic school" "widens the scope of politics to embrace the whole of human existence. It treats human thought and action as having social significance, and therefore as falling within the orbit of political action."[74] "The liberal approach," on the other hand, "assumes politics to be a matter of trial and error, and regards political systems as pragmatic contrivances of human ingenuity and spontaneity. It also recognizes a variety of levels of personal and collective endeavour, which are altogether outside the sphere of politics."[75] In Talmon, we see the full expression of the liberal turn away from regenerative politics, which is presumed to have been born in the excesses of the French Revolution and must be purged from the contemporary political world. A Rousseauian political system—the root of modern totalitarianism—is seen to collapse the human being into the political order, leaving people subjected entirely to the whims of their regime. Liberal protections of rights and freedoms, on the other hand, are presented as the solution to this collapse, leaving human beings outside of the political order, free to pursue their own desires.

Friedrich Hayek also "warned that embarking on 'collectivist experiments' would put countries on a slippery slope to fascism."[76] According to Hayek, the tradition of "Voltaire, Rousseau, Condorcet and the French Revolution" formed the roots of modern socialism; instead, Hayek wanted to invigorate the more "desirable political order" of liberalism.[77] Contrasting liberalism with the "anti-liberal" tradition of the French Revolution,[78] Hayek writes that the two "rest on altogether different philosophical foundations": "The first kind is consequently reverent of tradition and recognises that all knowledge and all civilisation rest on tradition, while the second type is contemptuous of tradition because it regards an independently existing reason as capable of designing civilisation. (Cf. the statement by Voltaire: 'If you want good laws, burn those you have and make new ones'.) The first is also an essentially modest creed, relying on abstraction as the only available means to extend the limited powers of reason, while the second refuses to recognise any such limits."[79]

Liberalism here is opposed to a regenerative politics that is presented as irrational and antithetical to individual rights and freedoms in its seemingly unlimited reconstitutive character. Using "government to achieve 'positive' (i.e., social or distributive) justice" leads to "the destruction of individual freedom";[80] instead, Hayek emphasizes the "basic principles of a liberal society," which he calls "the three great negatives: peace, justice, and liberty."[81]

Judith Shklar links the liberal preoccupation with negative freedom and human rights to the particular influence of American liberalism in the twentieth century, which "has been deeply marked by the general predominance of legal discourse and its language of claims and counter claims and of conflicting rights. It is not surprising that we all take rights seriously."[82] Here, Shklar is referencing the work of Ronald Dworkin, who writes in *Taking Rights Seriously* that "individual rights are political trumps held by individuals."[83] Considered inalienable and ineradicable facts about the human being, rights became the primary commitment of twentieth-century liberalism, which Shklar also sees as having been constituted through confrontations with "formidable ideological enemies abroad. They have done much to fortify the faith in human rights."[84] In his scholarship on human rights, Moyn sees this modern liberal commitment to rights detaching itself from nation-state and collective politics entirely in a "new politics of humanity."[85] Following from the UN Declaration of Human Rights in 1948, written in the wake of the Second World War, human rights are employed as extra-political universal standards to be leveled against particularized state collectivities.[86] The UN Declaration's imperative for the trump power of individual rights is in direct opposition to—and designed to be a protection from—the self-making regenerative politics perceived to be the hallmark of totalitarian regimes.[87]

THE PATH OF REGENERATION

Coterminous with the process of liberalism defining itself against Jacobinism, regeneration took on a life of its own in the wake of the French Revolution. Both Thomas Paine and Alexis de Tocqueville seized on the regenerative program of the revolutionary project as its historically transformative character. Paine had already noted the unique quality of the regeneration of man in the midst of the Revolution, writing in *The Rights of Man* (1791), "In the declaratory exordium which prefaces the Declaration of Rights, we see the solemn and majestic spectacle of a Nation opening its commission, under the auspices of the Creator, to establish a Government; a scene so new, and so transcendentally unequalled by any-thing in the European world, that the name of a Revolution is diminutive of its character, and it rises into a Regeneration of man."[88] Written as a direct refutation of Edmund Burke's attack on the revolutionary project, *The Rights of Man* states, "Had it confined itself merely to the destruction of flagrant despotism, perhaps Mr. Burke and some others had been silent. Their cry now is, 'It is gone too far': that is, it has gone too far for them. . . . Their fear discovers itself in their outrage, and they are but publishing the groans of wounded vice. But from such opposition, the French Revolution, instead of suffering, receives an homage. The more it is struck, the more sparks it will emit."[89]

For Paine, the core of the regenerative thrust of the revolutionary project is that the Revolution's regeneration in fact *regenerates itself*, pushing for further and future reconstitutions. Alexis de Tocqueville also saw this transformative movement in the Revolution, writing in *L'Ancien régime et la Révolution*, "Though the men who made the Revolution were more skeptical than our [American] contemporaries as regards the Christian verities, they had anyhow one belief, and an admirable one, that we today have not; they believed in themselves. Firmly convinced of the perfectibility of man, they had faith in his innate virtue, placed him on a pedestal, and set no bounds to their devotion to his cause. . . . They had a fanatical faith in their vocation—that of transforming the social system, root and branch, and regenerating the whole human race."[90] Thus, "the ideal the French Revolution set before it was not merely a change in the French social system but nothing short of a regeneration of the whole human race. It created an atmosphere of missionary fervor and, indeed, assumed all the aspects of a religious revival. . . . It would perhaps be truer to say that it developed into a species of religion," a religion that has "overrun the whole world."[91]

While Paine and Tocqueville highlighted this regenerative thrust to different ends—Paine to celebrate its novelty, Tocqueville to question, perhaps, its effects for modern politics—there is a shared sense on the part of these two liberals that something new had been summoned into the world: a transformative power that itself relies on the self-transformation of human beings. The affiliation of regeneration with the rights of man was, however, soon to dissipate, eventually to disintegrate entirely in the scientific and political developments of the nineteenth century. As liberalism emerged and envisioned itself as the proper inheritor of the Revolution's founding and rights-grounded principles, those who desired a more regenerative politics relied on different materials from the eighteenth century: its vitalist natural science and political philosophy.

Contemporary liberals like Isaiah Berlin see the turn to vitalism as a counter-Enlightenment movement. Recalling thinkers like Hamann and Herder, Romantic philosophers and poets like Schelling, Blake, and Shelley emphasized the idea of the creative self, which was, according to Berlin, the antithesis of the rational self of the Enlightenment. Berlin writes, "Hamann's theses rested on the conviction that all truth is particular, never general; that reason is impotent to demonstrate the existence of anything and is an instrument only for conveniently classifying and arranging data in patterns to which nothing in reality corresponds."[92] The later Romantic William Blake called on thinkers like Hamann to denounce the rationalism of those like Newton and Locke: Blake "accuses them of seeking to imprison the free human spirit in constricting, intellectual machines; when he says, 'A Robin Red breast in a Cage / Puts all Heaven in a Rage', the cage is none other than Newtonian physics, which crushes the life out of the free, spontaneous, untrammeled human spirit."[93] Berlin links this turn toward the vital spirit to the emphasis on a "future-directed dynamism of history" in which human beings become the creative masters of their own worlds and self-definitions.[94] This "doctrine of self-realisation [is] based on defiant rejection of the central theses of the Enlightenment, according to which what is true, or right, or good, or beautiful can be shown to be valid for all men by the correct application of objective methods of discovery and interpretation open to anyone to use and verify. In its full Romantic guise this attitude is an open declaration of war."[95] For Berlin, regenerative self-transformation is thus inherently counter-Enlightenment, while the Enlightenment proper protects the rational human being from the dangers of vitalism.

This Enlightenment/counter-Enlightenment discourse, whatever its merits, has made it more difficult to understand the genealogical development of regenerative political ideas. When thinkers were recalling regenerative eighteenth-century influences to reconstitute their politics in the nineteenth, their sources were predominantly natural-scientific—more specifically, it was to the palingenetic natural history of those like Buffon and Bonnet that the socialists turned when they accused the new liberals of abstracting man and harming the vitality of politics. Drawing on some of the most foundational works of the French Enlightenment, the antiliberal regenerative politics of the nineteenth century was not counter-Enlightenment but an alternative inheritance of the period's central ideas. Through the political conflicts of the nineteenth century, the once unified conception of the human being as self-regenerative— and thus rights-creating—fractured, with liberals critiquing the vitalism and dangerous regenerative commitments of socialism and socialists critiquing the abstraction of liberal rights. In these contestations, the "New Man"—*l'homme régénéré*—born in the French Revolution became antithetical to the static, rights-bearing human being.

At the beginning of the nineteenth century, the philosopher Pierre-Simon Ballanche spent the last part of his life writing his *Essais de palingénésie sociale (Essays on Social Palingenesis)*—an unfinished work that would become enormously influential for the emergence of socialism in France. For Ballanche, the French Revolution was a transformative event for both his own thinking and for human history. Arthur McCalla writes that Ballanche's idea of social palingenesis saw revolutionary upheavals as "the unfolding in time of the essence of humanity";[96] Ballanche was an "evolutionist" thinker, arguing that there is a shared "physiological and spiritual development of humanity" over time.[97] His evolutionism was explicitly rooted in the natural science of Charles Bonnet's 1770 work, *Palingénésie philosophique*, in which Bonnet offers a transformative natural history postulating that species undergo palingenetic modification over time. Ballanche's own palingenetic project was to take Bonnet's system of natural epochal change and apply it explicitly to social and political epochal shifts.

It is generally characteristic, McCalla writes, of nineteenth-century Romantics to hold the "conviction that humanity and nature share a common history of development. . . . Some Romantics limited the analogy to the gestation of the individual; thus, Lorenz Oken and Friedrich von Schelling asserted that individual ontogeny recapitulates the development of life on earth. Other Romantics extended the analogy to the history of humanity; thus Johann Wilhelm Ritter argued that the history of the earth is the history of humanity, and Johann Friedrich Blumenbach affirmed a meaningful parallel between geological periods and epochs of human change."[98] This geological and epochal historicism is an inheritance of eighteenth-century natural history like Buffon's, in which human beings are formed by and can form their natural surroundings. Ballanche, however, not only noted the geological codeterminism of the human being and nature but also, more importantly, seized on the distinctive palingenetic consciousness of the human being, exercised and made even more apparent through the regenerative action of the French Revolution.

McCalla believes that Ballanche is the first to have adopted *palingénésie* in the nineteenth century to describe social revolution: "Ballanche recalls that he was drawn to Bonnet's concept of palingenesis for its connotation of death and rebirth: 'I required, then, a name that, when applied to collective humanity, contained at once the idea of death and the idea of resurrection, or of a restitution of being.' "[99] In Ballanche's work, Bonnet's "revolutions of the globe" were "transformed from physical catastrophes into social upheavals. Old social orders die and new ones are born in what Ballanche calls ages of crisis, or epochs of end and renewal. . . . For Ballanche social revolutions providentially clear away obsolete orders so that new orders can unfold. Ballanche identifies the French Revolution as the latest such crisis."[100] Social palingenesis depends on the conscious activity of human beings, and "because evolution works through social institutions, only consciously social species evolve"; thus, "the evolution that, for Bonnet, operates throughout the entire chain of being, functions for Ballanche only from humanity upwards."[101]

Ballanche's social palingenesis was a defining concept for the Saint-Simonian socialists, influencing the thought of Pierre Leroux (cofounder of *Le Globe*), Charles Nodier, Jean Reynaud, and George Sand.[102] Following the July revolution of 1830 in France, "socialism" emerged as a movement and a political alternative in its opposition to liberalism. At this point, as Helena Rosenblatt writes, "accusations came from all around that liberals were incorrigibly selfish. They cared only about their own class and not at all about the poor. They were good at making speeches about equal rights, freedom, and reform, but were really only playing 'word games.' Liberals were devoid of any generosity, heart, or feeling. The policies they pursued, wrote one critic, were liberal only in appearance, but 'murderous' in reality."[103] Opposing liberals like François Guizot, the socialists imagined the possibility of a future palingenesis in which a revolution could once again transform how human beings exist in the world. It was in this highly charged historical period of conflict between liberals and the Saint-Simonians that Karl Marx and Friedrich Engels met in Paris in 1844, writing *The Communist Manifesto* in Brussels only four years later.

In 1844, Marx published "On the Jewish Question," his critique of the "so-called rights of man."[104] These rights, seen as "distinct from the rights of the citizen, are simply the rights of a member of civil society, that is, of egoistic man, of man separated from all other men and from the community. The most radical constitution, that of 1793, says: *Declaration of the Rights of Man and of the Citizen*: Article 2. 'These rights, etc. (the natural and imprescriptible rights) are: equality, liberty, security, property."[105] But, Marx continues, "liberty as a right of man is not founded upon the relations between man and man, but rather upon the separation of man from man. It is the right of such separation. The right of the circumscribed individual, withdrawn into himself."[106] For Marx, the consequence of French Revolutionary rights was the birth of bourgeois society and its attendant (mis)conception of the emancipatory possibilities of politics. When "the political community" is merely "a means for preserving those so-called rights of man," "man is far from being considered, in the rights of man, as a species-being; on the contrary, species-life itself—society—appears as a system which is external to the individual and as a limitation of his original independence."[107] In the bourgeois, liberal world, man as a member of civil society appears as the natural, egoistic man: he is authentic as opposed to political man, who is "abstract, artificial man, man as an allegorical, moral person. Thus man as he really is, is seen only in the form of egoistic man, and man in his true nature only in the form of the abstract citizen."[108] In this system, when there is a political revolution, there is only ever a political emancipation, or a return of man to his egoistic self—a self already predisposed to see itself as an abstraction, in and through abstract rights. For this reason, Marx argues that a liberal, political emancipation could never truly be a *human* emancipation, which would occur only when human beings have remade themselves, "when as an individual man, in his everyday life, in his work, and in his relationships, [man] has become a *species-being*; and when he has recognized and organized his own powers (*forces propres*) as social powers so that he no longer separates this social power from himself as political power."[109]

The distinction between abstract man and real or social man was defining for socialism and became central to the principles of late nineteenth- and early twentieth-century socialist thinkers. As Kevin Duong has written, "Modern French democracy won its conception of the citizen by abstracting away all social ascriptions. Socialism, in contrast, meant descending from 'abstract man' to 'real man' as he was embedded in concrete economic arrangements and from which he derived his interests. Hence, as Jeremy Jennings has put it, for *Le Mouvement socialiste*, 'syndicalism represented the victory of l'homme réel over l'homme abstrait of 1789.'"[110] Édouard Berth, a "contributor to *Le Mouvement socialiste* and future co-founder of the Cercle Proudhon" "railed against the state 'as an immense abstraction,' described parliamentary democracy as 'individualist, atomistic,' and [argued] that in modern life, 'Abstraction has destroyed reality—the abstract State, abstract morals, abstract law, abstract education: everything is abstract in the modern world.'"[111]

Among the contributors to *Le Mouvement socialiste* was Georges Sorel, who was indebted equally to Marx and to the philosopher Henri Bergson, whose *L'évolution créatrice* (*Creative Evolution*) (1907) continued the palingenetic social theory and vitalist philosophy of the eighteenth century and of Ballanche. As Duong writes, Sorel and his friends "came together under the sign of Henri Bergson to search for the sources of moral improvement and social regeneration in 'immediate experience,'" using Bergson to turn against liberal, rational universalism.[112] Bergson's philosophy envisioned human beings as the conscious and "motive principle of evolution."[113] All of life was for Bergson an *élan vital*, a vital force, that resists placing "the living into this or that one of our molds. All the molds crack. They are too narrow, above all too rigid, for what we try to put into them."[114] While it is the case that Bergson was transforming Charles Darwin's evolutionary theory in *Creative Evolution*, he stayed loyal to Darwin's fundamental principle: that the emergence of new forms over time was central to conceptualizing nature and the human being.[115] In his palingenetic view of creation and denial of classificatory natural science, however, Bergson was also returning to some of the core principles of the work of Buffon and Bonnet.

Bergson saw the human being as embedded in nature as part of its élan vital, which means that humans—like all other animals—have been and are subject to transformation. Echoing almost exactly the methodology of Buffon's "Initial Discourse," Bergson writes that philosophers "are right to attribute to man a privileged place in nature, to hold that the distance is infinite between the animal and man; but the history of life is there, which makes us witness the genesis of species by gradual transformation, and seems thus to reintegrate man in animality."[116] In his Darwinian antiteleological moments, Bergson denies the essences of species, instead postulating that patterns of continuity emerge historically: "The group must not be defined by the possession of certain characters, but by its tendency to emphasize them."[117] Though all natural life shares the vital force, Bergson—again, like Buffon—assigns the human being a distinction: "Life appears in its entirety as an immense wave which, starting from a centre, spreads outward and which on almost the whole of its circumference is stopped and converted into oscillation: at one single point the obstacle has been forced, the impulsion has passed freely. It is this freedom that the human form registers. Everywhere but in man, consciousness has had to come to a stand; in man alone it has kept on its way. Man, then, continues the vital movement indefinitely."[118] The freedom of the human being to enact "the creation of self by the self" and to be conscious of the capacity to do so makes man the "end" of evolution because amid consciousness as "the motive principle of evolution," the human being "comes to occupy a privileged place":[119] "we are seeking only the precise meaning that our consciousness gives to this word 'exist,' and we find that, for a conscious being, to exist is to change, to change is to mature, to mature is to go on creating oneself endlessly."[120]

The self-creating and palingenetic consciousness of the human being is, however, a double-edged sword. Our self-awareness is engaged through our self-understanding, which relies on the power of our intellect. But, Bergson writes, "precisely because it is always trying to reconstitute, and to reconstitute with what is given, the intellect lets what is *new* in each moment of a history escape. It does not admit the unforeseeable. It rejects all creation."[121] The intellect tends toward comprehension and abstraction; it desires knowable conclusions and prizes stability over change. For Bergson, this is why natural philosophers have privileged mechanistic explanations of the world: "The essence of mechanical explanation, in fact, is to regard the future and the past as calculable functions of the present, and thus to claim that *all is given*."[122] Bergson wants human beings to return to their instinct, which is "molded on the very form of life. While intelligence treats everything mechanically, instinct proceeds, so to speak, organically. If the consciousness that slumbers in it should awake, if it were wound up into knowledge instead of being wound off into action, if we could ask and it could reply, it would give up to us the most intimate secrets of life."[123] It is instinct that can access "vital processes" and "the generative force of life."[124] To regenerate themselves and to enact self-creation, human beings must fight the forces of their systematizing intellect to be free: "Our freedom, in the very movements by which it is affirmed, creates the growing habits that will stifle it if it fails to renew itself by a constant effort: it is dogged by automatism. The most living thought becomes frigid in the formula that expresses it. The word turns against the idea. The letter kills the spirit."[125]

Translated into the socialist movement, Bergson's intuitive life force became the source of the human will to overcome bourgeois abstraction.[126] Duong writes, "Between *Le Mouvement socialiste* and the *Cahiers de la Quinzaine*, the extraparliamentary left was creatively reimagining Bergson's philosophy into a political theory. In Lagardelle's hatred of 'merely political' democracy's 'abstract man,' in Péguy's protest against the deadening of 'mystique' into 'politique,' we can hear echoes of Bergson's dogged belief— so at odds with Hegel—that abstraction impoverished rather than enriched reality."[127] Duong continues, "Péguy believed that French youth needed to rediscover the sacred mystique of the Republic which its parliamentary form murdered. 'What we want to know is the tissue of the people in that heroic age . . . the marrow of our race, the cellular tissue. . . . All that we no longer see, all that we don't see nowadays.' 'There are,' Péguy believed, 'deeper forces and realities' to which we moderns have lost access."[128] Duong sees Georges Sorel as harnessing the Bergsonian creative life force to justify "the value of violence. No longer destructive, violence could be productive; not nihilistic, it could be value creating; the opposite of selfishness, it was a means of suppressing egoism for collective moral improvement. 'The strike is a phenomenon of war . . . in undertaking a serious, formidable, and sublime work, the socialists raise themselves above our frivolous society and make themselves worthy of pointing out new roads to the world.'"[129] From Sorel's regenerative Bergsonianism, we can draw a clear and direct link to modern fascism: "In Italy, 'Sorelismo' encouraged the reorganization of working class energy into nationalist forms of collectivism. Filippo Marinetti, who also called Sorel 'our master,' published his infamous 'The Foundation and Manifesto of Futurism' in *Le Figaro* on 20 February 1909.

It was a screed against history and the past, both deeply anti-establishment and ultranationalist. It exalted the existential rebirth of the 'new man' into the rebellious masses."[130] Duong writes, "Sorel's canonization as a member of fascism's intellectual pantheon was assured with Mussolini's proclamation that 'Who I am, I owe to Georges Sorel.' "[131]

Sorel was also deeply influenced by Friedrich Nietzsche, whose "will to power" has many affinities with Bergson's élan vital;[132] so, too, does Nietzsche's conception of the eternal recurrence reinvent the palingenetic or regenerative view of history and human life.[133] As Christopher Forth has written, "For many French writers, regeneration, nationalism, and Nietzschean thought seemed to go hand in hand, and all three had their immediate roots in the highly charged atmosphere of the early 1890s."[134] "The philosophy of Nietzsche," Forth writes, "inspired and legitimated a vitalistic desire for radical change" through a "rhetoric of regeneration" directed against the perceived decadence of the late nineteenth century.[135] This Nietzschean regeneration was activated in twentieth-century fascism in calls for a "New Man," growing out of the radicalized socialism of Sorel: "The utopia of building a New Man entailed a rupture with an avowedly decadent past . . . [which] was represented, above all, in the perceived materialism of liberal democracies and the looming threat of communism."[136] Mussolini and Hitler are the inheritors of the regenerative enterprise of Nietzsche, itself drawn into a connection with the French Revolution: "The project of fashioning a New Man in modern Europe outlived the French Revolution and was to find fertile terrain in the radical right universe."[137]

Circling back to its regenerative origin point in the French Revolution, the "New Man," or *l'homme régénéré*, of the Right is inextricably linked to the Terror. Fascism is conceived as a modern political movement that had been in the making ever since the Jacobins rejected the liberal and universalist principles of 1789 through their regenerative politics. In *Dangerous Minds*, Ronald Beiner presents Nietzsche's turn away from 1789 as transformative for modernity:

> The French Revolution represented the key moment of fundamental sea change in European consciousness and politics. To put it very crudely and simply, prior to 1789, one had a political world oriented fundamentally toward hierarchy; after 1789, one had a political world fundamentally oriented toward equality and the free judgments of individuals who

determine for themselves what their lives are about rather than having it dictated from above. That's an enormous change in the ordering of human society and the shape of moral consciousness! It's not an accident that the most virulent enemies of modern liberalism and modern democracy—such as Joseph de Maistre in the early nineteenth century and Nietzsche in the late nineteenth century—directed their most intense polemical energies against the French Revolution.[138]

Beiner sees the contemporary "neofascist revival" as rooted in "the fact that since the Enlightenment, a line of important thinkers has considered life in liberal modernity to be profoundly dehumanizing."[139] After all, it is Nietzsche himself who, in *Twilight of the Idols*, "affirms the need for cultural norms that are 'anti-liberal to the point of malice.'"[140] For Beiner, "the contemporary resurgence of far right thinkers," among whom Julius Evola and Alexander Dugin are especially dangerous, "forces us to command a heightened vigilance with respect to the directly practical implications of what Mark Lilla in 2001 called 'the reckless mind,' or what Georg Lukács in 1952 called 'the destruction of reason.'"[141]

Beiner is aligned here with Richard Wolin's analysis in *The Seduction of Unreason*, in which Wolin unifies the contemporary Far Right with the postmodern Left through their commitment to "the assault on humanism, [and] the dissolving of 'man.'"[142] There are, Wolin claims, "uncanny affinities between the Counter-Enlightenment and postmodernism," a movement in which most of its deepest thinkers were "inspired by Nietzsche's anticivilizational animus."[143] Postmodernists and poststructuralists—including Claude-Lévi Strauss, Michel Foucault, and Jacques Derrida—engage in a "neo-Nietzschean assault on 'reason' and 'truth,'"[144] aligning themselves with "one of fascism's avowed goals [which] was to put an end to the Enlightenment-derived nineteenth-century worldview: the predominance of science, reason, democracy, socialism, individualism, and the like. As Goebbels pithily observed a few months after Hitler's rise to power, 'The year 1789 is hereby erased from history.'"[145]

Two of Wolin's targets, Gilles Deleuze and Félix Guattari, in fact draw their antihumanism from the same polyp that inspired the revolutions in eighteenth-century philosophy: their "notion of a body without organs (BwO), developed in *A Thousand Plateaus* (1980), is explicitly linked by them to the work of the German biologist August Weismann who in turn had been influenced by the discourses and debates about the polyp."[146] They thus advanced what Keith Ansell-Pearson "calls a coherent philosophy of 'germinal life'"[147] and developed "rhizomatic thinking," which Christine Daigle and Terrance H. McDonald describe as a mode "of thinking that breaks down dualisms and moves beyond them."[148] Daigle goes so far as to draw the image of "polyp-being" out of Deleuze and Guattari:[149] a "concept of transubjectivity" that "acknowledges the mobility and permanent state of flux inherent in our being and in our very (self-)constitution."[150] This "polyp-being" is set against the presumed "humanist" identification of the human being, the "autonomous and free agent";[151] instead, a posthumanist philosophy will "challenge the anthropocentric world view by rejecting human exceptionalism and emphasizing the material embeddedness and interconnectivity of all beings."[152]

Deleuze and Guattari's regenerative philosophy moves the postmodern position further than the detachment from humanism, advocating—like Nietzsche's Übermensch ("overman")—for the transcendence of the "human" altogether. This position is, to say the least, conducive to a transhumanist vision that would forever abandon the constrictive rules of reason, rights, and the liberal world order of the Enlightenment. Deleuze and Guattari are often cited as influences—as are Nietzsche and Marx—in the broad swath of ideologies collected under the name "accelerationism," forming an amorphous Far Right antidemocratic movement advocating for the violent acceleration of the overcoming of modernity. In particular, Nick Land's Dark Enlightenment movement (associated with the neoreactionary movement, commonly abbreviated as "NRx") advocates supplanting liberalism and liberal democracy with a regenerated conception of human possibility that can be achieved only through authoritarianism. Land's writings in particular have been germinal in the disturbing and dangerous rise of an online-driven neofascist alt-right movement. I intend here not to legitimize, let alone advocate, any of these political movements, but rather to show how accelerationism and the Dark Enlightenment, along with all the other tributaries of the current Far Right rejection of liberalism, can be understood as issuing from broad intellectual-historical processes. As with all the other regenerative movements of today's Far Right—including those of Alain de Benoist, Guillaume Faye, and Daniel Forrest—such movements see the world as fundamentally divided between liberal stagnation and regenerative vitalism.

THE ARCHIMEDEAN POINT

From where we are now in the twenty-first century, it seems impossible for regenerative movements to be rights-protecting or for rights to have regenerative vitalism. Liberals see regenerative politics as their enemy; advocates of regenerative politics see the same in liberalism and rights. Both sides of this divide, however, relate back to the French Revolution for their self-understanding, opposing either 1789's universalism and rights or 1793's regenerative Terror. Having arrived at this Manichean condition, we have lost sight of the shared vision that instigated both the commitment to the universalism of rights and the vitalism of regenerative politics: the modern telic, or self-regenerating, human being, who saw that the world must be regenerated through the regeneration and reconstitution of the self. Rights were not stagnant, and regenerative politics was committed to universalism. But what was born in the eighteenth century as a new and transformative vision of the human being has bisected itself into two irreconcilable views of the self and of political possibility. If liberal rights remain as they are, they will stay static and unmoving, lacking the vitalism they require if they are meant to be expressions of self-constituting human beings. If regenerative political movements remain as they are, they will stay opposed by definition to any rights claim or rights-grounded regime.

Today's calls for regeneration from the Right and from the Left see human rights and liberalism as "hegemonic"—a word used by both Guillaume Faye and Sylvia Wynter.[153] For Wynter, this view implicitly rejects different "discursive formations" of what it means to be a human being.[154] For Faye, we must therefore be compelled to see that the "future remains open" "in order to regenerate history."[155] Facing these challenges to the liberal-democratic world, the temptation for liberals will be—as it has been—to respond as they always have before: to see these as illiberal and dangerous claims and to turn them into sources of unreason. The schism of liberal rights and regeneration has strengthened over time, but liberalism's enemies were clear from the beginning: regenerative and beastly Jacobins from whom individuals—and their rights and freedoms—had to be protected.

Defenders of liberal rights have thus latched onto the language of self-evidence as a bulwark against dangerously regenerative forms of politics. Where regeneration opens the door to self-reconstitution, self-evident rights close them forever—and intentionally so. Isaiah Berlin distinguishes liberal, negative freedom from its positive, self-determinative (and therefore dangerous) twin and grounds the self-evidence of this idea in Enlightenment reason.[156] His three principles of Enlightenment are rooted in the capacity of humans to discover truths about themselves that are sure, reasonable, and therefore incontrovertible. The first is that "all genuine questions can be answered, that if a question cannot be answered it is not a question"; "the second proposition is that all these answers are knowable"; and the third is that all of the answers "must be compatible with one another. . . . It is a logical truth that one true proposition cannot contradict another."[157] Berlin also claims that "there is only one way of discovering these answers, and that is by the correct use of reason. . . . That is the only way in which answers in general—true answers to serious questions—may be obtained. There is no reason why such answers, which after all have produced triumphant results in the worlds of physics and chemistry, should not equally apply to the much more troubled fields of politics, ethics, and aesthetics."[158]

The liberalism of those like Berlin commits us to a foundationally Cartesian conception of self-knowledge. To know ourselves, we must come to a clear and distinct idea of what we are that is self-evident and thus also be sure that this idea is a reasonable conclusion shared by all other reasoning and enlightened persons. As Descartes writes at the beginning of his second meditation, "I will stay on this course until I know something certain or, if nothing else, until I at least know for certain that nothing is certain. Archimedes sought but one firm and immovable point in order to move the entire earth from one place to another. Just so, great things are also to be hoped for if I succeed in finding just one thing, however slight, that is certain and unshaken."[159] Arriving at the clear and distinct idea of himself as a thinking thing, Descartes finds this Archimedean point in the self-evidence of his reason. In the Cartesian mode, liberalism presumes that its truths about the human being—its construction of humans as rights-possessors and its freedoms as protected only through negation—are so reasonably self-evident that any challenge to them must come *from* the unreasonable. The denial of rights is the denial of what is self-evidently human.

However, in the French Revolutionary period, a new Archimedean point was established. The question of how we as humans were to know ourselves was, to paraphrase Berlin, a true and serious question in the eighteenth century. But as we see in François d'Escherny's celebration of Rousseau's transformative effect on the revolutionary spirit, the Archimedean point had shifted: "Archimedes demanded one point to support the globe, to raise the world. What Rousseau said, what Rousseau did, executed it. . . . He seized upon a state that never existed, a state at odds with everything that exists; This is the state of nature, in which he finds his support. By making this metaphysical lever move, it raises and renews the whole system of our moral knowledge, [and] disrupts all of our ideas."[160] The Rousseauian image of human beings as self-regenerative and in possession of the universal *first right* by nature to change their conditions and change themselves gave rise to the regenerative claims of the Revolution—inspiring the Declaration of Rights, as well as its demise. It is the very lack of certainty about how human beings live in the world and our deep susceptibility to historical and political reconstitution that make it necessary to retain the first right to make and remake ourselves. This first right has been lost in today's conception of the rights of human beings. We have retained the universalism of the Declaration's aspirations but not the vitalism. The schism of rights and regeneration in modernity has detached the self-making and reconstituting force of rights claims from their affirmation and application. The liberal assertion of incontrovertible, self-evident rights is coupled with the relegation of regenerative claims to the realm of the illiberal, or the antihuman; but with it, the self-determinative core of rights is also relegated to a different and politically incompatible world.

Regenerative claims against liberal democracies and against human rights must be taken seriously—not because they challenge the liberal order from the outside but because they illuminate the defect in liberalism's self-understanding. Liberals continue to rely on conceptions of self-making when describing the rights and freedoms we possess. Alan Ryan writes, "Liberalism viewed as a doctrine for individuals can be understood in terms one might borrow from Immanuel Kant, Humboldt, Mill, Bertrand Russell, or Dewey, since a variety of formulations seize on the same points. The essence is that individuals are self-creating."[161] Despite Berlin's protestation to the contrary, even liberal claims for the purported self-evidence of human rights and freedom implicitly depend on this construction: that people by nature must be seen as capable of choosing their own life and creating the circumstances of their own existence. Freedom from totalizing control and from the imposition of positive freedom is the negative, liberal right of self-constitution.

The right of the individual to make itself in the world is, however, fundamentally a regenerative right. It is our first right. In turning against regenerative politics from its beginnings, the politics of liberal rights has always denied its own foundation. Rights now exist without their self-constituting power, and human beings are defined before they are allowed the freedom to define themselves. Still implicitly reliant on the modern telic conception of the human being, however, liberal regimes function through a presumed self-evident idea of the free and self-making individual that no longer has any referent in the world. As a consequence of the schism of rights and regeneration, there are no humans left in politics.

6

RESTORING OUR FIRST RIGHT

T he promise of universal rights in the French Revolution and
the genuine self-determination that was its founding vision and
force do not exist in the contemporary liberal-democratic world.
Citizens lack any real motive or self-determinative connection to the
rights their regimes are supposed to protect. Our polities, grounded as
they are on the assertion and affirmation of presumed and unquestionable rights, are without the conception of the regenerative self that would
bind human beings to their political life. With rights understood as possessions and the state as their attendant guarantor or suppressor, there is
no connection between assumed rights-bearers and the makers or protec-
tors of political rights. It is easy to see how the citizen of a contemporary
liberal democracy feels that there is no way out and no way of truly making one's own life in the world. Rights are seen not as tools of self-making
but as descriptions of a self that is already made—and now also subject
irrevocably to the manner in which selves are particularly constituted by
the state in which one lives.

If our normative commitment in a modern liberal democracy is to
the equal freedom of individuals, this conception of rights cannot stand.
Today's citizens exist in a state of psychic fissure between understanding themselves to be free and equal—self-evidently so—and seeing quite
clearly that in no sense are they in fact free and equal. Because we do not
see rights as creations that are the consequence and maintenance of active

human claims in the world, there is no link between the human beings seen to hold those rights and the political regimes presumably legitimized by their maintenance. If rights are not subject to regeneration by the very human beings who are their object, then no truly self-determinative act can be performed by the citizens of a state. The question of what it means to be human is always settled as the first premise of the liberal-democratic order, and a fully self-determinative human life is immediately foreclosed. For this reason, I have argued that there are no humans left in politics.

This diagnosis entails, or necessitates, the assertion of a universal human nature—that is, I do affirm that we can say something about what humans are and thus how they exist, or fail to, in relation to their political world. This universal nature is that of the self-regenerative human being. Seeing humans as self-regenerative requires the simultaneous commitment to a universal and unchanging, and a historical and changeable, conception of humanity. Drawing from Rousseau's political philosophy and Buffon's natural science, I have constructed this vision in a kind of dialectical image, with human lives suspended between the changeable arrangements of their social and political existence and the eternal and universal claim that they hold by nature to resist and transform those conditions. Adumbrated into the language of rights, Rousseau sees this arrangement as an ongoing relationship between political rights—which contain even those rights we would construct as and consider to be inalienable—and what he calls the *first right* to refuse those rights altogether. To be human is to retain the first right to make rights, or to revoke or regenerate them. For Rousseau, it is this regenerative right that serves as the primary foundation of all natural, inalienable, or self-evident rights that we see affirmed and asserted in more conventional social contract theories.

In the French Revolution, the revolutionaries saw and harnessed this regenerative first right in order to remake themselves into free and equal persons in the world. This first right also formed and reformed new iterations of the Declaration and formed new claims from women, slaves, and the colonies. The transformative power in asserting the ability to change the world was the act of self-regenerating human beings—as was the act of reconstructing the political world and making political rights anew, always seen simultaneously as the transformation and regeneration of the self. There was no free and equal person by nature or by right, except insofar as human beings regenerated themselves into rights-bearers by being rights-makers.

The attendant and constant risk in this capacity for self-determination was always present. It was understood that a world, and a conception of the human being, that could be altered through the regenerative power of humans was perpetually subject to further transformations, even in a degenerative direction. The fervor and panic of the Jacobin radicalism was in many ways a reaction to this consciousness of the palingenetic nature of the self and the world. Robespierre made every attempt to transform people into perfect and pure bastions of virtue so as to prevent moral and political degeneration; in this attempt, he committed unspeakable violence and terror, precipitating the decline of the regenerative promise of the Declaration's genesis all together. In an attempt to foreclose the political dangers of a Robespierrian politics, liberal political actors of the nineteenth century turned away from the self-regenerative image of the human being, resting instead on determinable, self-evident rights and constitutional solidity.

In the twenty-first century, it is no longer a question whether people have the right to freedom and equality—this is the foundational commitment of all liberal democracies and the UN Declaration of Human Rights. Many scholars want to interpret this outcome as a successful legacy of the Enlightenment, and of the French Revolutionary establishment of the "rights of man" in particular,[1] which Lynn Hunt sees as the inspiration for the 1948 UN Declaration: the "Declaration of the Rights of Man and of the Citizen incarnated the promise of universal human rights."[2] Like Anne Phillips,[3] Hunt sees the claim to self-evidence as the crucial and defining feature of human rights in the modern world. For Peter de Bolla, too, the self-evidence of human rights (inherited, he claims, from the Enlightenment's "rights of man") points to a noetic, as opposed to a political, architecture of rights in the modern world: one in which the universal rights of human beings serve as the foundational grammar of all things.[4]

Other scholars of human rights are much more skeptical about the connection of modern human rights to the eighteenth-century revolutionary period, and about their apparent self-evidence. James Tully has argued that we need to rethink our conception of rights, turning away from declarations of their existence as self-evident truths toward the affirmation of the democratic authority of persons as rights-makers. He bifurcates the tradition into two forms or modules of human rights:

the high Enlightenment model and the democratic Enlightenment model. The former consists of self-evident truths and universality; the latter is the more constructivist approach. The second module, preferred by Tully, is grounded in the "rejection of the premise that a set of unquestionable human rights and their equally unquestionable institutions and processes of socialization all precede democratic participation. It stands on the democratic premise that human rights and their institutions must always be co-articulated by the citizens who are subject to them."[5] For Tully, "to declare human rights as self-evident and to impose a rights regime unilaterally violates and undermines the dignity of human agency that human rights are supposed to recognize and enable. It robs human rights of their democratic authority."[6]

Samuel Moyn shares the project of questioning the lineage of today's self-evident human rights in the French Revolution or the Enlightenment period, arguing that there is no connection whatsoever between the rights of the eighteenth century and today's dominant human rights regime. Grounding today's universal rights in the emergence of a Cold War response to the Second World War—coming more prominently, he claims, from the Christian right than the secular left[7]—Moyn, like Tully, sees a vast disconnect between claims of the self-evidence of contemporary rights and any genuine form of self-determination. "Human rights rose," Moyn writes, "as self-determination fell," and there was "an exclusion of self-determination from early human rights ideas—up to and including the Universal Declaration of 1948."[8] Moyn sees a depoliticization of human rights in the contemporary world, with rights now functioning as a kind of moral utopia, and in this respect as claims that a person makes against politics as opposed to through it.[9] For Moyn, the turn away from self-determination was finalized in the Cold War period: "Creative agency had been liberalism's goal, and history its form of opportunity. The twentieth century changed all that."[10]

While in agreement about the exclusion of self-determination from claims of self-evidence in the contemporary rights regime, Moyn is nevertheless critical of Tully's confidence in the capacity of rights to hold up to a genuinely self-determinative commitment. As Moyn writes of Tully's construction of the so-called democratic Enlightenment tradition, "While inspiring, [it] omits that many of the most impressive proponents of human freedom and equality across modern history . . . have felt the need to break with rights altogether."[11] "What is self-evident about human rights," Moyn concludes, "turns out to be not very much."[12] The mode of problematizing rights as Tully constructs it is meant to avoid or overstep what he perceives to be the colonial inheritances of the universalizing conception of human rights that emerged in the dominant Enlightenment tradition, which exported rights as tools of domination over "less civilized" countries and persons while closing off sensitivities to pluralism and to the self-determinative needs of different cultures and communities. His turn toward the more self-determinative, and thus culturally contingent, mode of rights talk then walks head-first into what Moyn presents as the challenge of illiberalism (though he does not state it in such terms): that once you no longer assume the universal moral priority of human rights, there is no longer any claim—of nature, human nature, or self-evidence—you can make to defend rights against equally viable claims to self-determination that might undercut or destroy them.

Moyn sees this instability as a problem for human rights. And, in fact, rights—which are meant to protect the capacity of all human beings to freely determine the contours of their lives—have indeed become the symbols for many of the foreclosures of self-determination in the modern world. What Sylvia Wynter has termed "liberal monohumanism" precludes the possibility for human beings to make themselves, to question and reconstitute what it means to be human.[13] She aligns herself with Frantz Fanon and Aimé Césaire and is joined in this critique by many other Black, queer, Indigenous, and postcolonial scholars. As I outlined in chapter 1, a similar challenge to rights is being made by this progressive movement's antithesis: the Far Right. Daniel Forrest argues, for example, that human beings must awaken to their "historical consciousness," which will allow them to be the "*creator*[s] of a new future."[14] Echoing the language of the French Revolutionaries and the challenges of the critical Left, he claims that we must "promote a *historical regeneration*" of the human bring, opening ourselves up to novel reconstitutions and genuine self-determination.[15] For the Far Right, as for the Left, this regenerative project is set in explicit opposition to the modern liberal conception of rights. Wynter claims that "the very idea of human rights requires rethinking in order for authentic freedom to emerge for Black people,"[16] while Alain de Benoist, a founding member of the Nouvelle Droite, calls for the rejection of the "ideology of human rights."[17]

The challenges from both the Left and the Right to the modern reliance on the self-evidence of rights also result in foundationally regenerative political alternatives, which advocate new visions of what it means to be human in the world and reassert that human beings have a deeper right beyond rights to make themselves anew. The problem is not only, then, that rights face challenges to their self-evidence or to their historical roots but also that these challenges—resting as they do on deep claims to self-determination—contain the future possibility of the overturning of rights altogether. The response of liberal democrats seems to be simply to reject these regenerative claims as illiberal—to treat them as forces that make an attempt from the outside to overturn our founding commitment to freedom, which is maintained and protected by liberalism. This response is not sufficient. We must not dig our heels into the moral superiority, or the supposed self-evident and eternal universalism, of the rights of human beings. Against such a response, claims to self-determination will only grow stronger, the rights that we hold to be self-evident will degenerate, and only when it is too late will people recognize that the life of universal human rights is in fact contingently dependent on the constant regeneration of their existence in the world.

In a political environment increasingly hostile to the historical legacies and seemingly exclusionary boundaries of rights, I believe there is still potential for the regeneration of rights as opposed to their abandonment. But this possibility is counterintuitively constituted first in their loss. We must lose the reliance on our current conception of the universality of rights and their self-evidence. For those who are challenging liberal democracies, there is nothing at all self-evident about freedom and equality. This is a challenge that we need to understand and appreciate in full and see as a fundamental *human* claim against the current political order. The freedom and equality of human beings is never a presumption on which to rest; it is a universal claim that requires the vigilant regeneration of the self, and of the world, for its affirmation and survival. For rights to survive, the prospect of their degeneration, disappearance, or failure must therefore be omnipresent. The first right of human beings to renounce their political rights would maintain a priority in a truly self-determinative politics—and would mean that rights would always remain only one possible iteration of the human political experience in the world.

In a truly regenerative politics, the possibility of overturning rights would become a source of vitality instead of fear: the defenders of the liberal order would be compelled to regenerate their own human claim to and against their political rights. If all self-determinative claims—including those of the Far Right and Left—were seen as genuine claims of the first right of human beings to make themselves in the world, so too then would the liberal-democratic commitment to universal rights be required to justify its foundation in this first self-determinative and regenerative right. It would need to give itself life through perpetual reconstitution, instead of relying on the now rapidly degenerating affirmation that rights, once recognized and secured, can never be lost. A regenerative politics would demand that the human beings who know themselves to be universally free and equal make sure that they are free and equal in the world in fact.

As in the French Revolution, the genuine exercise of our first right against political rights would not come without risk. It is not a light—or even practical—demand for human beings to abandon the commitment to self-evidence. Exercising our first right would perpetually entail the possibility that rights may degenerate altogether. But this is an ever-increasingly real possibility, which remains whether or not we admit it into the political fact of our collective existence. We are already seeing the degeneration of the commitment to self-evident rights across the globe—and especially from within liberal democracies. The choice to consciously bring about their demise would allow us to—at the same time—embrace the regenerative, or palingenetic, consciousness of our own power to ensure the life and survival of rights through their reconstitution and active reaffirmation.

Opening ourselves up to all forms of human self-creation—and to our first right as human beings to make and remake our conventions—would regenerate our political rights and would once again make them vital in the world. This opening is what will allow for the reentry of human beings into their own political life, not merely of those on the Left and the Right who lack any self-determinative connection to their polities but also of the liberal democrats whose current conception of rights equally forecloses a genuinely free and self-made existence. The goal of my project—if there is one, practically speaking—is to reconnect people to their first right to determine their own lives and to reconnect the citizens of liberal

RESTORING OUR FIRST RIGHT 159

democracies to their political rights. The protection and maintenance of rights in the modern world would, in this view, be only one possible future for human beings; but it is one that must be kept alive if is to survive.

For those who see regenerative politics as illiberal—and especially as intimately bound to violence—this suggestion will be too much to bear: why would we want to abandon rights, the last possible bulwark against the descent of modern politics into fascism, terror, and violent upheaval, precisely at the moment when they appear to be the sole protection of human beings against these great dangers and injustices? So, too, will it seem to be going too far to forgo any claim (whether moral or otherwise) to the self-evidence of human rights: what would this entail? The destruction of modern bills of rights, of constitutions, of the basic protections of rights and freedoms? Why would we allow the forces of illiberalism to dismantle all that we hold dear, and all that keeps our politics legitimate and our citizens free?

On the charge of regeneration being intimately bound up with violence, I believe I have provided sufficient evidence and analysis to show that the regenerative conception of the self is fundamentally a claim about human nature and thus is not de facto tied to political violence or even to a particular way of being in the world, politically or apolitically. There is nothing inherently violent or fascist about a regenerative politics. The deeper question is whether there is something inherently illiberal about a regenerative politics that would render the assertion of rights its necessary antithesis, implying that opening the door to the former would mean the inevitable disintegration of the latter. The challenge of addressing this possibility is met with the historical story I have told here. There is nothing antithetical to a commitment to rights in a regenerative politics; in fact, the very idea of a universal right entailed at its inception in the French Revolutionary period a regenerative conception of the self and of politics.

What I see in the contemporary liberal-democratic world is an impoverished understanding of rights—an understanding that actively tries to construct regenerative reconstitution as the enemy of rights in order to suppress the reality that self-determinative human beings may choose to overturn their political rights altogether. In one sense, then, a truly regenerative politics would mean the disintegration of liberal rights, understood as self-evident prepossessions of human beings that are unquestionable facts. In another sense, however, to commit to an open regenerative politics would not mean abandoning rights at all. Allowing for human beings to assert their first right to make and choose their own lives would facilitate the conditions under which the rights that a state affirms are rights that its citizens actively hold to be true—both universally and in the contingent political world in which they find themselves.

This does mean, however, that we would open up the terms of legitimacy when it comes to envisioning how a self-determined human life ought to look. There are, and always will be, those who hold it to be true that the given political order does not facilitate human flourishing and those who would want to reconstitute the political order and the constitutions of the self that are conventionally accepted and protected. These are the challenges to rights that we see growing stronger day by day. The necessary response is not to assert with increasing certainty that claims against the liberal order are antithetical to a free and political human life. The correct reply, no matter how impractical it appears, is to embrace a genuinely regenerative politics, accepting that rights are only one self-determinative activation of the universal first right of human beings to be and determine themselves in the world.

In looking at eighteenth-century France in the time leading up to and including the French Revolution, we can see that rights conceived as active claims of human beings were themselves a form of regenerative politics—and so I hope they could be once again. As I discussed in chapter 1, the method of my argument is essentially what I have called a conceptual materialist claim. We do not need to abandon rights altogether to reinvigorate a regenerative spirit in citizens of liberal democracies, and in fact to do so would be foolish. The concept of rights is simply part of the modern parlance of politics and exists materially in the way we function in the modern liberal-democratic world. What needs to happen is that those who exist in the world believing they have universal human rights must be compelled—consistently and vigilantly—to make this a part of their political life.

For rights to be truly universal, they must be regeneratively affirmed, defended, and made by the very persons who currently hold their truth to be self-evident. The reality that there are those who do not believe that rights are evident to them has to remain a constantly present reality. These challenges cannot be rejected or ignored as illiberal aberrations, but must be accepted as opposing and legitimate human claims to determine the self both in and against the given political and conventional order. Only from the perpetual risk of loss could rights truly regain and retain the active engagement of the humans who are seen to possess them. In a regenerative political world, rights would be infused with the motive force and activity they need to be maintained, enabling the political life of rights-bearers by making them the true makers of their regimes and of themselves. The palingenetically conscious human being, recognizing and embracing its first right to regenerate the conditions of its own existence, would finally be determining itself in the world.

In "Human Rights and the Welfare State,"[18] Claude Lefort offers an account of French Revolutionary rights that, like my argument about regenerative rights, appears to be cohesive with Hannah Arendt's famous defense of the right to have rights. "By reducing the source of right to the human utterance of right," Lefort writes, the French Revolutionary Declaration "granted recognition of *the right to have rights* . . . and thus gave rise to an adventure whose outcome is unpredictable. In other words, the naturalist conception of right masked an extraordinary event: a declaration which was in fact a self-declaration, that is, a declaration by which human beings, speaking through their representatives, revealed themselves to be both the subject and the object of the utterance in which they named the human elements in one another."[19] What are now challenged as the "fictional universals" of the Enlightenment, according to Lefort, in fact brought into being only "the universality of the principle which reduces right to the questioning of right."[20] While appearing to operate in tandem with my analysis of rights, however, democratic agonists like Lefort actually help to reveal—through the distance between us—what is really at stake in a regenerative politics.

Lefort's take on the "political" as the site of the contestation of right, or the space where human beings make and determine themselves to be right-bearers through active declaration and reconstitution, has been enormously influential in radical democratic theory. The democratic, rights-protecting space is defined by its ability to be constituted by those who serve as both the object and subject of its definition. The agonistic democracy is characterized by the paradox that, in this regime, "there is no institution which can, by its very nature, guarantee the existence of a public space in which it is possible to question right on an increasingly broad basis" despite the fact that this is the very condition of a democracy's legitimacy.[21]

According to Sheldon Wolin, the space of human political life and activity is thus understood to be divided between "politics" and "the political": "I shall take the political to be an expression of the idea that a free society composed of diversities can nonetheless enjoy moments of commonality when, through public deliberations, collective power is used to promote or protect the well-being of the collectivity. Political refers to the legitimized and public contestation, primarily by organized and unequal social powers, over access to the resources available to the public authorities of the collectivity. Politics is continuous, ceaseless, and endless. In contrast, the political is episodic, rare."[22] Democracy is intimately bound up with the political: "In my understanding, democracy is a project concerned with the political potentialities of ordinary citizens, that is with their possibilities for becoming political beings."[23] Democracy, for Wolin, was born in revolutions and in transgressive acts, and it is "the means by which the demos makes itself political."[24] For both Lefort and Wolin, the openness of the capacity for human (re)constitution and self-making is preserved in the rare, but essential, true acts of democracy.

Chantal Mouffe also describes the political as a kind of "ontological condition" for human beings.[25] The agonistic confrontation that Mouffe wants to restore is a reinvigoration of the political element that is lacking in today's liberal-democratic institutions, a restoration of "the very condition of possibility for a pluralist form of human coexistence in which rights can exist *and* be exercised."[26] Mouffe concedes that "democracy is something uncertain and improbable and must never be taken for granted"[27]—an "always fragile conquest that needs to be defended"[28]— yet she presents the image of an agonistic democracy as a triumph of the political principle undergirding all human life. She denies the existence of an "undifferentiated human nature," rejecting "Enlightenment universalism,"[29] instead asserting a pluralist political essence to human activity: "Radical democracy demands that we acknowledge the difference—the particular, the multiple, the heterogeneous—in effect, everything that has been excluded by the concept of Man in the abstract."[30] Abandoning universalism thus appears to be liberating for human beings, freeing them to enact their pluralized identities in an open political sphere.

But in fact what Mouffe and other agonists have done is to commit human beings indefinitely to the definition of the conventional. The political and politics become all there is in the world; there is no claim that *humans* can make against it—only claims that human beings can make through and in it as implicitly democratic, agonistic creatures. Lefort's conception sees the human being *as political* revealing itself in the French Revolution. There is thus a natural form of government for human beings contained in this self-declaration: the rights-based democracy. For Lefort, human beings name the human elements in one another by recognizing the self in the democratic state, no matter how paradoxical its functionality might be. Wolin's fugitive human existence is also characterized by its political nature, functioning in and through the politics of its particular moment but in essence holding the ideals of a democratic political spirit. What presents itself as a novel emancipatory project in fact forecloses entirely the root cause and motive force of a genuinely emancipatory politics: the universal human claim that exists *against the political.*

While the distinction between these radical Leftist positions and what I am presenting as a regenerative politics might seem slight, the distance between them is in fact significant. Unlike the agonist argument, a truly regenerative politics does not take as its first principle the idea that human beings somehow necessarily *belong* in or to the political. "The political" is a conventional condition made by human beings, which can be remade or lost as easily as it can be reconstituted. Following Rousseau, while there could be some political condition that best facilitates a kind of independent and free existence for human beings, the completed existence of this condition is a logical impossibility. There can be no regime in which the exercise of political freedom precludes the exercise of human freedom; any shared existence is one of dependence, even if well constituted, and human beings always maintain a natural claim—a first right—against their own artifice. A regenerative politics sees that it is necessary to make human claims in and through the political, but it is only possible to do so, and to establish rights, because the human doing the claiming maintains the first right to do so. Human nature as such is universally understood as being constituted by a regenerative right to make the conditions of one's existence and to maintain a liberty from those conditions absolutely. It is the *freedom from the political* that grants the regenerative power, not the reduction of the human being to the political itself.

The vison of human nature that I have outlined in this book is essential to any genuinely regenerative politics. Respecting and restoring the first right of human beings to make and determine the conditions of their contingent historical existence requires an openness to all forms of self-determination, all remaking of convention, and most fundamentally the right to renounce and reconstitute the political in its entirety. What makes the regenerative vision of the human being a modern conception as opposed to an ancient one is the claim that human beings are not political by nature; what makes it not entirely modern is, at the same time, the claim that human beings have a nature that is directed in some way toward an end and oriented in some sense toward an idea of what is good for human life. This is what I have called the *modern telic*.

Such a conception of human nature must remain open to the possibility that political rights, or any given conception of inalienable rights, may not be the last word on what it means to be human in the world. If a good or desirable vision is on offer—perhaps a universal or universalizable vision—then it is worth the effort to preserve its life and to have human lives invested in its vitality. Rights must become one such vision, existing in the world as one among many and relying for their significance and maintenance on the regenerative vigor and commitment of self-regenerating human beings. There is no presumption of progress here, no affirmative complaisance that rights, once recognized, are eternally valued. The cyclical nature of regenerative politics relies instead on the persistent awareness that things could always be otherwise, that humans could just as easily constitute their political world differently, that there will always be human claims against the given political order. These claims must always be seen in the same way as claims for universal rights—as being made by self-regenerating human beings desiring self-determination in the world.

Today's idea of liberal progress, or the historical progress of rights, contains within itself the temporal implication of completion. It is this idea most of all of which today's critics of liberalism are most critical: the presumption that rights are a final statement on what it means to be human. It is my hope that a regenerative conception of rights would detach rights from this implicit finality. Seeing all (political) rights as subject to the first right of human beings to make and reconstitute them would mean that rights could become a liberating site of self-determination, even for those who do not currently see this potential in them. At its most practical, this conception of rights would mean that no right, under any condition, could be seen as irrevocable, as so self-evident that it would be immune from degeneration. No right gained could be invulnerable to loss, even political freedom and equality. The hope is that this would transform rights from passive declarations into active and regenerative assertions, and that human beings would once again see their life as more free and equal in the world, having determined that world, and thereby determined themselves, in the act of political (re)making.

But of course, great risks hang like shadows over this hopeful vision. Without the last bulwark of the claim to self-evidence, rights may not survive. The most significant fear regarding the overturning of rights comes from the rise of the Far Right, or the resurgence of fascism—that is, the rise of political worlds whose mission is to undo or eliminate human freedom(s) altogether. I am not claiming that this fear is illegitimate, nor am I trying to downplay its urgency or its danger. The risk of overturning rights and democracy is real. I am claiming, however, that only a regenerative politics can prevent the triumph of the political vision of the Far Right, by keeping the political world open to constant and dynamic reconstitution on the part of its members.

In the rise of today's Far Right, we see the attractiveness of a politics that allows citizens to believe (however falsely or unjustly the claim is constituted) that they are at last being given the opportunity to remake the world and to fight forces of oppression that they see as constraining their freedom and capacity to be equal to others. The force of this oppression is variously construed as the amorphous demon of "liberalism" and "rights," broadly understood. The perception is that people have been born into a world not of their own making or choosing, a world they would not make or choose for themselves. Wendy Brown has identified this as a "civilizational despair" exemplified in the stultifying and stagnating power of neoliberalism to crush the human spirit:[31] "Families become shells, ownership and savings vanish, marriages teeter and break, depression, anxiety, and other forms of mental illness are ubiquitous. . . . Nation, family, property, and the traditions reproducing gender and racial privilege, mortally wounded by deindustrialization, neoliberal reason, globalization, digital technologies, and nihilism, are reduced to affective remains. To date, these remains have been activated mostly by the Right."[32]

These remains and the palpable civilizational despair conjure images of stagnation—of a world left unmoving and citizens left unmoved. The Far Right has taken it upon themselves to cast their vision of the future as an alternative to this static reality. They present themselves as responsible for reinvigorating a sense of newness and movement and for reasserting differences that will propel change. Regenerative politics for the Far Right is an active and motive force that will supplant the still life of the modern liberal global order of human rights, and its accompanying Enlightenment-rooted universalism, with a new vision of the human being. Portraying themselves as the guardians of diversity, individualism, and novelty, the figures of the Far Right envision what they call a "metapolitical" future. In Guillaume Faye's terms,[33] *metapolitics* is defined as "the social diffusion of ideas and cultural values for the sake of provoking a profound long-term political transformation"[34]—it is the transformation of souls through the transformation of politics. Metapolitics is thus bound to the regenerative mode insofar as Far Right thinkers see political change as inextricably bound to changes in human psychology, mores, and thinking; that is, if human politics is made anew, so too will human beings be regenerated in a novel form.

The Far Right, however, embraces regenerative politics only as a temporary means to a far more sinister end. As the editor-in-chief of Arktos Media, John Bruce Leonard, reveals, the goal of a regenerative political world would be to "produce a society in which metapolitics . . . no longer exists."[35] For the Far Right, the regeneration or remaking of the human being would thus one day entail overcoming the need for political regeneration or remaking altogether. The envisioned change would transcend the political sphere to a meta-level: the transformation of humanity itself. For the Far Right, metapolitics is the overcoming of politics-as-such *through* political and social transformation, and the metapolitical vision in its end state eradicates the motive, regenerative project of the transformation of the world and of human beings. It is *this* final vision of the cessation of all political change, transformation, and novelty that is the most concerning facet of these thinkers on the Far Right, and the most problematic and ominous political force we have challenging liberal democracies today.

If we wish to avoid the triumph of one uncontested vision—the triumph of totalitarianism—our best chance is counterintuitively to embrace, rather than reject, regenerative politics. We must preserve the capacity of our future visions to change and to change over time—this is the very essence of what it means to be a self-regenerating and self-determining human being. To prevent the Far Right's metapolitical future, we must keep the genuinely political sphere of human action alive in the active power to regenerate, or remake, ourselves by regenerating, or remaking, our political worlds. To preserve the sphere of political action and the potential for positive change, the palingenetic nature of politics must be affirmed and maintained, which also requires that we look to the competing visions of our future and future selves that might propel regenerative transformations of our conditions.

It is only the possible success of the Far Right's metapolitics, and never a truly regenerative politics, that could end this necessary dynamism; and only a regenerative politics could prevent the ascendency of *one* vision, through maintaining a vigilant commitment to the presumption that human beings could always be, and make themselves, otherwise. This means that rights must become the constant subject of reimagining and remaking. Just as we reject the Far Right's vision of a metapolitical future, rights-affirming liberal democrats will be required to abandon all assertions of the stability or finality of self-evident human rights. Whether or not this means that human beings will stick with rights remains to be seen, but I believe that this is the best chance that rights have for survival in today's increasingly challenging political climate.

Making rights alive to human self-constitution would also, one can hope, make them alive and open to the challenges coming from critiques on the Left. This is precisely the kind of regenerative world that could accommodate Rinaldo Walcott's opposition to the linearity of "the logic of modernist freedom" that presumes a gradual perfection of "what it means to be human" in the system of rights.[36] For Walcott, rights belong to the realm of the "juridical" and thus predetermine the contours of humanity, allowing for political emancipation but never genuine human freedom. Following Sylvia Wynter, Walcott argues that "the very idea of the human requires rethinking in order for an authentic freedom to emerge for Black people."[37] His critique of the constraining capacity of today's liberal iteration of rights matches Dean Spade's account in

Normal Life of the limitations of the rights framework for trans politics and for lesbian, gay, feminist, and anti-racist politics.[38] Spade argues that "legal equality goals" in fact mask vast inequalities of treatment in the social and political world, facilitating injustices through the feigned neutrality and presumed universality of the liberal commitment to the freedom and equality of all persons.[39] Glen Coulthard argues in *Red Skin, White Masks* that attempting to achieve a peaceful coexistence of Western liberal democracies and Indigenous peoples through the "ideal of reciprocity or mutual recognition . . . in its contemporary liberal form [instead] promises to reproduce the very configurations of colonialist, racist, patriarchal state power that Indigenous peoples' demands for recognition have historically sought to transcend."[40] Reciprocity masks the attempt to distinguish between Indigenous and "legal" persons, establishing the same colonial power dynamic that it claims to overcome. Yann Allard-Tremblay sees us in the "Age of Man," in which the "Modern/Colonial Man presents himself as the universal subject, and thereby erases and disqualifies alternative ways of being human."[41] Tremblay seeks to "ground critical reflections about disjunctive alternatives to currently dominating practices, in ways that may support Indigenous self-determination and freedom."[42]

Rights reimagined, however, as a kind of dynamic consequence of regenerative agency, or of the first right of human beings, would be premised on the foundational commitment to the fact that, in the words of Walcott, "the question of the human . . . is not settled."[43] As he writes in *Queer Returns*, "In the case of a 'new world' for Indigenous and Blacks specifically, reconciliation can only be but a beginning towards a much more profound and challenging discussion of what it means to be human that rests upon multiple perspectives of humanness in which European concepts are but one among many. Reconciliation is a beginning: unimagined transformation is the desired outcome."[44] However unstable its practical realization might be, a regenerative politics would be grounded in the promise of unimaginable transformation. The normative commitment of a regenerative politics is to the preservation of this possibility and promise, to the desirability of upholding the political space in the world for human beings to constitute themselves and to feel and be truly self-determined. Here, as Walcott suggests, "new registers of life" could appear and be met on equal, human terms with others, standing together in the human position of a first right—against the political rights that

RESTORING OUR FIRST RIGHT   169

are subject to refashioning, maintenance, or abandonment.[45] This could be what Aimé Césaire called for, in a "humanism made to the measure of the world."[46] In their most recent book, *Undoing Gender*, Judith Butler has turned to precisely this mode of humanism, embracing the "necessity of keeping our notion of the human open to a future articulation [as] essential to the project of international human rights discourse and politics."[47] For Butler, the discourse of rights has emerged as a possible future, a mode of being for human beings who are "undone by each other."[48] Butler also sees this possible future as constituting "a loss, a disorientation" of what we know to be true about rights and about human beings "but one in which the human stands a chance of coming into being anew."[49]

In my account of the regenerative political enterprise, Jean-Jacques Rousseau has emerged as a theoretical forefather. While Rousseau's regenerative politics has in the past been associated with dangerous, violent, and illiberal politics, he appears here as a surprising friend to the project of reinvigorating the vitality of the liberal democracy and bolstering rights in the contemporary world. His foundational commitment to the first right of human beings to renounce all conditions of their dependence forms the bedrock of his construction of the *Social Contract* and of his position that the human always maintains a priority over the political, and nature over artifice. For Rousseau, any regime in which human beings cannot make a claim against the conditions of their own conventions loses its legitimacy, and this pertains especially to rights-based regimes in which the question of the human being is seen to be identifiable and settled.

Even in his own time, Rousseau was seen as a radical—for this reason, he is often portrayed as a counter-Enlightenment figure, averse to the otherwise rationalist and enlightening impulses of his contemporaries. There is nothing, in my accounting, that makes Rousseau 'counter' Enlightenment—he is very much of his time, embedded in the natural-scientific and political controversies of his day, and deeply influential to the human and political changes that culminated in the French Revolution. While he may be seen as an enemy of the more conventional account of rights we get in the likes of John Locke, he is no enemy to the project of establishing the rights of human beings in the world—as I have shown, his political philosophy was formative to the project of proclaiming the regenerative rights of the Declaration of the Rights of Man and of the Citizen in 1789.

Rousseau is once again being appropriated and studied for his progressive, radical potential. Charles Mills claimed Rousseau as his primary inspiration in both *The Racial Contract* and *Black Rights/White Wrongs* and retrieved Rousseau's work as "an alternative, radical democratic strain in contract theory" that may be able to reinvigorate "the liberalism that *should have been*."[50] Rousseau is also the hero of Jane Anna Gordon's *Creolizing Political Theory*,[51] which spearheaded the combinations of distinctive yet seemingly unconnected traditions, releasing new "emancipatory potential[s] of human inquiry."[52] Gordon brings together Rousseau and Frantz Fanon as thinkers who challenged "the way that reason had been used to advance the singularity of particular models of desirable political arrangements and ways of being human."[53] Like Fanon, Gordon argues, Rousseau liberated human beings from the constrictions of social and political convention: "For both Rousseau and Fanon the alternative to decadent culture is politically-legitimate-culture-in-the-making."[54] As Fanon writes in *Black Skin, White Masks*, "Truly what is to be done is to set man free."[55] This is exactly the sentiment of Rousseau's most radical work.

The historian Vincenzo Ferrone recognizes that this radical potential was always present in Rousseau and in the Enlightenment, contained in the vast project of establishing "a new humanism of rights" for a new world.[56] For Ferrone, Rousseau was responsible for "the definition of the natural right to freedom," making him the progenitor of "the original and authentic principle of the rights of man."[57] Rousseau appears here as a kind of lost radical, or—akin to Charles Mills's liberal that should have been—a lost radical of rights. In this respect, Ferrone's call to reinvigorate this old new humanism meets Kenan Malik's despair about our current "politics of defeat," epitomized in "disillusionment with the possibilities of social change."[58] According to Malik, we have abandoned the "radical intellectual tradition embodied" in the Enlightenment,[59] exemplified in the work of Jean-Jacques Rousseau. Malik presents Rousseau as engaged in a "dialectical approach to humanity" that sees "the universal and the particular as in a state of constant tension and dialogue."[60] In my construction, the affirmation of some universal nature to human beings, and the equal affirmation of the manner in which human beings are shaped by their particular historical circumstances, binds this radical Rousseauian conception of human nature to the essential preservation of the first right of human beings to change their particular social and political conditions.

Today's citizens of liberal democracies do not feel this ability to change their circumstances. The politics of defeat, the crushing forces of capitalism and neoliberalism, the increasing pessimism about the prospects of liberalism, the rise of the Far Right: these must all be met with some alternative, some hope for our future political lives. Wendy Brown has declared this the "task of the Left": "Tasked with the already difficult project of puncturing common neoliberal sense and with developing a viable and compelling alternative to capitalist globalization, the Left must also counter this civilizational despair. Our work on all three fronts is incalculably difficult, bears no immediate reward, and carries no guarantee of success."[61] Alex Zamalin has also recently called for a tentative new hope in his *Black Utopia*: "Elements of the mainstream political left seem stunted"; to counter this stagnation, "freedom must be reconstructed as an opening up of oneself to oneself and, by extension, the world."[62]

In *Critique and Praxis*, Bernard Harcourt presents our predicament as the consequence of "legal liberalism," which consists in "the idea that we should conform to the rule of law as a way to avoid political strife."[63] "This liberal view," he writes, "mostly solves the political quandary that we find ourselves in, halts the slippage into authoritarianism, and offers the most viable utopic vision. . . . Most people in advanced capitalist countries believe this. Most have faith in the rule of law and believe in its neutrality. . . . [But] it is the illusion of legal liberalism that renders many, here and now—in the United States at least—docile subjects."[64] It "stifles political action. There is also desperation, depression, a growing sense of futility, and problems of collective action. For many, there is a feeling that nothing will change anyway. There is a sense of powerlessness."[65] Helena Rosenblatt closes *The Lost History of Liberalism* with a similar call to shake up the decline of human agency in liberal democracies and wake up our fellow citizens: "Although liberalism today is widely regarded as the dominant political doctrine of the West, a kind of triumphalism coexists with pessimism. We often hear that liberalism is suffering from a crisis of confidence, a crisis made more intense by the rise of 'illiberal democracy' around the world. It is suggested that the problem could be solved if only liberals would agree about what they stood for and have the courage in their convictions. . . . Liberals should reconnect with the resources of their own tradition to recover, understand, and embrace its core values."[66] Samuel Moyn opens *Liberalism Against Itself* with a plea for today's liberals to depart from their Cold War inheritance: "Cold War liberalism left the liberal tradition unrecognizable and in ruins. For that reason, a better place to start in exploring liberalism's far reaches is with its nineteenth- and early twentieth-century versions, which will determine whether it deserves to survive in the twenty-first-century future. Emancipatory and futuristic before the Cold War, committed most of all to free and equal self-creation, accepting of democracy and welfare (though never enough to date), liberalism can be something other than the Cold War liberalism we have known."[67]

There is no doubt that there is a growing consensus that something needs to change. Human beings are no longer part of their politics. They are suffering, detached, and feeling hopeless and powerless despite the fact that we, as members of liberal democracies, are living in the most free and affluent age of human history. It is the double bind of acknowledging both the commitment and total failure to live up to the ideals of self-determination, of freedom and equality, that has frozen the liberal response to today's political pessimism. It is the fear of losing what has been gained that stops us from properly honoring the human need and desire to determine one's own life in the world.

But if we really do want things to change, we must be willing to change ourselves absolutely. This is the very essence of what it means to be a self-regenerating human being. Transforming ourselves in this case means that our rights must be lost entirely in order for them to be refound—made and maintained by the very human beings who both affirm and become the free and equal beings they hold themselves to be. The risk of the degeneration of rights will hang over any regenerative politics, but it will also be the source of political life. Only by restoring all human beings to their first right—in seeing ourselves as capable of changing our social and political conditions perpetually but not always progressively—will we be capable of keeping freedom and equality in the world, in and through us and through our political vigilance and action.

The prospect of losing some or all of our rights may be too heavy for the committed liberal democrat. At the risk of overstating the driving principle of my regenerative view of human beings and politics, my reply would simply be: nature always wins. Human beings want to determine themselves in the world, and the world is a perpetually shifting and regenerating space. If we do not remain open to the foundational human claim that people have against their conventional circumstance—their given, historical particularity—no political system or presumed universality will hold for long. It is only by remaining dynamic, open to regeneration and the regenerative claims and first right of all human beings, that we have any hope of our political rights surviving; without this dynamism, we are resigning ourselves to losing our rights and to perpetuating predetermined, closed human lives against our wills.

If there is a task for us, then, it is to remind ourselves actively, and by our own choosing, that no right we think we possess can be taken for granted or as settled by all persons in any given place or time. To bring human beings back into their own politics, that political space must be unceasingly open to self-regeneration and self-determination. It is the very instability and motive force of regenerative politics that will keep rights alive. Though there is risk, there is a world to win of free and equal human beings—for as long as we can make and keep it.

ACKNOWLEDGMENTS

For this book to become *Regenerative Politics*, it had to undergo many regenerations of its own. In this process, I have relied on the support, guidance, mentorship, and friendship of many. My work on regeneration began as part of my graduate studies at the University of Toronto, when I was fortunate to be part of a large and vibrant group of political theorists. My peers were knowledgeable and challenging interlocutors and are gifted and accomplished theorists. It is a privilege to have had this community. The rich student body at Toronto is a reflection of the outstanding faculty in the Political Science department. My work at Toronto would not have been possible without the unwavering encouragement I received from my supervisor, Peggy Kohn, who backed my project from its beginning and never doubted my capacity to think it through to its end. The members of my committee, Ronnie Beiner and Rebecca Kingston, also read every draft of every chapter and pushed the project into new spaces. Special thanks are owed, too, to my two examiners, Torrey Shanks and Jason Neidleman, and to Ed Andrew, Ryan Balot, Joe Carens, Simone Chambers, and Ruth Marshall for their support and challenging conversations. I am also grateful for the financial support of the Social Sciences and Humanities Research Council of Canada, the Ontario Graduate Scholarship Program, and the Northrop Frye Center at Victoria College, and for the intellectual communities at the Centre for Ethics and the Jackman Humanities Institute.

While in Toronto, I benefited from the mentorship of two people in particular who have now become dear friends. Teresa Bejan and I crossed paths at Toronto for only two years, but during that time I learned invaluable things from Teresa as her research assistant and from her academic mentorship. Since that time, we have seen each other across the world and through the developments of our lives. Mark Kingwell was one of the first professors of my undergraduate education, and when we reconnected during my graduate studies we became great friends. I am sure there will be many more decades of dry humor and discussion ahead. During my graduate studies, I also met Laura Rabinowitz, and I am so grateful for our continuing personal and intellectual friendship. It has been especially delightful to be able to get to know Silvie and Little Guy Joseph. Toronto remains a special place for me because the Balot/Rabinowitz clan is there and because my dear friends Tarek Dika and Constance de Font-Réaulx and my goddaughter, Saba, now also live there.

Before starting at Toronto, I completed an MA at McGill University in Montréal. During that time I was trained to be rigorous and disciplined in my scholarship. I would not be the scholar I am today without the mentorship of my supervisor there, Arash Abizadeh, and that of my readers and professors Jacob Levy and Christina Tarnopolsky. It was also at McGill where I first met Nina Valiquette Moreau, with whom I reconnected when I joined the Society of Fellows at the University of Chicago. Nina is a great friend and an even greater scholar, and we have had too many generative conversations about Rousseau and this book to count. I look forward to the day in the future when she turns her own incisive gaze from Plato to Rousseau.

My time as a fellow at Chicago was short but perhaps one of the most impactful of my life. My research there came alive through conversations with scholars across disciplines, pushing my work in new directions. Thanks especially to my fellow fellows Aaron Benanav, Miguel Caballaro Vazquez, Katie Kadue, Natacha Nsabimana, and Aaron Tugendhaft and to my great friends Daragh Grant and Sarah Johnson, whom I am thankful remain in Chicago—close enough to visit, though never often enough. Adom Getachew, Matt Landauer, and Emma Saunders-Hastings made my time in Chicago fun and memorable. Demetra Kasimis, Patchen Markell, John McCormick, Jennifer Pitts, Nathan Tarcov, Lisa Wedeen, Jim Wilson, and Linda Zerilli were and remain great models for me both in their teaching and their scholarship. I am especially grateful to Sankar Muthu, who was my official mentor as a fellow and who rendered his first judgment (of many) on *Regenerative Politics* in the proximity of the skeptical gaze of Linné. During my time at Chicago, I was also supported by the Social Sciences and Humanities Research Council of Canada, and I owe many thanks to Jim Sparrow and Lis Clemens for arranging this part of my fellowship.

From Chicago, I joined the Program of Liberal Studies (PLS) at the University of Notre Dame—a great books program composed of interdisciplinary tenured and tenure-track faculty and the most passionate and committed undergraduate students I have ever taught. At Notre Dame I have been afforded the time, resources, and intellectual environment to regenerate my historical work into this book—a book that I did not even know existed before my thinking began to expand through conversations, conferences, and new work. I am grateful for all of my colleagues in PLS (current and former): Francesca Bordogna, Eric Bugyis, Katie Bugyis, Chris Chowrimootoo, Tarek Dika, Steve Fallon, Robert Goulding, Jenny Martin, Julia Marvin, Felicitas Munzel, Clark Power, Andy Radde-Gallwitz, Gretchen Reydams-Schils, Matt Rickard, Denis Robichaud, Joseph Rosenberg, Arman Schwartz, Tom Stapleford, Henry Weinfield, and Heather Wiebe. Many of them have workshopped ideas with me, both formally and informally, for years, and the book would not exist if not for their support and the support of such a collegial department. Many thanks, too, to Becky Badger and Marie Revak, our departmental coordinators—they are the ones, along with Eric Bugyis, who have truly kept the department running. I also have wonderful colleagues and students in the political science department, yet another home to a robust political theory community of which I have had the good fortune to be a part.

The leave I was afforded in my fourth year at Notre Dame provided me the space and time to rewrite the book in its entirety. When I emerged from this process, Don Stelluto, then the executive director of the Kellogg Institute for International Studies, offered me generous financial support and much enthusiasm for workshopping the book at a conference. Along with the support of my department and the Institute for Scholarship in the Liberal Arts, we organized a book workshop at Kellogg for *Regenerative Politics* that was integral to its intellectual development. I will forever be grateful to my four external participants—Matt Kadane,

Sam Moyn, Sankar Muthu, and Denise Schaeffer—and to the six Notre Dame participants—Katlyn Carter, Bernard Forjwuor, Eileen Hunt, Phil Sloan, Tom Stapleford, and Don Stelluto—for taking two days of their time to think through this book with me. I hope that in its final form it lives up to the stimulating and challenging conversations we had. Thanks also to my three graduate students who attended and participated: Evy Behling, Makella Brems, and Linus Recht. I hope to be in a position someday soon to be thinking through your own books with you. The book also would not have been completed without the excellent work of my research assistant, Matt Foley, and my Kellogg research assistant, Gladys (Aimee) Umunyana. An extra thanks to Linus Recht, who offered great feedback on a tight timeline at the end.

In chapter 2, some material appears from "Regenerating Humanism," *History of European Ideas* 46, no. 3 (2020): 242–56; and in chapter 3 from "Homo Duplex: The Two Origins of Man in Rousseau's Second Discourse," *History of European Ideas* 47, no. 1 (2021): 71–90. Both are reprinted with permission from Taylor and Francis. The epigraph for the book comes from "And the Dogs Were Silent" from *The Complete Poetry of Aimé Césaire: Bilingual Edition* © 2024, translated by Clayton Eshleman and A. James Arnold and published by Wesleyan University Press. Used by permission.

I have presented arguments from or related to the book at the University of Chicago, London School of Economics and Political Science, and Stanford Political Theory workshops, the George Washington Forum, the Kellogg Institute, King's College, and Pomona College, and I am grateful for the invitations to do so. Thanks to the attendees of these workshops, and those on panels and in audiences at American Political Science Association and European Consortium for Political Research during which some of the book's ideas were developed.

For assisting with the intellectual development of the book across many years, and for supporting my work, of those not already mentioned I owe particular thanks to Mauro Caraccioli, Paul Cheney, Scott Dodds, Stefan Dolgert, Sue Donaldson, Christine Henderson, James Ingram, Leigh Jenco, Gary Kates, Simon Kow, Chandran Kukathas, Will Kymlicka, Sophie Marcotte Chenard, Martin McCallum, Alison McQueen, Darrin McMahon, Dan O'Neill, Taylor Putnam, Helena Rosenblatt, Avshalom Schwartz, John Scott, Michael Scott Thomas, Roy Scranton, Rob Sparling,

Céline Spector, Nick Stang, Zoltán Gábor Szűcs, Ann Ward, Paul Weithman, Richard Whatmore, David Lay Williams, and Caroline Winterer.

I am very thankful to have ended up with Columbia University Press working with Wendy Lochner, and with Amy Allen as part of the *New Directions in Critical Theory* series. It is not every press that will give a first-time author the platform to make a bold argument, and I am so appreciative of their confidence in my work. I am also immensely grateful for the prodigious copyediting of Kara Cowan, and for the financial support from The Institute for the Scholarship in the Liberal Arts, College of Arts and Letters, University of Notre Dame for the indexing of the book.

A few conversations have shifted my thinking entirely when building the argument of the book. My memories of these are vivid, and I describe them here in closing not only to express my thanks but also to remind readers just how important any one conversation can be. At a casual lunch, Jim McAdams persuaded me to think through the regenerative rhetoric of the Far Right for a conference at Notre Dame in 2019. Doing so altered the trajectory of my project permanently. A conversation over dinner with Mary Keys at a conference on Rawls convinced me that I had to do an equal amount of work looking into the regenerative claims of the critical Left for the argument to function. This was the tipping point in deciding to rewrite the book from the ground up over my research leave. During the COVID-19 lockdowns, I had the most formative conversation for the book with Dirk Schuck over Zoom from Germany. It was Dirk's confidence in the radical critical core of my argument and the angles from which he articulated it that made it clear that this was more than a historical project.

Two conversations occurred in downtown South Bend at the Central High apartment buildings, a converted high school that houses many Notre Dame faculty and, unfortunately, the occasional bat. Over dinner with my friends Tarek and Constance, Tarek told me that the genealogical story of the book didn't make sense. The comment has haunted me for years, and I hope I have solved this here. The most important moment for the book took place on the rooftop of Central High with my brother Jake, my friend Melissa, and her brother Levi. While enjoying our beer on this windy evening, I was asked what my book was about. Normally I might disengage from this kind of request in a social situation, but I obliged, explaining in brief my issue with how rights are conceptualized.

The conversation took off. Though they are not academics themselves, my argument resonated immediately with my friends' experiences of the world, and we had one of the most wide-ranging, real, and consequential discussions about the book's implications that I have had. When I begin to doubt the book's claims or usefulness, it is that night to which I return—to remind myself that connecting with people about what is at stake in the world and in politics is what thinking is for. It is also this night that reminds me that there is more to life than books and argument; that life is about the people you care about and who care enough about you to ask about your book on a rooftop. I am lucky to have wonderful friends in South Bend—Cassidy Fowler, Rich Fowler, Abby Gilmore, Stephanie Rizk, Melissa Rodriguez, and Levi Rodriguez—who have nothing at all to do with academia, and wonderful friends who do—Christina Bambrick, Abi Ocobock, Sara Marcus, Dana Moss, Sarah Shortall, and Josh Specht, among many others. We all share the South Bend spaces—the General Café (where this entire book was written), the Hammer and Quill, LangLab—with a great community of people who enrich my life. A special thanks is owed to Rich Fowler at Eco Owl Press, who completed the graphic design of the book cover's polyp.

It is a feature of the acknowledgments section that you end up writing about everyone else in the world as if they are somehow accessories to your own life experience or objective facts of the world against which you have forged your own unique locomotive and subjective path. Of course, this is not how life works. As much of the thesis of this book attests to, we are irreparably dependent on others and on the circumstances of our lives in ways that negate the idea of an absolute independent subjectivity. According to Rousseau, this dependence is a necessary feature of the world and one that in politics, at least, we ought to try to overcome. Contrary to politics, however, and perhaps contrary to Rousseau, a form of this dependence has not only been formative for my life but its greatest joy. We are not only born into the world but into our families—if we are lucky, as I have been, we are born into a family filled with love. All the things I am, have been, and will be is owed to them: to those here, gone, and to come.

In *The Human Condition*, Hannah Arendt allocates regeneration to the private sphere, to the realm of the family—here, she claims, is where regeneration belongs because it is in families where life is reproduced, where things are moving and cyclical. Everything about my life and about this book has led me to the opposite conclusion. Regeneration belongs to politics and the world, where things and people and ideas can change, where the distinction between independence and dependence is generative and productive. Family is where those distinctions dissolve—where change and cyclicality seem to stall and you return to a place where you, in some sense, have always been. My family has been a place of stability, a dependence and dependability, that I wouldn't trade for the world.

To Jake, Lucy, Eila, Emily and baby Alice, Steve; to Oona, to Paul;

And to my parents, Leah and Zdravko, to whom I dedicate this book. They are distinguished not only for having brought me into the world and for being my source of dependence and love but also for being the sources from which I had to regenerate myself in the world as a thinker and a scholar. For me, they are and have been everything—the root of both my dependence and my independence—and this is a special gift.

NOTES

1. NO HUMANS LEFT

1. Jean-Yves Camus, "Alain de Benoist and the New Right," in *Key Thinkers of the Radical Right: Behind the New Threat to Liberal Democracy*, ed. Mark Sedgwick (Oxford: Oxford University Press, 2019), 73–90; Guillaume Faye, *Why We Fight: Manifesto of the European Resistance*, trans. Michael O'Meara (London: Arktos, 2011); Arthur Versluis, "A Conversation with Alain de Benoist," *Journal for the Study of Radicalism* 8, no. 2 (2014): 79–106.
2. Faye, *Why We Fight*, 173.
3. Faye, *Why We Fight*, 173–74.
4. Faye, *Why We Fight*, 174.
5. Versluis, "A Conversation," 97.
6. Versluis, "A Conversation," 95.
7. Daniel S. Forrest, *Suprahumanism: European Man and the Regeneration of History* (London: Arktos, 2014), 29.
8. Michel Foucault, *The Order of Things: An Archaeology of the Human Sciences*, trans. Alan Sheridan (New York: Vintage, 1994), xxiii.
9. Foucault, *The Order of Things*, 340.
10. Sylvia Wynter, interview with Katherine McKittrick. In Katherine McKittrick, ed., *Sylvia Wynter: On Being Human as Praxis* (Durham, NC: Duke University Press, 2015), 31.
11. Wynter in McKittrick, *Sylvia Wynter*, 73.
12. Wynter in McKittrick, *Sylvia Wynter*, 21, 31.
13. Wynter in McKittrick, *Sylvia Wynter*, 63.
14. Zakiyyah Iman Jackson, *Becoming Human: Matter and Meaning in an Antiblack World* (New York: New York University Press, 2020), 4, 21.
15. Jackson, *Becoming Human*, 28.

16.   Angela Y. Davis, *The Meaning of Freedom: And Other Difficult Dialogues* (San Francisco: City Lights, 2012); Ta-Nehisi Coates, *Between the World and Me* (Melbourne: Text, 2015); Rinaldo Walcott, *The Long Emancipation: Moving Toward Black Freedom* (Durham, NC: Duke University Press, 2021); Rinaldo Walcott, *Queer Returns: Essays on Multiculturalism, Diaspora, and Black Studies* (London, ON: Insomniac, 2016); Achille Mbembe, *Necropolitics* (Durham, NC: Duke University Press, 2019).

17.   Walcott, *The Long Emancipation*, 56.

18.   Mbembe, *Necropolitics*, 160–61.

19.   Aimé Césaire, *Discourse on Colonialism*, trans. Joan Pinkham (New York: Monthly Review, 2001), 74. Here, Césaire recalls Marx's rejection of the bourgeois rights of man in Marx's "On the Jewish Question."

20.   Césaire, *Discourse on Colonialism*, 74, 37.

21.   Kenan Malik, *The Meaning of Race: Race, History, and Culture in Western Society* (New York: New York University Press, 1996), 221.

22.   Stuart Hall, "The West and the Rest: Discourse and Power," in *Essential Essays*, vol. 2 (Durham, NC: Duke University Press, 2018), cited in Malik, *The Meaning of Race*, 222.

23.   Carl L. Becker, *The Heavenly City of the Eighteenth-Century Philosophers*, ed. Johnson Kent Wright (New Haven, CT: Yale University Press, 1932), 129.

24.   Patrick J. Deneen, *Regime Change: Toward a Postliberal Future* (New York: Sentinel, 2023).

25.   For more on the connection to Nietzsche on the Far Right, see Ronald Beiner, *Dangerous Minds: Nietzsche, Heidegger, and the Return of the Far Right* (Philadelphia: University of Pennsylvania Press, 2018).

26.   Forrest, *Suprahumanism*, 14.

27.   Forrest, *Suprahumanism*, 25–26.

28.   Faye, *Why We Fight*, 127.

29.   Faye, *Why We Fight*, 127.

30.   Faye, *Why We Fight*, 165.

31.   Faye, *Why We Fight*, 162.

32.   Wynter in McKittrick, *Sylvia Wynter*, 11.

33.   Alexander G. Weheliye, *Habeas Viscus: Racializing Assemblages, Biopolitics, and Black Feminist Theories of the Human* (Durham, NC: Duke University Press, 2014), 21. The critique of Man, too, follows from Michel Foucault's argument in *The Order of Things*.

34.   Jackson, *Becoming Human*, 4, 21.

35.   Dean Spade, *Normal Life: Administrative Violence, Critical Trans Politics, and the Limits of Law* (Durham, NC: Duke University Press, 2015); Lee Edelman, *No Future: Queer Theory and the Death Drive* (Durham, NC: Duke University Press, 2004).

36.   Mbembe, *Necropolitics*, 187.

37.   Walcott, *The Long Emancipation*, 5.

38.   Walcott, *The Long Emancipation*, 7.

39.   Wynter in McKittrick, *Sylvia Wynter*, 11.

40.   Jackson, *Becoming Human*, 21.

41.   Jackson, *Becoming Human*, 28.

42.   Jackson, *Becoming Human*, 36.

43. Walcott, *The Long Emancipation*, 15.

44. Coates, *Between the World and Me*, 115.

45. See, for example, Stephen Holmes, *The Anatomy of Antiliberalism* (Cambridge, MA: Harvard University Press, 1993).

46. Patrick J. Deneen, *Why Liberalism Failed* (New Haven, CT: Yale University Press, 2018).

47. See, for example, Duncan Bell, "What Is Liberalism?," *Political Theory* 42, no. 6 (2014): 682–715.

48. I will say more about the emergence of this liberal vision in chapter 5. For recent defenses of the self-evidence of these rights, see Danielle Allen, *Our Declaration: A Reading of the Declaration of Independence in Defense of Equality* (New York: Liveright, 2014), and Anne Phillips, *Unconditional Equals* (Princeton, NJ: Princeton University Press, 2021).

49. Alan Ryan, *The Making of Modern Liberalism* (Princeton, NJ: Princeton University Press, 2012), 35.

50. This is, in effect, the argument made by Samuel Moyn in his most recent book about the Cold War liberal abandonment of human self-creativity: Samuel Moyn, *Liberalism Against Itself: Cold War Intellectuals and the Making of Our Times* (New Haven, CT: Yale University Press, 2023).

51. Pierre Manent, *Natural Law and Human Rights: Toward a Recovery of Practical Reason*, trans. Ralph C. Hancock (Notre Dame, IN: University of Notre Dame Press, 2021); Alasdair MacIntyre, *After Virtue: A Study in Moral Theory*, 3rd ed. (Notre Dame, IN: University of Notre Dame Press, 2007); Leo Strauss, *Natural Right and History* (Chicago: University of Chicago Press, 1965); Leo Strauss, *What Is Political Philosophy?* (Glencoe, IL: Free Press, 1959).

52. Judith Butler, *Undoing Gender* (New York: Routledge, 2004); Judith Butler, *Gender Trouble: Feminism and the Subversion of Identity* (New York: Routledge, 2006); Foucault, *The Order of Things*; Michel Foucault, *Madness and Civilization: A History of Insanity in the Age of Reason*, trans. Richard Howard (New York: Vintage, 1965); Donna Haraway, *Simians, Cyborgs, and Women: The Reinvention of Nature* (New York: Routledge, 1990).

53. See, for example, Ernesto Laclau, *On Populist Reason* (London: Verso, 2007); Ernesto Laclau and Chantal Mouffe, *Hegemony and Socialist Strategy: Towards a Radical Democratic Politics* (London: Verso, 2014); Chantal Mouffe, *The Return of the Political* (London: Verso, 2020); Chantal Mouffe, *The Democratic Paradox* (London: Verso, 2009); Jacques Rancière, *Hatred of Democracy*, trans. Steven Corcoran (London: Verso, 2014); Jacques Rancière, *Dissensus: On Politics and Aesthetics*, trans. Steven Corcoran (New York: Continuum, 2010). I will return to these arguments in chapter 6.

54. Throughout the book, I often use the term *man* to mean "human being" (and thus also employ "he," "him," and "his"). This is in part because of the historical focus of the book, which is grounded in the French Enlightenment and French revolutionary period. In that context, *l'homme* means "human being." I do acknowledge the implications of this gendered language, particularly in chapter 4 in relation to Olympe de Gouges, but I believe it is best to maintain a faithful translation. Adhering to use of the masculine noun and pronouns also offers a connection to the critiques of the Enlightenment period's conception of "Man" (also meaning "human being" but of course from the perspective of critique).

55.   Archives parlementaires, première série (1787 à 1799), tome VIII, du mai 1789 au 15 septembre 1789, Assemblée nationale, présidence de M. le comte de Clermont-Tonnerre. Accessed via the ARTFL Project of the University of Chicago, https://artfl-project.uchicago .edu/archives-parlementaires.

56.   Phillips, *Unconditional Equals*, 57.

57.   Marie-Luisa Frick, *Human Rights and Relative Universalism* (New York: Palgrave Macmillan, 2019), 15.

58.   Frick, *Human Rights*, 53.

59.   Phillips, *Unconditional Equals*, 46.

60.   Mark Goodale, *Reinventing Human Rights* (Stanford, CA: Stanford University Press, 2022), 5, also citing Jack Donnelly, "Human Rights as Natural Rights," *Human Rights Quarterly* 4, no. 3 (1982): 391–405.

61.   Manent, *Natural Law*, 8.

62.   Manent, *Natural Law*, 10, 13.

63.   The split between ancient and modern is most often attributed to Leo Strauss, although it also appears in much different guises in the works of, for example, Michel Foucault (*The Order of Things*), and Arthur O. Lovejoy (*The Great Chain of Being: A Study of the History of an Idea* [Cambridge, MA: Harvard University Press, 1976]).

64.   On this, I agree with Claude Lefort. He writes that in the French revolutionary declaration, a unique conception of the human being came into existence. With the "rights of man," we get a "naturalist conception of right," which is in fact an event: "a declaration which was in fact a self-declaration, that is, a declaration by which human beings, speaking through their representatives, revealed themselves to be both the subject and the object of the utterance in which they named the human elements in one another" (Claude Lefort, *Democracy and Political Theory* [Minneapolis: University of Minnesota Press, 1988], 38). In this respect, "naturalism and historicism are equally inappropriate tools for conceptualizing the rights of man" (38).

65.   Unless otherwise noted, translations of Buffon are my own. All citations to Buffon's *Histoire naturelle* are to Georges-Louis LeClerc, comte de Buffon, *Histoire naturelle, générale et particulière, avec la description du Cabinet Du Roy* (Paris: Imprimerie royale, 1749–1789). Here from vol. 12, iv. The volumes of Buffon's *Histoire* were published over the course of the second half of the eighteenth century. The most cited volumes in this book are volumes 1 to 4, of which the first three were published together in 1749 and the fourth in 1753. I occasionally use William Smellie's translation; when I do, this will be noted: Georges-Louis LeClerc, comte de Buffon, *Natural History, General and Particular*, trans. William Smellie (London: W. Strahan and T. Cadell, 1781).

66.   This image is related to what Vincenzo Ferrone has described as "the new humanism of rights," founded in the work of Buffon, Diderot, and Rousseau: Vincenzo Ferrone, *The Enlightenment: History of an Idea*, trans. Elisabetta Tarantino (Princeton, NJ: Princeton University Press, 2017), xiii.

67.   Charles Bonnet, *La palingénésie philosophique, ou Idées sur l'état passé et sur l'état futur des êtres vivans* (Geneva: Claude Philibert and Barthélemy Chirol, 1770).

68. For all references to the *Social Contract* and *Second Discourse*, I use Victor Gourevitch's translations: Jean-Jacques Rousseau, *The Discourses and Other Early Political Writings*, 2nd ed., trans. and ed. Victor Gourevitch (Cambridge: Cambridge University Press, 2019), and Jean-Jacques Rousseau, *The Social Contract and Other Later Political Writings*, trans. and ed. Victor Gourevitch (Cambridge: Cambridge University Press, 1997). In addition to these works, I also consulted the French.

69. Ronald Dworkin, *Taking Rights Seriously* (Cambridge, MA: Harvard University Press, 1978); see also Ronald Dworkin, "Rights as Trumps," in *Theories of Rights*, ed. C. L. Ten (Burlington, VT: Ashgate, 2006), 153–67. Thanks to illuminating discussions with Francisco Urbina, I am now aware of a large movement in legal scholarship also committed to offering an alternative to this conception of rights as trumps. I will return to this argument in chapter 6. See Bradley W. Miller et al., eds., *Legislated Rights: Securing Human Rights Through Legislation* (Cambridge: Cambridge University Press, 2018).

70. Ryan, *The Making of Modern Liberalism*, 27, citing Robert Nozick, *Anarchy, State, and Utopia* (New York: Basic Books, 1974).

71. Jürgen Habermas, *Between Facts and Norms: Contributions to a Discourse Theory of Law and Democracy*, trans. William Rehg (Cambridge: Polity, 1996); Rainer Forst, "The Basic Right to Justification: Toward a Constructivist Conception of Human Rights," *Constellations* 6, no. 1 (1999): 49.

72. Roger Griffin, *The Nature of Fascism* (New York: Psychology, 1993), 47.

73. Griffin, *The Nature of Fascism*, 33.

74. Griffin, *The Nature of Fascism*, 47.

75. In this respect, too, I also disagree with Kevin Duong's recent account of the regenerative project of the Jacobins in the French Revolution, which he locates explicitly in violence, and, following the revolution, in political projects that desire the violent upheaval of "the social." See Kevin Duong, *The Virtues of Violence: Democracy Against Disintegration in Modern France* (Oxford: Oxford University Press, 2020), and Kevin Duong, "The People as a Natural Disaster: Redemptive Violence in Jacobin Political Thought," *American Political Science Review* 111, no. 4 (2017): 786–800.

76. Helena Rosenblatt, *The Lost History of Liberalism: From Ancient Rome to the Twenty-First Century* (Princeton, NJ: Princeton University Press, 2018); Judith N. Shklar, *After Utopia: The Decline of Political Faith*, ed. Samuel Moyn (Princeton, NJ: Princeton University Press, 2020); Samuel Moyn, *The Last Utopia: Human Rights in History* (Cambridge, MA: Belknap, 2012); Samuel Moyn, *Liberalism Against Itself*.

77. Isaiah Berlin, "Two Concepts of Liberty," in *Four Essays on Liberty* (Oxford: Oxford University Press, 1969), 118–172.

78. Rosenblatt, *The Lost History*, 272.

79. Mouffe in particular (along with Laclau) denies a connection to Rousseau. On this, though, see Kevin Inston, *Rousseau and Radical Democracy* (New York: Continuum, 2010), in which the author claims that Mouffe and Laclau share many affinities with Rousseau's arguments despite their claims to the contrary.

80. Mouffe, *The Return of the Political*, 6.

81. Mouffe, *The Democratic Paradox*, 10–11.

82. Lefort, *Democracy and Political Theory*, 19.

83. Mouffe, *The Return of the Political*, 13.

84. This idea is similar to that found in the work of Sheldon Wolin and Jacques Rancière, both of whom build much of their work from the distinction of *politics* from *the political*, the former being (roughly speaking) the day-to-day mechanism of the settled order and the latter being the truly motive, and self-determinative, praxis of the people *against* the claims of politics. As in Mouffe's work, this conflict is restricted to something political against something political. There are no humans here, either, which I address in chapter 6. See, for example, Sheldon Wolin, "Fugitive Democracy," in *Fugitive Democracy and Other Essays*, ed. Nicholas Xenos (Princeton, NJ: Princeton University Press, 2016), 100–113, and Rancière, *Hatred of Democracy*.

85. Rinaldo Walcott claims in *The Long Emancipation* that the notion of progress is itself the greatest injustice committed against Black freedom: "The conditions of a potential Black freedom remain outside of modernity's imagining. There is a tension within the logic of modernist freedom, which assumes a linearity—that one perfects *what it means to be human* in a linear fashion" (2–3).

86. Amy Allen, *The End of Progress: Decolonizing the Normative Foundations of Critical Theory*, New Directions in Critical Theory (New York: Columbia University Press, 2016).

87. Tyler Stovall makes a similar claim about freedom in *White Freedom*: "The idea that freedom is a universal value transcending race is now the default standard in modern societies, and it is hard to imagine that changing any time soon" (Tyler Stovall, *White Freedom: The Racial History of an Idea* [Princeton, NJ: Princeton University Press, 2021], 320). He thus argues that the concept of freedom must be reimagined away from the intertwining of race and freedom and toward a reconfigured yet still universal conception.

88. This understanding certainly has echoes in Hannah Arendt's concept of the "right to have rights," a connection that Lefort also draws to his own work. See also Alastair Hunt et al., *The Right to Have Rights* (London: Verso, 2018). I discuss this notion further in chapter 6.

89. In chapter 6, I will address more substantively the recent turns toward thinking about the transformative potential in the idea of rights, and I will also address the postmodern critiques. It is important to note from the outset that the argument I offer here is complemented by the account of rights that Judith Butler supplies in *Undoing Gender*. They write, "The necessity of keeping our notion of the human open to a future articulation is essential to the project of international human rights discourse and politics. . . . When we start with the human as a foundation, then the human at issue in human rights is already known, already defined" (36–37). The reconstitution of the human "will constitute a loss, a disorientation, but one in which the human stands a chance of coming into being anew" (38–39).

90. This fallacy may be a quality of what is more specifically known as "Cold War liberalism," or twentieth-century liberalism, which was imagined in a particularly minimalist fashion following the upheavals of communism and fascism in the twentieth century. I will discuss this further in chapter 5.

91. Moyn would agree with this account of rights claims in the contemporary world. As he writes in *Human Rights and the Uses of History*, "Human rights rose as self-determination fell." Samuel Moyn, *Human Rights and the Uses of History*, 2nd ed. (London: Verso, 2017), 108.

92. Walcott, *The Long Emancipation*, 73.

93. Forrest, *Suprahumanism*, 14.

94. Wendy Brown, *In the Ruins of Neoliberalism: The Rise of Antidemocratic Politics in the West* (New York: Columbia University Press, 2019), 181, 188.

95. Wendy Brown, *Undoing the Demos: Neoliberalism's Stealth Revolution* (New York: Zone, 2017), 222.

96. Brown, *Undoing the Demos*, 222.

97. Rosenblatt, *The Lost History of Liberalism*, 277.

98. Moyn, *Liberalism Against Itself*, 175.

99. Charles W. Mills, *Black Rights/White Wrongs: The Critique of Racial Liberalism* (Oxford: Oxford University Press, 2017), 215, 10.

100. Césaire, *Discourse on Colonialism*, 73. Frantz Fanon cites Césaire in the conclusion to his *Black Skin, White Masks*, writing that man must be "an affirmation" (Frantz Fanon, *Black Skin, White Masks*, trans. Richard Philcox [New York: Grove, 2008], 197). Rinaldo Walcott also calls for "a new humanism" (Walcott, *The Long Emancipation*, 7, following Fanon and Wynter), and Achille Mbembe calls for a new way of "becoming-human-in-the-world" (Mbembe, *Necropolitics*, 187).

101. Forrest, *Suprahumanism*, 239.

102. Charles Bonnet, "Essai de psychologie," in *Oeuvres d'histoire naturelle et de philosophie de Charles Bonnet*, vol. 17 (Neuchatel: Samuel Fauche, 1783), 1–444, section LXVII.

103. Buffon, *Histoire naturelle*, XII, iv.

104. François Furet, *Interpreting the French Revolution* (Cambridge: Cambridge University Press, 1981); Mona Ozouf, *L'Homme régénéré: Essais sur la Révolution française* (Paris: Gallimard, 1989).

105. Archives parlementaires, tome premier états généraux, Cahiers des sénéchaussées et baillages; Cahiers des sénéchaussées et baillages, Cahiers contenant les pouvoirs et instructions remi, etc. Accessed via the ARTFL Project of the University of Chicago, https://artfl-project.uchicago.edu/archives-parlementaires.

106. Darrin M. McMahon, *Enemies of the Enlightenment: The French Counter-Enlightenment and the Making of Modernity* (Oxford: Oxford University Press, 2002), 165.

107. William Selinger, *Parliamentarism: From Burke to Weber*, Ideas in Context (Cambridge: Cambridge University Press, 2019). See also Gregory Conti, *Parliament the Mirror of the Nation: Representation, Deliberation, and Democracy in Victorian Britain*, Ideas in Context (Cambridge: Cambridge University Press, 2019); Lucia Rubinelli, *Constituent Power: A History*, Ideas in Context (Cambridge: Cambridge University Press, 2020).

108. Selinger, *Parliamentarism*, 5.

109. Annelien de Dijn, *Freedom: An Unruly History* (Cambridge, MA: Harvard University Press, 2020), 3.

110. Duong, *The Virtues of Violence*, 139.

111.   Cited in Duong, *The Virtues of Violence*, 160.

112.   Beiner, *Dangerous Minds*, 4, 21.

113.   J. L. Talmon, *The Origins of Totalitarian Democracy* (London: Mercury, 1961), 1, 6.

2. THE PALINGENETIC CONSCIOUSNESS

1.   Stephen Holmes, *The Anatomy of Antiliberalism* (Cambridge, MA: Harvard University Press, 1993), 14. Graeme Garrard has more recently discussed the counter-Enlightenment impulses of the antiliberals. Garrard is critical of what he sees as an oversimplification of the antiliberals' "Enlightenment" as it is presented in Holmes's account but is also in basic agreement with Holmes that the Enlightenment is often the target. See Graeme Garrard, "Illiberalism and Opposition to the Enlightenment," in *Routledge Handbook of Illiberalism*, ed. András Sajó, Renáta Uitz, and Stephen Holmes (New York: Routledge, 2021), 33–42.

2.   As J. G. A. Pocock has written, there may "no longer be 'The Enlightenment,' a unitary and universal phenomenon with a single history either celebrated or condemned, but instead a family of discourses arising about the same time in a number of European cultures." Pocock's "Enlightenment" versus "Enlightenments" comes from "The Tell-Tale Article: Reconstructing (. . .) Enlightenment" (plenary address to the 29th annual meeting of the American Society for Eighteenth-Century Studies, University of Notre Dame, Notre Dame, IN, April 2, 1998). See also Sankar Muthu, *Enlightenment Against Empire* (Princeton, NJ: Princeton University Press, 2003); James Schmidt, "What Enlightenment Project?," *Political Theory* 28, no. 6 (2000): 734–57.

3.   Arthur O. Lovejoy, *The Great Chain of Being: A Study of the History of an Idea* (Cambridge, MA: Harvard University Press, 1976), 227.

4.   Lovejoy, *The Great Chain of Being*, 59, 104.

5.   Georges-Louis LeClerc, comte de Buffon, *Histoire naturelle, générale et particulière, avec la description du Cabinet Du Roy* (Paris: Imprimerie royale, 1749–1789), vol. 1, 12–13.

6.   Buffon, *Histoire naturelle*, vol. 1, 12.

7.   Lovejoy, *The Great Chain of Being*, 329.

8.   Buffon, *Histoire naturelle*, vol. 1, 12–13.

9.   See also William Max Nelson's excellent book, *The Time of Enlightenment: Constructing the Future in France, 1750 to Year One* (Toronto, ON: University of Toronto Press, 2021), which is largely about Buffon's remaking of time in the eighteenth century.

10.   John Lyon, introduction to "The 'Initial Discourse' to Buffon's *Histoire naturelle*: The First Complete English Translation," *Journal of the History of Biology* 9, no. 1 (1976): 135.

11.   Phillip R. Sloan, "The Buffon-Linnaeus Controversy," *Isis* 67, no. 3 (1976): 359.

12.   Sloan, "The Buffon-Linnaeus Controversy," 358.

13.   Lovejoy, *The Great Chain of Being*, 227.

14.   Aristotle is a complicated figure and can also be invoked as a predecessor of the second camp of scientific inquiry. While he did classify living things according to species and genera, and thus was an inspiration for taxonomists like Linnaeus, he also, as Lovejoy

discusses, acknowledged that such classification invariably reveals the manners in which "nature refuses to conform to our craving for clear lines of demarcation" (Lovejoy, *The Great Chain of Being*, 56). See also Justin E. H. Smith, ed., introduction to *The Problem of Animal Generation in Early Modern Philosophy*, Cambridge Studies in Philosophy and Biology (Cambridge: Cambridge University Press, 2006), in which Smith argues that "no matter how much [these philosophers] were motivated in many respects by a fierce rejection of Aristotelianism, [they] remained Aristotelian at least to the extent that their results were seen as bearing on a cluster of distinctly philosophical questions inherited from the Greeks concerning the nature and origins of substances or beings" (2).

15. Margaret J. Osler, "John Locke and the Changing Ideal of Scientific Knowledge," *Journal of the History of Ideas* 31, no. 1 (1970): 3. She also groups Francis Bacon with Aristotle and Descartes.

16. Osler, "John Locke," 3.

17. Aristotle, *Posterior Analytics*, in *The Basic Works of Aristotle*, ed. Richard McKeon (New York: Modern Library, 1941), 111–12; cited in Osler, "John Locke," 3.

18. René Descartes, *Descartes: Selected Philosophical Writings*, trans. John Cottingham and Robert Stoothoff (Cambridge: Cambridge University Press, 1988), 30.

19. Descartes, *Selected Philosophical Writings*, 30.

20. See, for example, G. A. J. Rogers, "Locke's Essay and Newton's Principia," *Journal of the History of Ideas* 39, no. 2 (1978): 217–32; A. Rupert Hall, *Philosophers at War: The Quarrel Between Newton and Leibniz* (Cambridge: Cambridge University Press, 1980); Ernst Cassirer, "Newton and Leibniz," *Philosophical Review* 52, no. 4 (1943): 366–91.

21. Osler, "John Locke," 6.

22. Ernan McMullin, "The Impact of Newton's Principia on the Philosophy of Science," *Philosophy of Science* 68, no. 3 (2001): 281.

23. McMullin, "The Impact," 286.

24. Isaac Newton, *Principia*, trans. Andrew Motte, ed. Florian Cajorli (Berkeley: University of California Press, [1726] 1996), 547; cited in McMullin, "The Impact," 290.

25. Osler, "John Locke," 9.

26. Osler, "John Locke," 11.

27. Osler, "John Locke," 13.

28. James Farr, "The Way of Hypotheses: Locke on Method," *Journal of the History of Ideas* 48, no. 1 (1987): 56, citing John Locke, *An Essay Concerning Human Understanding* (London, 1690), book 4, chapter 12, section 13. Farr emphasizes that while Locke uses hypotheses and finds them useful for human understanding, he continually reminds the reader that they are merely conjectures. In this, Locke's philosophy coheres with David Hume's *An Inquiry Concerning Human Understanding* (London: Andrew Millar, 1748) (published as *The Philosophical Essays Concerning Human Understanding*).

29. McMullin, "The Impact," 280. On real and nominal essences, and their relationship to Locke's method and philosophy, see also Torrey Shanks, *Authority Figures: Rhetoric and Experience in John Locke's Political Thought* (University Park: Pennsylvania State University Press, 2014). Shanks writes that Locke's emphasis on the *humanness* of nominal essences makes human knowledge dependent on language and thus rhetoric: "How to

identify a substance depends upon its name and definition, that is, its nominal essence. God may create such entities, but humans author the words used to organize them" (57). This is very similar to Buffon putting humans at the center of his natural science.

30. G. W. Leibniz, *Discourse on Metaphysics and the Monadology*, trans. George R. Montgomery, ed. Albert R. Chandler (Mineola, NY: Dover, [1714] 2005), 58. See also Justin E. H. Smith, *Divine Machines: Leibniz and the Sciences of Life* (Princeton, NJ: Princeton University Press, 2011).

31. Leibniz, *Discourse*, 58.

32. Virginia P. Dawson, *Nature's Enigma: The Problem of the Polyp in the Letters of Bonnet, Trembley and Réaumur* (Philadelphia: American Philosophical Society, 1987), 43.

33. Dawson, *Nature's Enigma*, 44.

34. This is a vastly simplified restatement of Leibniz's "principle of sufficient reason," which, in an also vastly simplified version, serves as the foundation of the argument that we can know God exists because we have sufficient reason to know he exists through the order of the universe. The principle of sufficient reason also associates Leibniz with Baruch Spinoza. Lovejoy links Leibniz's nominalistic philosophy with Spinoza's denial of final causes: "The 'good,' then, for the sake of which, and by reason of which, things exist, is simply existence itself—the actualization of essence; and the world that in the eternal nature of things was necessitated to be, was. . . . Thus the difference between Leibniz's nominal assertion and Spinoza's denial of final causes approaches a vanishing point" (Lovejoy, *The Great Chain of Being*, 180).

35. Lovejoy, *The Great Chain of Being*, 3.

36. Gottfried Wilhelm Leibniz, letter to Pierre Varignon, June 20, 1702, quoted in Lovejoy, *The Great Chain of Being*, 145.

37. This argument is repeated by Jean le Rond d'Alembert: "Since everything in nature is linked together," since "beings are connected with one another by a chain of which we perceive some parts as continuous, though in the greater number of points the continuity escapes us," the "art of the philosopher consists in adding new links to the separated parts, in order to reduce the distance between them as much as possible. But we must not flatter ourselves that gaps will not remain in many places" (Jean le Rond d'Alembert, "Cosmologie," in *Encyclopédie* [Paris: 1751–1752], 4, 294), cited in Lovejoy, *The Great Chain of Being*, 232.

38. Locke, *An Essay Concerning Human Understanding*, book 3, chapter 6, section 12; cited in Lovejoy, *The Great Chain of Being*, 185.

39. Cited in Lovejoy, *The Great Chain of Being*, 250.

40. Gottfried Wilhelm Leibniz, *De Rerum Originatione Radicali* (1697), quoted in Lovejoy, *The Great Chain of Being*, 257.

41. Lovejoy, *The Great Chain of Being*, 198.

42. Lovejoy, *The Great Chain of Being*, 198.

43. Alexander Pope, "An Essay on Man," in *Moral Essays and Satires* (London: Cassell, [1734] 1891), Second Epistle.

44. Lovejoy, *The Great Chain of Being*, 259.

45. Lovejoy, *The Great Chain of Being*, 269.

46. Cited in Robert J. Cribb, Helen Gilbert, and Helen Tiffin, *Wild Man from Borneo: A Cultural History of the Orangutan* (Honolulu: University of Hawai'i Press, 2014), 10.

47. Cited in Cribb, Gilbert, and Tiffin, *Wild Man*, 14.

48. Carl Linnaeus, "Letter, 25 February 1747, Uppsala, to Johann Georg Gmelin, St. Petersburg," February 25, 1747, letter 0783, Uppsala University Library, Linnaean Correspondence.

49. Claude Blanckaert, "Buffon and the Natural History of Man: Writing History and the 'Foundational Myth' of Anthropology," *History of the Human Sciences* 6, no. 1 (1993): 30.

50. E. C. Spary, *Utopia's Garden: French Natural History from Old Regime to Revolution* (Chicago: University of Chicago Press, 2000), 111.

51. This experiment was performed on November 25, 1740. The story is cited and discussed in Virginia Dawson's *Nature's Enigma*, a thorough accounting of the letters exchanged among Trembley, Réaumur, and Bonnet concerning the discovery of the polyp.

52. Cited in Aram Vartanian, "Trembley's Polyp, La Mettrie, and Eighteenth-Century French Materialism," *Journal of the History of Ideas* 11, no. 3 (1950): 271.

53. Vartanian, "Trembley's Polyp," 270.

54. Virginia P. Dawson, "Regeneration, Parthenogenesis, and the Immutable Order of Nature," *Archives of Natural History* 18, no. 3 (1991): 309.

55. Keith R. Benson, "Observation Versus Philosophical Commitment in Eighteenth-Century Ideas of Regeneration and Generation," in *A History of Regeneration Research: Milestones in the Evolution of a Science*, ed. Charles E. Dinsmore (Cambridge: Cambridge University Press, 1991), 96, citing Aram Vartanian, "Review of *Abraham Trembley of Geneva: Scientist and Philosopher* by John R. Baker," *Isis* 44, no. 4 (1953): 388. For more on the regenerative polyp, see also Charles E. Dinsmore, "Animal Regeneration: From Fact to Concept," *Bioscience* 45, no. 7 (1995): 484–92.

56. Dawson, *Nature's Enigma*, 37.

57. Dawson, *Nature's Enigma*, 40.

58. Aristotle, *Generation of Animals*, in *The Basic Works of Aristotle*, ed. Richard McKeon (New York: Random House, 1970), 641b.

59. Aristotle, *Generation*, 642a.

60. *Histoire de l'Académie royale des sciences* (Paris: Imprimerie royale, 1744), 33–34; cited in Shirley A. Roe, *Matter, Life, and Generation: Eighteenth-Century Embryology and the Haller–Wolff Debate* (Cambridge: Cambridge University Press, 1981), 10.

61. Some were less enthusiastic about the polyp, such as Voltaire who declared it "much more like a carrot or an asparagus than an animal" (cited in John R. Baker, *Abraham Trembley of Geneva: Scientist and Philosopher, 1710–1784* [London: Edward Arnold, 1952], 45).

62. Buffon, *Histoire naturelle*, vol. 2, 320–21.

63. Jacques Roger, *Buffon: A Life in Natural History*, trans. Sarah Lucille Bonnefoi (Ithaca, NY: Cornell University Press, 1997), 128. For more on Buffon and the polyp, see Lovejoy, *The Great Chain of Being*; Phillip R. Sloan, "Buffon, German Biology, and the Historical Interpretation of Biological Species," *British Journal for the History of Science* 12, no. 2 (1979): 109–53; Devin Vartija, "Revisiting Enlightenment Racial Classification: Time and the Question of Human Diversity," *Intellectual History Review* 31, no. 4 (2021): 603–25.

64. Reinvigorating a vitalist sense of nature in the eighteenth century is a project I share with Phil Sloan, whose work on Buffon is cited here. He has also recently produced some fascinating work on metaphysics, "vital" materialism, and the influence of Émilie du Châtelet. See Phillip R. Sloan, "Metaphysics and Vital Materialism: Émilie du Châtelet and the Origins of French Vitalism," in *Philosophy of Biology Before Biology*, ed. Cécilia Bognon-Küss and Charles T. Wolfe (London: Routledge, 2019), 48–65.

65. Buffon, *Histoire naturelle*, vol. 2, 324.

66. All citations to Bonnet's *Contemplation* are to Charles Bonnet, *The Contemplation of Nature: Translated from the French of C. Bonnet*, 2 vols. (London: T. Longman, 1766). Here from vol. 1, xxvi. In addition to this work, I also consulted the French.

67. Bonnet, *Contemplation*, vol. 1, 23. For more on Charles Bonnet, see Lorin Anderson, *Charles Bonnet and the Order of the Known*, Studies in the History of Modern Science, vol. 11 (Dordrecht: Reidel, 1982).

68. Bonnet, *Contemplation*, vol. 1, 16.

69. Bonnet, *Contemplation*, vol. 1, 191.

70. Bonnet, *Contemplation*, vol. 1, 183.

71. Bonnet, *Contemplation*, vol. 1, 209.

72. Bonnet, *Contemplation*, vol. 1, 188, 191.

73. Bonnet, *Contemplation*, vol. 1, 191.

74. Bonnet, *Contemplation*, vol. 1, 187.

75. Bonnet, *Contemplation*, vol. 1, 211. For more on Bonnet and the polyp, see Michel Foucault, *The Order of Things: An Archaeology of the Human Sciences*, trans. Alan Sheridan (New York: Vintage, 1994) (in which he also discusses Buffon); Lovejoy, *The Great Chain of Being*; Katia Sainson, " 'Le régénérateur de la France': Literary Accounts of Napoleonic Regeneration 1799–1805," *Nineteenth-Century French Studies* 30, no. 1 (2001): 9–25.

76. See, in particular, Denis Diderot, "Letter on the Blind," in *Diderot's Early Philosophical Works*, ed. Margaret Jourdain (Chicago: Open Court, 1916), 68–141; Claude Adrien Helvétius, *De l'esprit: Or, Essays on the Mind and Its Several Faculties* (New York: Burt Franklin, 1972); Paul Henri Thiry Holbach, *The System of Nature: Or, Laws of the Moral and Physical World*, trans. H. D. Robinson, 2 vols. (New York: Burt Franklin, 1970); Julien Offray de La Mettrie, "Man a Machine," in *Machine Man and Other Writings*, trans. Ann Thomson (Cambridge: Cambridge University Press, 1996).

77. Holbach, *The System of Nature*, vol. 1, 47.

78. Holbach, *The System of Nature*, vol. 1, 11.

79. Holbach, *The System of Nature*, vol. 1, 47.

80. Holbach, *The System of Nature*, vol. 1, 88.

81. Holbach, *The System of Nature*, vol. 2, 174.

82. Buffon, *Histoire naturelle*, vol. 1, 12.

83. Buffon, *Histoire naturelle*, vol. 2, 443.

84. Buffon, *Histoire naturelle*, vol. 4, 69.

85. Buffon, *Histoire naturelle*, vol. 4, 69.

86. Buffon, *Histoire naturelle*, vol. 4, 38.

87. Buffon, *Histoire naturelle*, vol. 4, 69.

88. Buffon, *Histoire naturelle*, vol. 4, 32.

89. Buffon, *Histoire naturelle*, vol. 4, 51.

90. Buffon, *Histoire naturelle*, vol. 4, 109–10 (French), as translated by William Smellie.

91. Buffon, *Histoire naturelle*, vol. 5, 237.

92. Buffon, *Histoire naturelle*, vol. 5, 237.

93. Buffon, *Histoire naturelle*, vol. 5, 253.

94. Unless otherwise noted, translations of Bonnet are my own. All citations to Bonnet's *Palingénésie* are to Charles Bonnet, *La palingénésie philosophique, ou Idées sur l'état passé et sur l'état future des êtres vivans* (Geneva: Claude Philibert and Barthelémy Chirol, 1770). Here from 234.

95. Charles Bonnet, "Essai de psychologie," in *Oeuvres d'histoire naturelle et philosophie de Charles Bonnet*, vol. 17 (Neuchatel: Samuel Fauche, 1783), LXVII. Translations are my own.

96. Bonnet, *Contemplation*, vol. 2, 27.

97. Bonnet, *Contemplation*, vol. 1, 5.

98. Bonnet, *Contemplation*, vol. 2, 120.

99. Bonnet, *Contemplation*, vol. 2, 121.

100. Bonnet, *Palingénésie*, 315. *Perfectible* is a term he borrows from Rousseau.

101. Bonnet, *Contemplation*, vol. 1, 20.

102. Bonnet, "Essai de psychologie," VIII.

103. Bonnet, *Contemplation*, vol. 2, 182.

104. Bonnet, *Contemplation*, vol. 1, 72.

105. Bonnet, *Contemplation*, vol. 1, 67.

106. Buffon, *Histoire naturelle*, vol. 12, iv.

107. Buffon, *Histoire naturelle*, vol. 12, xv.

108. Buffon, *Histoire naturelle*, vol. 13, iv.

109. Buffon, *Histoire naturelle*, vol. 4, 215–16 (French), as translated by William Smellie.

110. The doctrine of original prototypes is, curiously, a position that Lovejoy ascribes to Jean-Baptiste Robinet, who wrote *De la nature* in 1761, more than a decade after the publication of Buffon's first volumes: "Robinet finds, that there must be a single anatomical type-form common to all living things—which is to say, to all things. And this must, of course, be a particular form, distinct from all other possible forms; so that the 'fullness' of nature is limited to the realization of all possible variations upon a single prototype" (Lovejoy, *The Great Chain of Being*, 277). Lovejoy also claims that Robinet borrows the language of prototypes from Denis Diderot, who writes in 1754 (also following Buffon) of the "successive metamorphoses of the envelope of the prototype . . . by insensible degrees" (279).

111. Buffon's account of the effects of the domestication of animals is not unique for this period. For more examples, see Harriet Ritvo, "At the Edge of the Garden: Nature and Domestication in Eighteenth- and Nineteenth-Century Britain," *Huntington Library Quarterly* 55, no. 3 (1992): 363–78; Spary, *Utopia's Garden*.

112. Buffon, *Histoire naturelle*, vol. 11, 353.

113. The mouflon (*Ovis Orientalis*) is still considered one of two ancestors of all domesticated breeds of sheep. The allusions to Rousseau's account of the natural state (and natural

man) are also unmistakable here, concerning the strength and vigor of the "original" stock. Relations to Rousseau are conspicuous throughout Buffon's *Histoire naturelle*, especially, and perhaps most importantly, in Buffon's account of the degeneracy of human beings (XI, 363–64).

114.   Buffon, *Histoire naturelle*, vol. 11, 365, my emphasis.

115.   Buffon, *Histoire naturelle*, vol. 11, 369.

116.   Buffon, *Histoire naturelle*, vol. 11, 369.

117.   Buffon, *Histoire naturelle*, vol. 9, 102.

118.   Buffon, *Histoire naturelle*, vol. 9, 103.

119.   Justin E. H. Smith, *Nature, Human Nature, and Human Difference: Race in Early Modern Philosophy* (Princeton, NJ: Princeton University Press, 2015), 139, citing Thomas Jefferson, *Notes on the State of Virginia* (1787). See also Lee Alan Dugatkin, *Mr. Jefferson and the Giant Moose: Natural History in Early America* (Chicago: University of Chicago Press, 2009).

120.   Buffon, *Histoire naturelle*, vol. 9, 103–104.

121.   Andrew S. Curran, *The Anatomy of Blackness: Science and Slavery in an Age of Enlightenment* (Baltimore: Johns Hopkins University Press, 2013), 222.

122.   Michèle Duchet, *Anthropologie et histoire au siècle des lumières: Buffon, Voltaire, Rousseau, Helvétius, Diderot* (Paris: Flammarion, 1978); Blanckaert, "Buffon and the Natural History of Man"; Carl Niekerk, "Buffon, Blumenbach, Herder, Lichtenberg, and the Origins of Modern Anthropology," in *Johann Friedrich Blumenbach: Race and Natural History, 1750–1850*, ed. Nicolaas Rupke and Gerhard Lauer (London: Routledge, 2018), 27–52.

123.   Michel-Rolph Trouillot, *Silencing the Past: Power and the Production of History* (New York: Beacon, 2015), 78. See also Claude-Olivier Doron, "Race and Genealogy: Buffon and the Formation of the Concept of 'Race,'" *Humana. Mente Journal of Philosophical Studies* 5, no. 22 (2012): 75–109; Jean-Frédéric Schaub and Silvia Sebastiani, "Between Genealogy and Physicality: A Historiographical Perspective on Race in the Ancien Régime," *Graduate Faculty Philosophy Journal* 35, no. 1 (2014): 23–51; Sloan, "Buffon, German Biology"; Sloan, "The Buffon-Linnaeus Controversy"; Phillip R. Sloan, "The Idea of Racial Degeneracy in Buffon's *Histoire naturelle*," *Studies in Eighteenth-Century Culture* 3, no. 1 (1974): 293–321.

For arguments against Buffon having developed a racist conception of human beings, see Curran, *The Anatomy of Blackness*; Thierry Hoquet, "Biologization of Race and Racialization of the Human: Bernier, Buffon, Linnaeus," in *The Invention of Race: Scientific and Popular Representations*, ed. Nicolas Bancel, Thomas David, and Dominic Thomas (New York: Routledge, 2014), 17–32; Nelson, *The Time of Enlightenment*; E. C. Spary, "Climate Change and Creolization in French Natural History, 1750–1795," in *Johann Friedrich Blumenbach: Race and Natural History, 1750–1850*, ed. Nicolaas Rupke and Gerhard Lauer (New York: Routledge, 2018), 53–79; Spary, *Utopia's Garden*. While Andrew Curran does not see Buffon's science as inherently "racist" in the modern sense of the term, he argues in *The Anatomy of Blackness* that Buffon's work had an unintended consequence: "Buffon's degeneration-based ethnography would ultimately give way to a new and more brutal version of the story of human sameness" once it was "perused and interpreted by a new generation of anatomists and more materially oriented pro-slavery writers" (116). Foucault also argues in *The Order of Things* that it was not until the nineteenth century that scientific racism truly emerged, following from Cuvier's scientific anatomy.

124. Claude Lévi-Strauss, "Jean-Jacques Rousseau, Founder of the Sciences of Man," in *Structural Anthropology*, vol. 2, trans. Monique Layton (Chicago: University of Chicago Press, 1983), 33–43.

125. Asher Horowitz, "'Law and Customs Thrust Us Back Into Infancy': Rousseau's Historical Anthropology," *Review of Politics* 52, no. 2 (1990): 215–41; Arthur O. Lovejoy, "The Supposed Primitivism of Rousseau's 'Discourse on Inequality,'" *Modern Philology* 21, no. 2 (1923): 165–86; Roger D. Masters, "Jean-Jacques Is Alive and Well: Rousseau and Contemporary Sociobiology," *Daedalus* 107, no. 3 (1978): 93–105; Robert Wokler, "Perfectible Apes in Decadent Cultures: Rousseau's Anthropology Revisited," *Daedalus* 107, no. 3 (1978): 107–34. For those who see Rousseau's conflation of natural man and the orangutan in a negative light, usually as contributing to the racialized animalization of the human, see (to some degree) Charles W. Mills, *The Racial Contract* (Ithaca, NY: Cornell University Press, 1999); Gustav Jahoda, *Images of Savages: Ancient Roots of Modern Prejudice in Western Culture* (New York: Routledge, 1998); Elizabeth Liebman, "Unspeakable Passions: The Civil and Savage Lessons of Early Modern Animal Representation," in *Representing the Passions: Histories, Bodies, Visions*, Issues and Debates, ed. Richard Meyer (Los Angeles: Getty Research Institute, 2003), 137–62; Muthu, *Enlightenment Against Empire*; Silvia Sebastiani, "Enlightenment Humanization and Dehumanization, and the Orangutan," in *The Routledge Handbook of Dehumanization*, Routledge Handbooks in Philosophy, ed. Maria Kronfeldner (London: Routledge, 2021), 64–82.

126. Michel-Rolph Trouillot, "Anthropology and the Savage Slot: The Poetics and Politics of Otherness," in *Global Transformations: Anthropology and the Modern World* (New York: Palgrave Macmillan, 2003), 7–28.

127. For more on Rousseau and the noble savage tradition, see Muthu, *Enlightenment Against Empire*.

128. Curran, *The Anatomy of Blackness*, 222.

129. Spary, "Climate Change," 53.

130. Spary, "Climate Change," 54.

131. Sloan, "The Idea of Racial Degeneracy," 294.

132. Sloan, "The Idea of Racial Degeneracy," 310.

133. Doron, "Race and Genealogy," 82.

134. Smith, *Nature, Human Nature*, 266.

135. Smith is not overwhelmingly critical of Buffon, however. He writes that Buffon's "unified account of the causes of variation throughout living nature" presented human variation "simply as a local instance of this vastly more comprehensive scheme" (*Nature, Human Nature*, 119).

136. Kenan Malik, *The Meaning of Race: Race, History, and Culture in Western Society* (New York: New York University Press, 1996), 54.

198 2. THE PALINGENETIC CONSCIOUSNESS

137. Hoquet, "Biologization of Race," 23.

138. Spary, "Climate Change," 54.

139. Spary, "Climate Change," 64.

140. Spary, "Climate Change," 62.

141. Spary, "Climate Change," 63.

142. Nelson, *The Time of Enlightenment*, 106.

143. Buffon, *Histoire naturelle*, vol. 9, 127, my emphasis.

144. Buffon, *Histoire naturelle*, vol. 13, iii–iv.

145. Muthu, *Enlightenment Against Empire*; Jennifer Pitts, *A Turn to Empire: The Rise of Imperial Liberalism in Britain and France* (Princeton, NJ: Princeton University Press, 2006).

146. Alyssa Goldstein Sepinwall, *The Abbé Grégoire and the French Revolution: The Making of Modern Universalism* (Berkeley: University of California Press, 2005), 7.

147. For the dangerous turn toward "anatomy" in the nineteenth century, see especially Curran, *The Anatomy of Blackness*; Foucault, *The Order of Things*; Hoquet, "Biologization of Race."

148. Blanckaert, "Buffon and the Natural History of Man," 30.

149. Vincenzo Ferrone, *The Enlightenment and the Rights of Man* (Liverpool: Voltaire Foundation in association with Liverpool University Press, 2019), 244.

150. Ernst Cassirer, *The Philosophy of the Enlightenment*, trans. Peter Gay (Princeton, NJ: Princeton University Press, 1951), 264.

3. THE RIGHT TO RENOUNCE DEPENDENCE

1. While I have done much work on Rousseau elsewhere and acknowledge that many texts pertain to the analysis I provide in this chapter, here I am restricting myself to the *Second Discourse* and the *Social Contract* (though I also briefly examine "Considerations on the Government of Poland"). In particular, elements of Rousseau's *Emile* could be integrated into the argument, but I have chosen to save that for another time. All citations to the *Second Discourse* and *Social Contract* are to the following: Jean-Jacques Rousseau, *The Discourses and Other Early Political Writings*, 2nd ed., trans. and ed. Victor Gourevitch (Cambridge: Cambridge University Press, 2019), and Jean-Jacques Rousseau, *The Social Contract and Other Later Political Writings*, trans. and ed. Victor Gourevitch (Cambridge: Cambridge University Press, 1997). Hereafter, these works will be cited as SD and SC, respectively, followed by the corresponding reference to Jean-Jacques Rousseau, *Oeuvres complètes* (Paris: NRF-Éditions de la Pléiade, 1965–1995), in the following form: OC volume number, page number.

2. Rousseau also cites and engages with the works of many others in the social contract tradition, including Jean-Jacques Burlamaqui's *Principes du droit naturel* (1747) and *Principes du droit politique* (1751); Hugo Grotius's *The Rights of War and Peace* (1625), as translated by Jean Barbeyrac in 1724, and Samuel Pufendorf's *Le droit de la nature et des gens* (1672), as translated by Barbeyrac in 1706.

3. Thomas Hobbes, *Leviathan: With Selected Variants from the Latin Edition of 1668*, ed. Edwin Curley (Indianapolis, IN: Hackett, 1994), part I, chapter XI, section 1.

4. Hobbes, *Leviathan*, part I, chapter XI, section 2.

5. Hobbes, *Leviathan*, part I, chapter XIII, section 6.

6. Hobbes, *Leviathan*, part I, chapter XIV, section 1.

7. Hobbes, *Leviathan*, part I, chapter XIV, section 3.

8. The story is of course more complex than this. For my interpretation of the logic of Hobbes's social covenant, see Emma Planinc, "The Creation of Man: Linguistic Reformation and the Necessity of the State in the Work of Thomas Hobbes," in *Polis, Nation, Global Community* (India: Routledge, 2021), 47–66.

9. John Locke, *Second Treatise of Government*, ed. C. B. Macpherson (Indianapolis, IN: Hackett, 1980), chapter 2, section 6.

10. Locke, *Second Treatise*, chapter 2, section 7.

11. Locke, *Second Treatise*, chapter 2, section 13.

12. Locke, *Second Treatise*, chapter 8, section 95.

13. This is an interpretation of the *Second Discourse* that I share with David Lay Williams, who writes in *Rousseau's Platonic Enlightenment*, "The heart of the *Second Discourse* is a critique of social contract theory." David Lay Williams, *Rousseau's Platonic Enlightenment* (University Park: Pennsylvania State University Press, 2007), 79.

14. Whether this entails a rejection of natural law on Rousseau's part is a matter of debate. On this, see C. E. Vaughan, ed., introduction to *The Political Writings of Jean-Jacques Rousseau* (Cambridge: Cambridge University Press, [1915] 1962), 1–117; Helena Rosenblatt, *Rousseau and Geneva: From the First Discourse to the Social Contract, 1749–1762*, Ideas in Context (Cambridge: Cambridge University Press, 1997); Williams, *Rousseau's Platonic Enlightenment*, 76–88.

15. Rousseau, SD 129; OC vol. 3, 125.

16. Rousseau, SD 129; OC vol. 3, 125.

17. Rousseau, SD 129; OC vol. 3, 125.

18. Rousseau, SD 129; OC vol. 3, 126.

19. Rousseau, SD 135; OC vol. 3, 132.

20. Rousseau, SD 128; OC vol. 3, 124.

21. Rousseau, SD 130; OC vol. 3, 126.

22. Scholars like Eileen Hunt draw our attention to the question of gender in Rousseau's invocation of a natural standard meant to serve as a universal. Hunt claims that over the course of his life, Rousseau moved from an early "egalitarian feminism" to a fully "patriarchal" view of the relations between men and women. See Eileen Hunt Botting, "Rousseau and Feminism," in *The Rousseauian Mind*, ed. Eve Grace and Christopher Kelly (New York: Routledge, 2019): 463–73. Like Susan Okin, Carol Pateman, and Penny Weiss, Hunt views the *Second Discourse* and the *Social Contract* as inherently sexist and is thus critical of Rousseau's use of the term "natural *man*." While this interpretive body of work yields fascinating insights into Rousseau's work, and challenges some of the core tenets of his philosophy, on the whole I do not agree with this reading. Rousseau takes great pains to insist that men and women are equal in the state of nature, to the point

of reaching almost comical conclusions about how this equality would affect offspring (perhaps echoing the comedy of the equality of men and women in Plato's *Republic*). Further, nowhere in *Social Contract* do I see Rousseau excluding women from sovereignty, citizenship, or any discussion of politics. Every interpretation of Rousseau's sexism reads the sexual politics of *Emile* into the *Second Discourse* and the *Social Contract*. Textual evidence from *Emile* is often interspersed with exegesis of the *Second Discourse* or *Social Contract* as if they were interchangeable texts. That Rousseau offers a gendered account in *Emile* is undeniable. The purpose of this in relation to the text as a whole and to the rest of his corpus is, I think, subject to variable interpretation. For the gendered reading, see Susan Moller Okin, "Rousseau's Natural Woman," *Journal of Politics* 41, no. 2 (1979): 393–416; Carole Pateman, *The Sexual Contract* (Stanford, CA: Stanford University Press, 1988); Penny A. Weiss, *Gendered Community: Rousseau, Sex, and Politics* (New York: New York University Press, 1993). For more, see Lynda Lange, ed., *Feminist Interpretations of Jean-Jacques Rousseau*, Re-Reading the Canon (University Park: Pennsylvania State University Press, 2002); Eileen Hunt Botting, "The Early Rousseau's Egalitarian Feminism: A Philosophical Convergence with Madame Dupin and 'The Critique of the Spirit of the Laws,'" *History of European Ideas* 43, no. 7 (2017): 732–44.

23. Rousseau, SC 45; OC vol. 3, 356.
24. Rousseau, SD 129; OC vol. 3, 125.
25. Rousseau, SD 135; OC vol. 3, 132.
26. Rousseau, SD 137; OC vol. 3, 134.
27. Rousseau, SD 136; OC vol. 3, 133.
28. Rousseau, SD 143; OC vol. 3, 140.
29. Rousseau, SD 162; OC vol. 3, 162.
30. Rousseau, SD 137; OC vol. 3, 134.
31. Rousseau, SD 145; OC vol. 3, 143.
32. Rousseau, SD 146; OC vol. 3, 144.
33. Rousseau, SD 129; OC vol. 3, 126.
34. Rousseau, SD 178; OC vol. 3, 178.
35. Rousseau, SD 178; OC vol. 3, 177–78.
36. Rousseau, SC 41; OC vol. 3, 351.
37. Rousseau, SC 49–50; OC vol. 3, 360.
38. Rousseau, SC 44; OC vol. 3, 355.
39. Rousseau, SC 45; OC vol. 3, 356.
40. As Ernst Cassirer writes, "Rousseau considers man a political being . . . but not a political *animal*, not a *zoon politikon*." Ernst Cassirer, *The Question of Jean-Jacques Rousseau*, trans. and ed. Peter Gay (Bloomington: Indiana University Press, 1963), 126.
41. Seeing natural man in the *Second Discourse* as a kind of transformative image is a vision I share with John T. Scott and Denise Schaeffer. See Denise Schaeffer, "Moral Motivation and Rhetoric," in *The Rousseauian Mind*, ed. Eve Grace and Christopher Kelly (New York: Routledge, 2019), 267–77; Denise Schaeffer, *Rousseau on Education, Freedom, and Judgment* (University Park: Pennsylvania State University Press, 2014); John T. Scott, *Rousseau's Reader: Strategies of Persuasion and Education* (Chicago: University of

Chicago Press, 2020); John T. Scott, *Rousseau's God: Theology, Religion, and the Natural Goodness of Man* (Chicago: University of Chicago Press, 2023).

42. Rousseau, SD 130; OC vol. 3, 126.
43. Rousseau, SD 135; OC vol. 3, 132.
44. Rousseau, SD 131; OC vol. 3, 127.
45. Rousseau, SD 135; OC vol. 3, 133.
46. Rousseau, SD 126; OC vol. 3, 122.
47. Rousseau, SD 194; OC vol. 3, 195. Rousseau is citing Georges-Louis LeClerc, comte de Buffon, *Histoire naturelle, générale et particulière, avec la description du Cabinet Du Roy* (Paris: Imprimerie royale, 1749), vol. 4, 151.
48. Rousseau and Buffon maintained an intellectual friendship throughout Rousseau's life (not an easy feat when it came to Rousseau), and Rousseau is said to have actively sought out every new volume of *Histoire naturelle* as they were published. In the spring of 1770, Buffon hosted Rousseau: "According to tradition, Rousseau went down on his knees at the entrance of the small building in the park where Buffon had installed his office. An inscription would for a long time recall the event: 'Passerby, bow down; it is before this retreat/ That the author of *Émile* fell at the great Buffon's feet." Jacques Roger, *Buffon: A Life in Natural History*, trans. Sarah Lucille Bonnefoi (Ithaca, NY: Cornell University Press, 1997), 350. Following the posthumous publication of Rousseau's *Confessions*, however, Buffon reversed his fondness for Rousseau, writing to Hérault de Séchelles, "I like him fairly well; but when I saw the *Confessions*, I ceased admiring him. His soul revolted me" (Roger, *Buffon*, 350). For more on Rousseau's relationship with Buffon, see Otis Fellows, "Buffon and Rousseau: Aspects of a Relationship," *PMLA* 75, no. 3 (1960): 184–96.
49. Rousseau, SD 126; OC vol. 3, 122.
50. Rousseau, SD 126; OC vol. 3, 123.
51. Rousseau, SD 126; OC vol. 3, 122.
52. Rousseau, SD 126; OC vol. 3, 123.
53. Buffon, *Histoire naturelle*, vol. 1, 12.
54. Buffon, *Histoire naturelle*, vol. 1, 12.
55. Rousseau, SD 137; OC vol. 3, 134.
56. Rousseau, SD 137; OC vol. 3, 134–35.
57. Rousseau, SD 146; OC vol. 3, 144.
58. Rousseau SD 141; OC vol. 3, 138.
59. For a thorough account of the travel literature upon which Buffon's and Rousseau's descriptions of the great apes were based, see Francis Moran III, "Of Pongos and Men: *Orangs-Outang* in Rousseau's *Discourse on Inequality*," *Review of Politics* 57, no. 4 (1995): 641–64, in which Moran establishes that the description of the pongo and orang-outang were grounded in Antoine-François, l'abbé Prévost, *Histoire générale des voyages* (Paris, 1746–1789), itself drawing on Samuel Purchas's *Hakluytus Posthumus* of 1625. See also Claude Blanckaert, "Premier des singes, dernier des hommes?," *Alliage* 7, no. 8 (1991): 113–28; Odile Gannier, "De l'usage des notes dans le *Discours sur l'inégalité* de Rousseau: Récits de voyages et ethnogrophie," *Loxias* 27, no. 2 (2009),

http://revel.unice.fr/loxias/index.html?id=3169; Jean Morel, "Recherches sur les sources du *Discours de l'inégalité*," *Annales de la Société Jean-Jacques Rousseau* 5 (1909): 119–98. Silvia Sebastiani has also done wonderful work locating the satyr-orangutan in negotiations of the human and nonhuman in the eighteenth century. See Silvia Sebastiani, "Challenging Boundaries: Apes and Savages in the Enlightenment," in *Simianization: Apes, Gender, Class, and Race*, ed. Wulf D. Hund, Charles W. Mills, and Silvia Sebastiani (Zurich: Lit Zurlag, 2015): 105–37; Silvia Sebastiani, "La caravane des animaux," in *Mobilités creatrices: Hommes, savoirs et pratiques en mouvement (XVIe–XIXe siècle)*, ed. Catherine Brice, *Diasporas* 29 (2017).

60.   Rousseau, SD 211–12; OC vol. 3, 209.

61.   Rousseau, SD 213; OC vol. 3, 210.

62.   Robert Wokler, "Perfectible Apes in Decadent Cultures: Rousseau's Anthropology Revisited," *Daedalus* 107, no. 3 (1978): 128. See also Asher Horowitz, "'Law and Customs Thrust Us Back Into Infancy': Rousseau's Historical Anthropology," *Review of Politics* 52, no. 2 (1990): 215–41; Arthur O. Lovejoy, "The Supposed Primitivism of Rousseau's 'Discourse on Inequality,'" *Modern Philology* 21, no. 2 (1923): 165–86; Roger D. Masters, "Jean-Jacques Is Alive and Well: Rousseau and Contemporary Sociobiology," *Daedalus* 107 (1978): 93–105. Contrary to the evolutionary reading, see Francis Moran III, "Between Primates and Primitives: Natural Man as the Missing Link in Rousseau's *Second Discourse*," *Journal of the History of Ideas* 54, no. 1 (1993): 37–58; Moran, "Of Pongos and Men," 641–64.

63.   Hermann Samuel Reimarus, *The Principal Truths of Natural Religion Defended and Illustrated, in Nine Dissertations: Wherein the Objections of Lucretius, Buffon, Maupertuis, Rousseau, La Mettrie, and Other Ancient and Modern Followers of Epicurus Are Considered, and Their Doctrines Refuted* (London: B. Law, [1755] 1766), 316.

64.   "Lettre de Voltaire à Jean-Jacques Rousseau, 30 August 1755," OC vol. 3, 1379–81, 1379.

65.   Buffon, *Histoire naturelle*, vol. 2, 443.

66.   Buffon, *Histoire naturelle*, vol. 4, 22.

67.   Rousseau, SD 144; OC vol. 3, 142.

68.   Rousseau, SD 143; OC vol. 3, 141.

69.   Rousseau, SD 143; OC vol. 3, 141–42.

70.   Rousseau, SD 143; OC vol. 3, 141.

71.   Rousseau, SD 144; OC vol. 3, 141–42.

72.   Rousseau, SD 144; OC vol. 3, 142. There is much debate over two aspects of this argument: (1) some claim that Rousseau replaces freedom with perfectibility, while others claim that perfectibility requires an already present free will, and (2) some claim that the entire aspect of Rousseau's discussion of freedom or free will and any claims that would substantiate a metaphysical dualism are detachable from Rousseau's thought. This second argument is attributable to Roger D. Masters, *The Political Philosophy of Rousseau* (Princeton, NJ: Princeton University Press, 1968). I disagree with the second point, siding with Robin Douglass, who aligns himself with Timothy O'Hagan in claiming that whatever Rousseau's metaphysical dualism is, it is substantially related to his picture of the human being. See Robin Douglass, "Free Will and the Problem of Evil:

Reconciling Rousseau's Divided Thought," *History of Political Thought* 31, no. 4 (2010): 639–55; Timothy O'Hagan, *Rousseau* (New York: Routledge, 2003). On the first point, the waters are a bit murkier. The replacement of perfectibility with freedom in order to avoid metaphysical (and theological) debates is an argument that has been made by O'Hagan, as well as Masters, and can be traced back to Leo Strauss, *Natural Right and History* (Chicago: Chicago University Press, 1965). Lee MacLean, also following O'Hagan, has written that any account of perfectibility implies the presence of free will. See Lee MacLean, *The Free Animal: Rousseau on Free Will and Human Nature* (Toronto, ON: University of Toronto Press, 2013). Rousseau's trepidation about the use of freedom is often seen as rooted in a desire to avoid theological disagreements about free will. However, I also take him to be trepidatious because animals can be described as free in many respects. Rousseau thus sees *freedom* as either a dangerous or useless term when it comes to describing human distinction and so comes up with *perfectibility*, which is what others (including the natural scientist Charles Bonnet) began using following the publication of the *Second Discourse*. *Freedom* and *perfectibility* describe the same phenomenon—a feature that distinguishes humans from animals—and it is this phenomenon that I am trying to unpack here. I will stick with Rousseau's *perfectibility* to describe whatever this distinction is while remaining committed to taking any claims of metaphysical dualism seriously, following O'Hagan and Douglass. Both *perfectibility* and *free will* can accommodate the more interesting fact, in my view, that Rousseau borrows from Buffon the interior distinction of sentiment of one's present existence from a consciousness of the self (the latter of which is the metaphysical principle).

73. Rousseau, SD 144; OC vol. 3, 142.

74. Rousseau has an exchange about this with "Philopolis"—a pen name of Charles Bonnet's—in which Bonnet accuses Rousseau of confusing the ape with natural man in his *Second Discourse*. See "Lettre de M. Philopolis au sujet du discours de M. J. J. Rousseau de Genève, sur l'origine et fondemens de l'inégalité parmi les hommes," in Jean-Jacques Rousseau, *Oeuvres complètes* (Paris: NRF-Éditions de la Pléiade, 1965–1995), vol. 3, 1383–1386 [1755]; and Rousseau's reply: Jean-Jacques Rousseau, "Letter to Philopolis," in *The Discourses and Other Early Political Writings*, trans. and ed. Victor Gourevitch (Cambridge: Cambridge University Press, 2007), 223–28.

75. Rousseau, SD 145; OC vol. 3, 143.

76. Even Leo Strauss wants to make a version of this claim, writing that natural man without perfectibility would thus seem to be "subhuman." Strauss, *Natural Right and History*, 271.

77. Robert Wokler, "From *l'homme physique* to *l'homme moral* and Back: Towards a History of Enlightenment Anthropology," *History of Human Sciences* 6, no. 1 (1993): 121–38.

78. See Timothy O'Hagan, "Taking Rousseau Seriously," *History of Political Thought* 25, no. 1 (2004): 73–85; O'Hagan, *Rousseau*.

79. Douglass is referencing "The Profession of Faith of the Savoyard" here. See Jean-Jacques Rousseau, *Emile: or On Education*, trans. Allan Bloom (New York: Basic Books, 1979). Douglass also relies on other texts for evidence, including Jean-Jacques Rousseau, *Fiction or Allegorical Fragment on Revelation*, in *On Philosophy, Morality, and Religion*, trans. and ed. Christopher Kelly (Hanover, NH: Dartmouth College Press, 2004), 63–72.

80.   Douglass, "Free Will," 652.

81.   Frederick Neuhouser, *Rousseau's Critique of Inequality: Reconstructing the Second Discourse* (Cambridge: Cambridge University Press, 2014), 48–49.

82.   Some have described the link between Rousseau and Buffon in some detail (see, for example, Jean Starobinski, *Transparency and Obstruction* [Chicago: University of Chicago Press, 1998]; Céline Spector, *Rousseau*, Classic Thinkers [Cambridge: Polity, 2019]; Robert Wokler, "The *Discours sur l'inégalité* and Its Sources" [PhD diss., University of Oxford, 1976], chap. 3; MacLean, *The Free Animal*) but never in terms of their accounts of human nature. For more on how I view the relationship between Rousseau and Buffon, see Emma Planinc, "Homo Duplex: The Two Origins of Man in Rousseau's *Second Discourse*," *History of European Ideas* 47, no. 1 (2021): 71–90.

83.   Buffon, *Histoire naturelle*, vol. 4, 69.

84.   Buffon, *Histoire naturelle*, vol. 4, 70.

85.   Buffon, *Histoire naturelle*, vol. 4, 39.

86.   Buffon, *Histoire naturelle*, vol. 4, 51.

87.   Rousseau, SD 146; OC vol. 3, 143.

88.   The reading of Rousseau as the first step into "modernity" comes from interpreters who see Rousseau as "the father of progressive history." Matthew D. Mendham, "Gentle Savages and Fierce Citizens Against Civilization: Unraveling Rousseau's Paradoxes," *American Journal of Political Science* 55, no. 1 (2011): 185.

89.   Rousseau, SD 127; OC vol. 3, 123.

90.   In the work of both Buffon and Rousseau, it is undeniable that this bears some resemblance to a Platonic form. Certainly, the idea of a universal nature or original prototype is the aspect of their thought that I would tie to the ancient, or telic, mode of understanding the human being. David Lay Williams also sees the power of Rousseau's normative critique in his ties to the ancient world and to ancient philosophy. He writes that Rousseau's "commitment to transcendent ideas is as essential to his philosophy as his critique" and is what "allows him to level the critique as persuasively as he does" (Williams, *Rousseau's Platonic Enlightenment*, 238).

91.   Rousseau, SD 192; OC vol. 3, 192–93.

92.   Rousseau, SD 141; OC vol. 3, 138.

93.   Rousseau, SD 127; OC vol. 3, 123. The various interpretations of Rousseau's conception of the passing of time in his "hypothetical history" are well described in Christopher Kelly, "Rousseau's 'Peut-Être': Reflections on the Status of the State of Nature," *Modern Intellectual History* 3, no. 1 (2006): 75–83.

94.   In this respect, I agree with Strauss's reading of Rousseau that he "realized that to the extent to which the historical process is accidental, it cannot supply man with a standard, and that, if that process has a hidden purpose, its purposefulness cannot be recognized except if there are transhistorical standards." Strauss, *Natural Right and History*, 274.

95.   As Jonathan Marks puts it, "Nature is not a beginning but an end of perfection." Jonathan Marks, "Who Lost Nature? Rousseau and Rousseauism," *Polity* 34, no. 4 (2002): 478. This position is echoed by Ernst Cassirer, who claims that the goodness of man is not an origin, properly understood, but a "destiny of man's will," a destiny that requires the

activity of man to reach its goal. While "Rousseau deplored the gift of 'perfectibility,' which differentiated man from all the other living creatures, he also knew that it alone can bring ultimate deliverance." Cassirer, *The Question of Jean-Jacques Rousseau*, 104, 78. See also Richard Velkley, "The Measure of the Possible: Imagination in Rousseau's Philosophical Pedagogy," in *The Challenge of Rousseau*, ed. Eve Grace and Christopher Kelly (Cambridge: Cambridge University Press, 2013), 217–29. In *The Theology of Liberalism*, Eric Nelson ties Rousseau to the roots of liberalism insofar as Rousseau's work was a Pelagian theodicy—that is, in denying original sin, Nelson claims that Rousseau put a "Pelagian insistence on human freedom" and identified the "corrosive force of social convention," placing him at the beginnings of the liberal commitment to human self-making. Eric Nelson, *The Theology of Liberalism: Political Philosophy and the Justice of God* (Cambridge, MA: Belknap, 2019), 3, 4.

96. Buffon, *Histoire naturelle*, vol. 12, iv.
97. Rousseau, SD 162–63; OC vol. 3, 162.
98. Rousseau, SD 158; OC vol. 3, 157.
99. Rousseau, SD 165; OC vol. 3, 164.
100. Rousseau, SD 166; OC vol. 3, 165; Rousseau, SD 142; OC vol. 3, 140.
101. The claim that climate alters human beings is not unique to Buffon, of course, but can also be found in the work of many eighteenth-century philosophes, including Montesquieu's *Spirit of the Laws*.
102. Rousseau, SD 166; OC vol. 3, 165.
103. Rousseau, SD 166; OC vol. 3, 165.
104. Rousseau, SD 169; OC vol. 3, 168.
105. Rousseau, SD 169; OC vol. 3, 168.
106. Rousseau, SD 170; OC vol. 3, 169.
107. Rousseau, SD 170; OC vol. 3, 170.
108. Rousseau, SD 171; OC vol. 3, 171, 170.
109. Rousseau, SD 172; OC vol. 3, 171.
110. Rousseau, SD 175; OC vol. 3, 174–75.
111. Rousseau, SD 177; OC vol. 3, 177.
112. Rousseau, SD 177; OC vol. 3, 177.
113. Rousseau, SD 178; OC vol. 3, 177–78.
114. Rousseau, SD 178; OC vol. 3, 178.
115. Rousseau, SD 181; OC vol. 3, 181.
116. Rousseau, SD 181; OC vol. 3, 181.
117. Rousseau, SD 182; OC vol. 3, 182.
118. Rousseau, SD 191–92; OC vol. 3, 191–92.
119. Rousseau, SD 192; OC vol. 3, 192–93.
120. This is why, I would argue, Rousseau claims that the happiest epoch for man is not the pure state of nature but a condition in which human beings are in fact sociable and dependent on one another in small, naturally just communities. This also makes the human being, properly speaking, both a creature of *amour-de-soi-même* and *amour-propre*.
121. Rousseau, SC 41; OC vol. 3, 351.

122.   Rousseau, SC 41; OC vol. 3, 352.

123.   Rousseau, SD 185; OC vol. 3, 186.

124.   Rousseau, SD 130; OC vol. 3, 126.

125.   Rousseau, SD 131; OC vol. 3, 127.

126.   Rousseau, SC 50; OC vol. 3, 360.

127.   This is my translation of *premiers droits*, which Gourevitch translates as "original rights." Rousseau, SC 50; OC vol. 3, 360.

128.   Rousseau, SC 50; OC vol. 3, 360.

129.   Rousseau, SC 45; OC vol. 3, 356.

130.   Locke, *Second Treatise*, chapter 8, section 119.

131.   Hobbes, *Leviathan*, book I, chapter XIV, section 5.

132.   Rousseau, SC 50; OC vol. 3, 360.

133.   Rousseau, SC 50; OC vol. 3, 361.

134.   Rousseau, SC 50; OC vol. 3, 360.

135.   J. L. Talmon, *The Origins of Totalitarian Democracy* (London: Mercury, 1961). See also James Swenson, *On Jean-Jacques Rousseau: Considered as One of the First Authors of the Revolution* (Stanford, CA: Stanford University Press, 2000).

136.   Rousseau, SC 50; OC vol. 3, 361.

137.   Rousseau, SD 185; OC vol. 3, 186.

138.   Rousseau, SC 120; OC vol. 3, 436.

139.   Rousseau, SC 53; OC vol. 3, 364.

140.   Rousseau, SC 78; OC vol. 3, 391.

141.   Rousseau, SD 192; OC vol. 3, 192.

142.   Rousseau, SD 184; OC vol. 3, 184.

143.   Rousseau, SD 116; OC vol. 3, 111.

144.   Rousseau, SD 126; OC vol. 3, 123.

145.   Rousseau, SD 126; OC vol. 3, 123.

146.   Here, I am not engaging in a discussion of the Lawgiver, the figure in Rousseau's *Social Contract* assigned the role of transforming human beings by preparing them for law and government. However, elsewhere I have argued that Rousseau is himself the Lawgiver and that the transformation occurs when one reads the *Second Discourse*. See Emma Planinc, "The Figurative Foundations of Rousseau's Politics," *Modern Intellectual History* 20, no. 1 (2023): 1–26.

147.   Rousseau, SC 41; OC vol. 3, 351, 352.

148.   Here again is alignment with Strauss, who writes that, for Rousseau, human beings always "have a reservation against society in the name of the state of nature" that is undetermined (Strauss, *Natural Right and History*, 294).

149.   Rousseau, SC 41; OC vol. 3, 352.

150.   Rousseau, SC 44; OC vol. 3, 355.

151.   Rousseau, SC 50; OC vol. 3, 361; Rousseau, SC 53; OC vol. 3, 364.

152.   Rousseau, SC 54; OC I vol. 3, II 364; Rousseau, SC 53; OC vol. 3, 364.

153.   Rousseau, SC 50; OC vol. 3, 360.

154.   Rousseau, SD 174; OC vol. 3, 174.

155.   Rousseau, SD 172; OC vol. 3, 171.

156.   Rousseau, SD 177; OC vol. 3, 177.

157.   Rousseau, SC 56; OC vol. 3, 367.

158.   Rousseau, SD 190–91; OC vol. 3, 191.

159.   Rousseau, SD 126; OC vol. 3, 123.

160.   Rousseau, SC 56n; OC vol. 3, 367.

161.   Rousseau, SC 50; OC vol. 3, 361.

162.   Rousseau, SC 50; OC vol. 3, 360. Here, I maintain my translation of *premiers droits* as "first rights" (as opposed to Gourevitch's "original rights").

163.   Rousseau, SC 91–92; OC vol. 3, 405–406.

164.   *L'an I des droits de l'homme: Controverses et débats de 1789 autour de la Déclaration des droits de l'homme*, ed. Antoine de Baecque (Paris: CNRS, 1988), 94.

165.   François Furet, "Rousseau and the French Revolution," in *The Legacy of Rousseau*, ed. Clifford Orwin and Nathan Tarcov (Chicago: University of Chicago Press, 1997), 179.

166.   This is a reading that is in most respects compatible with Sankar Muthu's concept of "humanity as cultural agency" in the thought of Rousseau (and Diderot, among others): "The understanding of the human subject that such an account presupposes is that human beings are *cultural agents*; that is, humans are partly shaped by and situated in cultural contexts, yet are also able to consciously and freely transform themselves and their surroundings." Sankar Muthu, *Enlightenment Against Empire* (Princeton, NJ: Princeton University Press, 2003), 11, 67.

167.   This argument about Rousseau is also made by Ernst Cassirer: "The idea of inalienable rights, which in the theory of natural law was designed to draw a clear and precise line of demarcation between the sphere of the individual and that of the state and to preserve the independence of the former from the latter, is now asserted by Rousseau to belong to the sphere of the state." Ernst Cassirer, *The Philosophy of the Enlightenment*, trans. Peter Gay (Princeton, NJ: Princeton University Press, 1951), 264.

168.   Sankar Muthu presents this pessimism as a tragedy, much as Judith Shklar does in *Men and Citizens*. The prospect of human beings fixing themselves, writes Muthu, "seems vanishingly thin"; Rousseau's general will "illustrates from a distinctive and genuinely all-encompassing global perspective, the profoundly tragic sensibility of his social and political thought." Sankar Muthu, "On the General Will of Humanity: Global Connections in Rousseau's Political Thought," in *The General Will: The Evolution of a Concept*, ed. James Farr and David Lay Williams (Cambridge: Cambridge University Press, 2015): 270–306. See also Judith N. Shklar, *Men and Citizens: A Study of Rousseau's Social Theory* (Cambridge: Cambridge University Press, 1969). While Rousseau is certainly not a champion of human progress as such, I do not think that he is resigned to a completely tragic view of human possibilities. For more on Rousseau as tragic or pessimistic, see Jason Neidleman, "Politics and Tragedy: The Case of Rousseau," *Political Research Quarterly* 73, no. 2 (2020): 464–75; Michael E. Winston, *From Perfectibility to Perversion: Meliorism in Eighteenth-Century France* (New York: P. Lang, 2005). Winston also explicitly contrasts Rousseau's general pessimism with Buffon's optimism about the prospect of improving the human species.

169. Rousseau, SC 109; OC vol. 3, 424. Here, Rousseau is seemingly drawing on an argument from Augustine's *The City of God*—"No sooner do we begin to live in this dying body, than we begin to move ceaselessly toward death" (XIII.10, 419)—though Marcus Dods acknowledges that Augustine took this from Seneca. Augustine, *The City of God*, trans. Marcus Dods (New York: Modern Library, 1950).

170. Rousseau, SC 109; OC vol. 3, 424.

171. Rousseau, SC 109; OC vol. 3, 424.

172. Jean-Jacques Rousseau, "Considerations on the Government of Poland," in *The Social Contract and Other Later Political Writings*, trans. and ed. Victor Gourevitch (Cambridge: Cambridge University Press, 1997), 192; OC vol. 3, 969.

173. Charles Bonnet, "Essai de psychologie," in *Oeuvres d'histoire naturelle et philosophie de Charles Bonnet*, vol. 17 (Neuchatel: Samuel Fauche, [1755] 1783).

174. Rousseau, "Considerations," 193; OC vol. 3, 970.

175. Rousseau, "Considerations," 183; OC vol. 3, 959.

176. Rousseau, "Considerations," 178; OC vol. 3, 954.

177. Rousseau, "Considerations," 193; OC vol. 3, 970, my emphasis.

4. REGENERATION AND REVOLUTION

1. Alyssa Goldstein Sepinwall, *The Abbé Grégoire and the French Revolution: The Making of Modern Universalism* (Berkeley: University of California Press, 2005), 57. Emma Spary also notes that many terms underwent similar changes in eighteenth-century France, all relying on the natural foundations of subsequent political and social shifts: "Many political terms, such as *constitution*, *régénération*, and *corruption*, were simultaneously medical, natural historical, and agricultural, and Revolutionary reformers presented themselves as facilitators of the formation of a new society in France based upon natural laws." E. C. Spary, *Utopia's Garden: French Natural History from Old Regime to Revolution* (Chicago: University of Chicago Press, 2000), 4. Sepinwall also cites, and relies on, the important analyses of Antoine de Baecque, *The Body Politic: Corporeal Metaphor in Revolutionary France, 1770–1800*, trans. Charlotte Mandell (Stanford, CA: Stanford University Press, 1997) and Mona Ozouf, *L'homme régénéré: Essais sur la Révolution française* (Paris: Gallimard, 1989).

2. *Dictionnaire de l'Académie française*, 4th ed. (Paris, 1762). All entries accessed via the ARTFL Project of the University of Chicago.

3. Scholars have focused on various aspects of the regenerative root as it transformed into its political use in the eighteenth century. Antoine de Baecque's *The Body Politic* focuses on the corporeal metaphor, focusing on the regeneration of the *body* of the state. Lucien Jaume concentrates on the religious origins, denying both any significant influence of the scientific sense of the term and its philosophic import among the lumières. Its usage is "strictly religious." Lucien Jaume, *Le religieux et le politique dans la Révolution française: L'idée de régénération* (Paris: Presses universitaires de France, 2015), 7. Gilles Barroux swings the opposite way, drawing a line of heritage from the political and social

regeneration of the revolutionary period solely to the natural sciences and developments in biological regeneration, not to theology. Gilles Barroux, *Philosophie de la régénération: Médicine, biologie, mythologies* (Paris: Harmattan, 2009). Taken together, these works explain many pieces of the heritage of regeneration, but they do not to my mind add up in their particulars to a general account of the whole, nor do they articulate the reimagination of human nature that occurred in the century leading up to the Revolution.

4.   Roger Griffin, *The Nature of Fascism* (New York: Psychology, 1993), 33.

5.   Griffin, *The Nature of Fascism*, 32, 33.

6.   Griffin, *The Nature of Fascism*, 40, 41, 41.

7.   Griffin, *The Nature of Fascism*, 41.

8.   Waller R. Newell, *Tyranny: A New Interpretation* (Cambridge: Cambridge University Press, 2013), 450.

9.   Bertrand Russell, *A History of Western Philosophy and Its Connection with Political and Social Circumstances from the Earliest Times to the Present Day* (New York: Simon and Schuster, 1945), 696.

10. Russell, *A History of Western Philosophy*, 701. For a recent discussion of this argument, see Anthony Gottlieb, *The Dream of Enlightenment: The Rise of Modern Philosophy* (New York: Liveright, 2016), chapter 8.

11. François Furet, "Rousseau and the French Revolution," in *The Legacy of Rousseau*, ed. Clifford Orwin and Nathan Tarcov (Chicago: University of Chicago Press, 1997), 179.

12. Sean Quinlan, "Physical and Moral Regeneration After the Terror: Medical Culture, Sensibility and Family Politics in France, 1794–1804," *Social History* 29, no. 2 (2004): 146.

13. Sepinwall, *The Abbé Grégoire*, 134. On the fountain and the festival's regenerative function, see William Max Nelson, *The Time of Enlightenment: Constructing the Future in France, 1750 to Year One* (Toronto, ON: University of Toronto Press, 2021); Quinlan, "Physical and Moral Regeneration," 139–40.

14. *Archives parlementaires, première série (1787 à 1799)*, tome LXXIV, du 12 septembre 1793 au 22 septembre 1793. Accessed via the ARTFL Project of the University of Chicago, https://artfl-project.uchicago.edu/archives-parlementaires.

15. *Archives parlementaires, première série (1787 à 1799)*, tome LXXII, du 11 août 1793 au 24 août 1793. Accessed via the ARTFL Project of the University of Chicago, https://artfl-project.uchicago.edu/archives-parlementaires.

16. Ozouf, *L'homme régénéré*; as cited in Katia Sainson, " 'Le régénerateur de la France': Literary Accounts of Napoleonic Regeneration 1799–1805," *Nineteenth-Century French Studies* 30, no. 1 (2001): 10.

17. Lynn Hunt, "Revolutionary Time and Regeneration," *Diciottesimo Secolo* 1 (2016): 70.

18. Nelson, *The Time of Enlightenment*, 124.

19. Matthew D. Mendham, "Gentle Savages and Fierce Citizens Against Civilization: Unraveling Rousseau's Paradoxes," *American Journal of Political Science* 55, no. 1 (2011): 185.

20. Asher Horowitz, " 'Law and Customs Thrust Us Back Into Infancy': Rousseau's Historical Anthropology," *Review of Politics* 52, no. 2 (1990): 219; Arthur M. Melzer, *The Natural Goodness of Man: On the System of Rousseau's Thought* (Chicago: University of Chicago Press, 1990), 50.

21.   Cited in Fayçal Falaky, "Reverse Revolution: The Paradox of Rousseau's Authorship," in *Rousseau and Revolution*, Continuum Studies in Political Philosophy, ed. Holger Ross Lauritsen and Mikkel Thorup (New York: Continuum, 2011), 85.

22.   George Armstrong Kelly, "A General Overview," in *The Cambridge Companion to Rousseau*, ed. Patrick Riley (Cambridge: Cambridge University Press, 2001), 43.

23.   Citied in Henri Peyre, "The Influence of Eighteenth Century Ideas on the French Revolution," *Journal of the History of Ideas* 10, no. 1 (1949): 63–87.

24.   Kevin Duong, *The Virtues of Violence: Democracy Against Disintegration in Modern France* (Oxford: Oxford University Press, 2020), 12. In its interpretation of the French Revolution, Duong's *The Virtues of Violence* associates the regenerative political calls of the Jacobins only with roots in violent natural disasters: "By lifting regicide out of classical theories of tyrannicide and reinscribing it in Enlightenment conceptions of natural disaster, this language imbued 'the people' with nature's own catastrophic, regenerative agency" (23). Duong also incorrectly identifies regeneration in Buffon's work as being grounded in the "agency" of lightning: "Marat outlined the regenerative, purifying effects of lightning for the atmosphere. He built his analysis on the insights of popular naturalists like the Comte de Buffon, who had discussed lightning as a spontaneous manifestation of the earth's universal heat and energy in his widely read *Histoire naturelle*" (43); "The connection between lightning and social regeneration was a widespread motif of revolutionary political culture" (43). See also Kevin Duong, "The People as a Natural Disaster: Redemptive Violence in Jacobin Political Thought," *American Political Science Review* 111, no. 4 (2017): 786–800.

25.   Darrin M. McMahon, *Enemies of the Enlightenment: The French Counter-Enlightenment and the Making of Modernity* (Oxford: Oxford University Press, 2002), 96.

26.   Marcel Gauchet, *Robespierre: The Man Who Divides Us the Most*, trans. Malcolm DeBevoise (Princeton, NJ: Princeton University Press, 2022), 168, 167.

27.   Mona Ozouf, "Regeneration," in *A Critical Dictionary of the French Revolution*, ed. François Furet and Mona Ozouf (Cambridge, MA: Belknap, 1989), 789. This is Ozouf's own reuse of a portion of *L'homme régénéré*.

28.   Ozouf, "Regeneration," 781.

29.   Ozouf, "Regeneration," 790, 789.

30.   François Furet, *Interpreting the French Revolution* (Cambridge: Cambridge University Press, 1981), 63.

31.   Furet, *Interpreting*, 61.

32.   Furet, *Interpreting*, 77.

33.   Furet, *Interpreting*, 62–63.

34.   Dan Edelstein, "Nature or Nation? Rights Conflicts in the Age of the French Revolution," in *Rethinking the Age of Revolutions: France and the Birth of the Modern World*, ed. David Bell and Yair Mintzker (Oxford: Oxford University Press, 2018), 32. See also Dan Edelstein, *The Terror of Natural Right: Republicanism, the Cult of Nature, and the French Revolution* (Chicago: University of Chicago Press, 2010).

35.   Isaiah Berlin, "The Counter-Enlightenment," in *Against the Current: Essays in the History of Ideas*, 2nd ed., ed. Henry Hardy (Princeton, NJ: Princeton University Press, 2013), 24, 4.

36. Berlin, "The Counter Enlightenment," 32.

37. William Max Nelson provides a similar account of this transformation: "The practical understanding of the constructability of the future developed well before the Revolution, and in fact it helped make the Revolution possible. The Revolution, then, was only the event that brought forth this understanding and radicalized it by triggering individuals to state it explicitly and forcefully, while also enacting it in a wide variety of practices that pushed the constructability of the future to new extremes." Nelson, *The Time of Enlightenment*, 112.

38. Archives parlementaires, tome premier États Généraux, Cahiers des Sénéchaussées et Baillages, Cahiers Contenant les Pouvoirs et Instructions Remi, etc. Accessed via the ARTFL Project of the University of Chicago, https://artfl-project.uchicago.edu /archives-parlementaires.

39. Archives parlementaires, première série (1787 à 1799), tome VII, du 5 mai 1789 au 15 septembre 1789. Accessed via the ARTFL Project of the University of Chicago, https:// artfl-project.uchicago.edu/archives-parlementaires.

40. Archives parlementaires, première série (1787 à 1799), tome quatrième États Généraux, 1789, from the Third Estate of Seneschales of Nimes to be taken to the États generale. Accessed via the ARTFL Project of the University of Chicago, https://artfl-project .uchicago.edu/archives-parlementaires.

41. Archives parlementaires, première série (1787 à 1799), tome XVI, Assemblée Nationale Constituante du 31 mai 1790 au 8 juillet 1790, M. Camus. Accessed via the ARTFL Project of the University of Chicago, https://artfl-project.uchicago.edu /archives-parlementaires.

42. Archives parlementaires, première série (1787 à 1799), tome XXIC, du 10 mars 1791 au 12 avril 1791. Accessed via the ARTFL Project of the University of Chicago, https:// artfl-project.uchicago.edu/archives-parlementaires.

43. Archives parlementaires, première série (1787 à 1799), tome XXVI, du 12 mai au 5 juin 1791, M. Duport. Accessed via the ARTFL Project of the University of Chicago, https:// artfl-project.uchicago.edu/archives-parlementaires.

44. Archives parlementaires, première série (1787 à 1799), tome XXXIX, du 22 février au 14 mars 1792. Accessed via the ARTFL Project of the University of Chicago, https:// artfl-project.uchicago.edu/archives-parlementaires.

45. Archives parlementaires, première série (1787 à 1799), M. Lavigne, Assemblée Nationale Législative. Accessed via the ARTFL Project of the University of Chicago, https:// artfl-project.uchicago.edu/archives-parlementaires.

46. Archives parlementaires, première série (1787 à 1799), tome XXXVII, du 2 au 28 janvier 1792. Accessed via the ARTFL Project of the University of Chicago, https://artfl-project .uchicago.edu/archives-parlementaires.

47. Cited in de Baecque, *The Body Politic*, 140.

48. Cited in C. E. Vaughan, "Introduction," in Jean-Jacques Rousseau, *The Political Writings of Jean-Jacques Rousseau*, vol. 1, trans. and ed. C. E. Vaughan (New York: John Wiley, 1962), 17–18.

49. Vaughan, "Introduction," 18.

50. Archives parlementaires, tome premier États Généraux, Cahiers des Sénéchaussées et Baillages; Cahiers des Sénéchaussées et Baillages, Cahiers Contenant les Pouvoirs et Instructions Remi, etc. Accessed via the ARTFL Project of the University of Chicago, https://artfl-project.uchicago.edu/archives-parlementaires.

51. Joan McDonald, *Rousseau and the French Revolution, 1762–1791* (London: Athlone, 1965), 67.

52. McDonald, *Rousseau and the French Revolution*, 68.

53. McDonald, *Rousseau and the French Revolution*, 70.

54. For other "Rousseau influence deniers," see Robert Derathé, *Jean-Jacques Rousseau et la science politique de son temps* (Paris: Vrin, 1970); Samuel Taylor, "Rousseau's Contemporary Reception in France," *Studies on Voltaire and the Eighteenth Century* 27 (1963): 1545–74.

55. James Swenson, *On Jean-Jacques Rousseau: Considered as One of the First Authors of the Revolution* (Stanford, CA: Stanford University Press, 2000), 193.

56. Judith N. Shklar, *Men and Citizens: A Study of Rousseau's Social Theory* (Cambridge: Cambridge University Press, 1969), 222.

57. Gary Kates, *The Cercle Social, the Girondins, and the French Revolution* (Princeton, NJ: Princeton University Press, 1985), 77.

58. Cited in Kates, *The Cercle Social*, 78.

59. Kates, *The Cercle Social*, 80.

60. Kates, *The Cercle Social*, 80.

61. De Baecque, *The Body Politic*, 144. Mercier also engaged in utopian fiction, publishing *L'an 2440, rêve s'il en fut jamais* in 1770. Mercier's tale involves a Frenchman falling asleep and waking up in a future Paris that has fulfilled many of the goals of Rousseau's natural man.

62. François d'Escherny, "Éloge de J. J. Rousseau," in *La philosophie de la politique, ou Principes généraux sur les institutions civiles, politiques, et religieuses* (Paris, [1790] 1796). "Éloge" serves as the introduction to *La philosophie de la politique*, in which d'Escherny discusses the *Social Contract* at length. The citations in notes 63 to 72 are all from this volume, and translations are my own. D'Escherny was a member of the Encyclopedic Circle and a great friend of Rousseau's until 1768, when they seemingly fell out over d'Escherny's attempt to introduce Rousseau to a publisher who had rejected Rousseau's work some years before.

63. D'Escherny, "Éloge de J. J. Rousseau," iii.

64. D'Escherny, "Éloge de J. J. Rousseau," vi.

65. D'Escherny, "Éloge de J. J. Rousseau," xiii–xiv.

66. D'Escherny, "Éloge de J. J. Rousseau," liv.

67. D'Escherny, "Éloge de J. J. Rousseau," liv.

68. D'Escherny, "Éloge de J. J. Rousseau," lxxxvi.

69. D'Escherny, "Éloge de J. J. Rousseau," xciv.

70. D'Escherny, "Éloge de J. J. Rousseau," xcv.

71. D'Escherny, "Éloge de J. J. Rousseau," lvii.

72. D'Escherny, "Éloge de J. J. Rousseau," lvii.

73. Ozouf, *L'homme régénéré*, 157. Translation is my own.
74. "The Declaration of the Rights of Man and of the Citizen," 1789, https://www.elysee.fr/en/french-presidency/the-declaration-of-the-rights-of-man-and-of-the-citizen.
75. Cited in de Baecque, *The Body Politic*, 137.
76. Stephen Gaukroger also connects Buffon and Nicolas de Condorcet through Condorcet's account of scientific knowledge and his *Equisse d'un tableau historique des progrès de l'esprit humain*, in which Condorcet (like Buffon) divides historical and human progress into epochs, ending with the "Future Progress of Mankind"; "experience of the past enables [man] to foresee, with considerable probability, future appearances." Stephen Gaukroger, *The Natural and the Human: Science and the Shaping of Modernity, 1739–1841*, Science and the Shaping of Modernity (Oxford: Oxford University Press, 2016), 25, 61. But Condorcet's *Esquisse d'un tableu historique des progress de l'esprit humain* was not written until 1794 and only published posthumously in 1795. The earlier epochal invocations thus could not have been drawn from Condorcet's account but must have been from Buffon's.
77. Cited in William H. Sewell Jr., *A Rhetoric of Bourgeois Revolution: The Abbé Sieyes and What Is the Third Estate?* (Durham, NC: Duke University Press, 1994), xvii. It was not uncommon for revolutionaries to speak of Rousseau and Buffon together. See, for example, M. Hérault Séchelle, "Parallele de J. J. Rousseau et de M. de Buffon," *Journal encyclopédique* 3 (1786): 329–30.
78. In this, I am in agreement with Sophia Rosenfeld's excellent analysis in *A Revolution in Language*. See especially Sophia Rosenfeld, "Revolutionary Regeneration and the Politics of Signs," in *A Revolution in Language: The Problem of Signs in Late Eighteenth-Century France* (Stanford, CA: Stanford University Press, 2001), chap. 4, 123–80.
79. It is very probable, for example, that thinkers such as Montesquieu, Sièyes, and their predecessors are more central than Rousseau to the development of certain clauses of the Declaration and to the particular laws that were generated and refined. As Quinlan writes in "Physical and Moral Regeneration After the Terror," Montesquieu had a reputation for being a philosopher of "comparative politics" and, in Keegan Callanan's wording, of political particularism. Keegan Callanan, "Liberal Constitutionalism and Political Particularism in Montesquieu's *The Spirit of the Laws*," *Political Research Quarterly* 67, no. 3 (2014): 589–602. It is true that much of Montesquieu's work emphasizes the legislation appropriate to each regime and to the peoples that make up each regime. In this respect, he is far more particular than Rousseau. But Montesquieu and Rousseau share many philosophical premises and an emphasis on the legislation that can shift men's *moeurs* and virtue; so, in one way, it is unjust to classify Montesquieu as unqualifiedly opposed to Rousseau. Nevertheless, Rousseau's work aims higher, and is more universal, than Montesquieu's in constructing a philosophically grounded account of human nature. As Rebecca Kingston writes, "In general, [Montesquieu's] work demonstrates an ongoing attempt to find a moral basis for politics, not in any pre-social or meta-political framework, but through a close examination of the dynamics of human association and the conventions to which it gives rise." Rebecca Kingston, *Montesquieu and the Parlement of Bordeaux* (Geneva: Librairie Droz, 1996), 26. Montesquieu also devoted much of his work to particular recommendations, and Kingston emphasizes the legal language

with which he was familiar and in which he was operating as a means of understanding his "new language of politics" (Kingston, *Montesquieu*, 11). His emphasis on the effective means of governance, political moderation, and legal and jurisprudential language and norms certainly distances him from Rousseau, and it is a distance that emphasizes political particularities as opposed to natural-political regeneration of the sort discussed here. For an interpretation that places Rousseau in the same legal language, see Derathé, *Jean-Jacques Rousseau et la science politique de son temps*. Sièyes, who wrote the most famous and most read pamphlet leading up to the first phase of the Revolution, *What Is the Third Estate?*, employed Rousseau's political philosophy and applied it to representative government. Swenson writes that while "Sièyes links the sovereignty to the people in Rousseauian terms," he turns it into a "representative Rousseauianism" (Swenson, *On Jean-Jacques Rousseau*, 198, 201). And while Alexandre-Joseph de Falcoz, a deputy from Dauphiné, wrote in a letter "that the principles of Sièyes's text 'were almost entirely drawn from the *Contrat Social*'" (Swenson, *On Jean-Jacques Rousseau*, 164, citing Stéphane Rials, *La Déclaration des droits de l'homme et du citoyen* [Paris: Hachette, 1988], 37), many scholars have sought to establish that Sièyes's political thought, and thus its influence on political debates, was distinct from Rousseau's thinking insofar as Sièyes was more legally minded and concerned with the practicality of political representation. See, for example, Bronislaw Baczko, "The Social Contract of the French: Sièyes and Rousseau," *Journal of Modern History* 60 (1988): 98–125; Murray Forsyth, *Reason and Revolution: The Political Theory of the Abbé Sièyes* (New York: Holmes and Meier, 1987); Stephanie Frank, "The General Will Beyond Rousseau: Sièyes' Theological Arguments for the Sovereignty of the Revolutionary National Assembly," *History of European Ideas* 37, no. 3 (2011): 337–43.

80. Selections from the archival materials cited above, notes 38–46.
81. Quinlan, "Physical and Moral Regeneration," 146.
82. Sepinwall, *The Abbé Grégoire*, 4.
83. Sepinwall, *The Abbé Grégoire* 194.
84. Sepinwall, *The Abbé Grégoire*, 7.
85. William Max Nelson, "Colonizing France: Revolutionary Regeneration and the First French Empire," in *The French Revolution in Global Perspective*, ed. Suzanne Desan, Lynn Hunt, and William Max Nelson (Ithaca, NY: Cornell University Press, 2013), 75.
86. Sepinwall ties this natural-scientific reimagining of regeneration to Charles Bonnet (Sepinwall, *The Abbé Grégoire*, 59). William Max Nelson also connects Grégoire to Buffon. See Nelson, "Colonizing France."
87. "Rousseau remained a particular inspiration to Grégoire"; "When Grégoire commented on the Convention's educational projects, he also drew heavily from Rousseau. For example: 'We cannot inculcate enough a truth that is proved by experience: man is in large part the product of his education, or as J. Jacques said, man is good, men are mean.'" Sepinwall, *The Abbé Grégoire*, 128–29.
88. *Oeuvres de l'Abbé Grégoire*, 2:187, cited in Julia V. Douthwaite, *The Wild Girl, Natural Man, and the Monster: Dangerous Experiments in the Age of Enlightenment* (Chicago: University of Chicago Press, 2002), 176.

89. Sepinwall, *The Abbé Grégoire*, 182.

90. Cited in David Patrick Geggus, ed., *The Haitian Revolution: A Documentary History* (Indianapolis, IN: Hackett, 2014), 48.

91. Sepinwall, *The Abbé Grégoire*, 91.

92. For more on the dynamic of "worldmaking" by harnessing universalism from the revolutionary period onward, see Adom Getachew, *Worldmaking After Empire: The Rise and Fall of Self-Determination* (Princeton, NJ: Princeton University Press, 2019).

93. Geggus, *The Haitian Revolution*, 49.

94. See, in particular, Petion de Villeneuve's address in Geggus, *The Haitian Revolution*, 52.

95. Archives nationales, Paris, section moderne, AA 53 d.1490, August 29, 1793; cited in Geggus, *The Haitian Revolution*, 125.

96. Archives nationales, Paris, section moderne, AE II 1375, August 25, 1793; cited in Geggus, *The Haitian Revolution*, 124.

97. This has been a quick discussion of the Haitian Revolution. For more detail, see Laurent Dubois, *Avengers of the New World: The Story of the Haitian Revolution* (Cambridge, MA: Belknap, 2005); Geggus, *The Haitian Revolution*; Kevin Olson, *Imagined Sovereignties: The Power of the People and Other Myths of the Modern Age* (Cambridge: Cambridge University Press, 2016).

98. Sepinwall writes of Grégoire that his "revolutionary universalism was made possible only through the mechanism of regeneration." Sepinwall, *The Abbé Grégoire*, 7.

99. Olympe de Gouges, "Declaration of the Rights of Woman (September 1791)," in *The French Revolution and Human Rights: A Brief Documentary History*, trans. and ed. Lynn Hunt (Boston: Bedford, 1996): 124–29. For more on feminism in the French Revolution, see Jane Abray, "Feminism in the French Revolution," *American Historical Review* 80, no. 1 (1975): 43–62; Quinlan, "Physical and Moral Regeneration"; Leonora Cohen Rosenfield, "The Rights of Women in the French Revolution," *Studies in Eighteenth-Century Culture* 7, no. 1 (1978): 117–37; Joan Wallach Scott, "French Feminists and the Rights of 'Man': Olympe de Gouges's Declarations," *History Workshop Journal* 28, no. 1 (1989): 1–21; Janie Vanpée, "Performing Justice: The Trials of Olympe de Gouges," *Theatre Journal* 51, no. 1 (1999): 47–65.

100. Jacques Rancière, *Hatred of Democracy*, trans. Steve Corcoran (London: Verso, 2014), 61.

101. Rancière, *Hatred of Democracy*, 61–62.

102. Griffin, *The Nature of Fascism*, 41.

103. Gauchet, *Robespierre*, 169.

104. Gauchet, *Robespierre*, 186–87.

105. The Declarations can be found in John Hall Stewart, *A Documentary Survey of the French Revolution* (Ann Arbor: University of Michigan Press, 1951), 112–15, 230–32, 454–58, 571–612.

106. Ruth Scurr, *Fatal Purity: Robespierre and the French Revolution* (New York: Metropolitan, 2006).

107. Bernard E. Harcourt, *Critique and Praxis* (New York: Columbia University Press, 2020), 244.

108. Jean-Jacques Rousseau, "The Social Contract," in *The Social Contract and Other Later Political Writings*, trans. and ed. Victor Gourevitch (Cambridge: Cambridge University Press, 1997), 109; OC vol. 3, 424.

109.   Berlin, "The Counter-Enlightenment," 4.
110.   Gauchet, *Robespierre*, 190.
111.   Gauchet, *Robespierre*, 191.

5. AFTER ENLIGHTENMENT

1.   August 10 was the assault on the Tuileries after which followed the replacement of the Legislative Assembly with the Convention and the abolishment of the monarchy on September 21.

2.   Paul Huot, *Les prisonniers d'Orléans : Épisode révolutionnaire* (Strasbourg: C. Decker, 1868), 8. Translation is my own.

3.   Matthew Senior claims that this is said to have occurred at around the time Phillipe Pinel opened the *loges* and released the inmates. Matthew Senior, ed., *A Cultural History of Animals in the Age of Enlightenment* (Oxford: Berg, 2009), 21. Like the story about the Jacobins, the tale about Pinel has been questioned. It may have been a myth invented by Pinel's son, Scipion, to enhance his father's reputation as the founder of humane psychiatric care in France. The story can be found in Scipion Pinel, *Traité complet du régime sanitaire des aliénés* (Paris: Mauprivez, 1836). See also Michel Foucault, *Madness and Civilization: A History of Insanity in the Age of Reason*, trans. Richard Howard (New York: Vintage, 1965).

4.   Louise E. Robbins, *Elephant Slaves and Pampered Parrots: Exotic Animals in Eighteenth-Century Paris* (Baltimore: Johns Hopkins University Press, 2002), 214.

5.   Laura Mason, *Singing the French Revolution: Popular Songs and Revolutionary Politics, 1787–1799* (Princeton, NJ: Princeton University Press, 1990), 318.

6.   All references to Barruel's *Memoirs* are from Augustin Barruel, *Memoirs, Illustrating the History of Jacobinism: A Translation from the French of the Abbé Barruel*, trans. Robert Clifford (London: T. Burton, 1798). Here vol. 2, 144.

7.   Joseph de Maistre, "Étude sur la souveraineté," in *Collection : Les archives de la Révolution française* (Bibliothèque nationale, Oxford: Pergamon, 1989), 6.3.270, vol. 1, 407. Translation is my own.

8.   De Maistre, "Étude sur la souveraineté," 407. Translation is my own.

9.   Jean-Thomas-Élisabeth Richer de Sérizy, *Accusateur public*, no. 2, 22, lines 19 and 20; as cited in De Maistre, "Étude sur la Souveraineté," 404. Translation is my own.

10.   Barruel, *Memoirs*, vol. 1, ix.

11.   Barruel, *Memoirs*, vol. 1, xi.

12.   Barruel, *Memoirs*, vol. 2, 130.

13.   Barruel, *Memoirs*, vol. 2, 144.

14.   Hermann Samuel Reimarus, *The Principal Truths of Natural Religion Defended and Illustrated, in Nine Dissertations: Wherein the Objections of Lucretius, Buffon, Maupertius, Rousseau, La Mettrie, and Other Ancient and Modern Followers of Epicurus Are Considered, and Their Doctrines Refuted* (London: B. Law, [1755] 1766), 316.

15. Hippolyte Taine, *The Ancient Regime*, trans. John Durand (New York: Henry Holt, 1876), 226.

16. Darrin M. McMahon, *Enemies of the Enlightenment: The French Counter-Enlightenment and the Making of Modernity* (Oxford: Oxford University Press, 2002), 102.

17. McMahon, *Enemies*, 105.

18. McMahon, *Enemies*, 96, 50.

19. Edmund Burke, *A Letter from the Right Honourable Edmund Burke to a Noble Lord, on the Attacks Made Upon Him and His Pension, in the House of Lords, by the Duke of Bedford and the Earl of Lauderdale* (London: Leopold Classic Library, 1796).

20. Burke, *A Letter*, 27.

21. Burke, *A Letter*, 32.

22. Burke, *A Letter*, 11.

23. Edmund Burke, *Reflections on the Revolution in France*, ed. F. G. Shelby (London: Macmillan, 1890), 96.

24. Samuel Moyn, *Liberalism Against Itself: Cold War Intellectuals and the Making of Our Times* (New Haven, CT: Yale University Press, 2023).

25. Moyn, *Liberalism*, 51, 54.

26. Isaiah Berlin, "The Counter-Enlightenment," in *Against the Current: Essays in the History of Ideas*, 2nd ed., ed. Henry Hardy (Princeton, NJ: Princeton University Press, 2013), 4.

27. Isaiah Berlin, *The Roots of Romanticism*, 2nd ed., ed. Henry Hardy and John Gray (Princeton, NJ: Princeton University Press, 2013), 137–38.

28. Isaiah Berlin, "Two Concepts of Liberty," in *Four Essays on Liberty* (Oxford: Oxford University Press, 1969), 165.

29. Berlin, "Two Concepts," 166.

30. Berlin, "Two Concepts," 162.

31. McMahon, *Enemies*, 14. For more on the radicals of the Enlightenment and counter-Enlightenment, see Matthew Kadane, *The Enlightenment and Original Sin* (Chicago: University of Chicago Press, 2024).

32. McMahon, *Enemies*, 14.

33. McMahon, *Enemies*, 50. See also James Schmidt, "Inventing the Enlightenment: Anti-Jacobins, British Hegelians, and the *Oxford English Dictionary*," *Journal of the History of Ideas* 64, no. 3 (2003): 421–43.

34. McMahon, *Enemies*, 95.

35. Graeme Garrard, *Counter-Enlightenments: From the Eighteenth Century to the Present*, Routledge Studies in Social and Political Thought 44 (New York: Routledge, 2006), 36.

36. Jean-Yves Pranchère, "The Negative of Enlightenment, the Positive of Order," in *Joseph de Maistre and the Legacy of Enlightenment*, Oxford University Studies in the Enlightenment, ed. Carolina Armenteros and Richard Lebrun (Oxford: Voltaire Foundation, 2011), 51.

37. Helena Rosenblatt, *The Lost History of Liberalism: From Ancient Rome to the Twenty-First Century* (Princeton, NJ: Princeton University Press, 2018), 48–49.

38. Rosenblatt, *The Lost History*, 65.

39. Rosenblatt, *The Lost History*, 52.

40.   Rosenblatt, *The Lost History*, 51.

41.   McMahon, *Enemies*, 96.

42.   McMahon, *Enemies*, 165.

43.   McMahon, *Enemies*, 165.

44.   Immanuel Kant, *What Is Enlightenment?*, trans. Mary C. Smith ([1784] 2014, last updated March 24, 2021), https://www.constitution.org/2-Authors/kant/enlightenment.html.

45.   McMahon, *Enemies*, 167.

46.   McMahon, *Enemies*, 169.

47.   McMahon, *Enemies*, 169.

48.   Rosenblatt, *The Lost History*, 72.

49.   Rosenblatt, *The Lost History*, 69.

50.   Aurelian Crăiuțu, *Liberalism Under Siege: The Political Thought of the French Doctrinaires*, Applications of Political Theory (Lanham, MD: Lexington, 2003), 58.

51.   Crăiuțu, *Liberalism Under Siege*, 80.

52.   William Selinger, *Parliamentarism: From Burke to Weber*, Ideas in Context (Cambridge: Cambridge University Press, 2019). See also Gregory Conti, *Parliament the Mirror of the Nation: Representation, Deliberation, and Democracy in Victorian Britain*, Ideas in Context (Cambridge: Cambridge University Press, 2019).

53.   Selinger, *Parliamentarism*, 5.

54.   Selinger, *Parliamentarism*, 3.

55.   Annelien de Dijn, *Freedom: An Unruly History* (Cambridge, MA: Harvard University Press, 2020), 3.

56.   De Dijn, *Freedom*, 3.

57.   See Duncan Bell, "What Is Liberalism?," *Political Theory* 42, no. 6 (2014): 684.

58.   Raymond Geuss, "Liberalism and Its Discontents," *Political Theory* 30, no. 3 (2002): 322.

59.   Geuss, "Liberalism," 323.

60.   Alan Ryan, *The Making of Modern Liberalism* (Princeton, NJ: Princeton University Press, 2012), 24.

61.   Rosenblatt, *The Lost History*, 110. On the misplaced reception of Mill in the liberal canon, see Menaka Philips, *The Liberalism Trap: John Stuart Mill and Customs of Interpretation* (Oxford: Oxford University Press, 2023).

62.   John Stuart Mill, *On Liberty and Utilitarianism* (New York: Bantam Classics, 2008), 13–14.

63.   Bell, "What Is Liberalism?," 689–90.

64.   Bell, "What Is Liberalism?," 698–99.

65.   Bell, "What Is Liberalism?," 699.

66.   Bell, "What Is Liberalism?," 699.

67.   Ryan, *The Making of Modern Liberalism*, 29.

68.   Moyn, *Liberalism*, 39.

69.   Moyn, *Liberalism*, 21.

70.   Moyn, *Liberalism*, 1.

71.   Moyn, *Liberalism*, 3–4.

72.   Moyn, *Liberalism*, 43.

73. Moyn, *Liberalism*, 51.

74. J. L. Talmon, *The Origins of Totalitarian Democracy* (London: Mercury, 1961), 2.

75. Talmon, *The Origins*, 1.

76. Rosenblatt, *The Lost History*, 263.

77. F. A. Hayek, "The Principles of a Liberal Social Order," in *The Collected Works of F. A. Hayek*, ed. Paul Lewis, vol. 18, *Essays on Liberalism and the Economy* (Chicago: University of Chicago Press, 2022), 273, 272.

78. Hayek, "The Principles," 273.

79. Hayek, "The Principles," 274.

80. Hayek, "The Principles," 285.

81. Hayek, "The Principles," 291. See also Chandran Kukathas, "Hayek and Liberalism," in *The Cambridge Companion to Hayek*, Cambridge Companions to Philosophy, ed. Edward Feser (Cambridge: Cambridge University Press, 2006), 182–207; Chandran Kukathas, *Hayek and Modern Liberalism* (Oxford: Oxford University Press, 1989).

82. Judith N. Shklar, "Rights in the Liberal Tradition," *Political Studies* 71, no. 2 (2023): 288. On the Americanism of rights, see Duncan Bell, *Reordering the World: Essays on Liberalism and Empire* (Princeton, NJ: Princeton University Press, 2016); Rosenblatt, *The Lost History*.

83. Ronald Dworkin, *Taking Rights Seriously* (Cambridge, MA: Harvard University Press, 1978), ix.

84. Shklar, "Rights," 292.

85. Samuel Moyn, *The Last Utopia: Human Rights in History* (Cambridge, MA: Belknap, 2012), 227.

86. As Moyn acknowledges, too, human rights can be used to the end of redesigning states (see Samuel Moyn, *Human Rights and the Uses of History*, 2nd ed. [London: Verso, 2017], 180), but for him this would require a reimagining of how rights currently function in the world. Authors of recent legal scholarship are trying to change this functionality, however; see John Tasioulas, "Saving Human Rights from Human Rights Law," *Vanderbilt Journal of Transnational Law* 52, no. 5 (2019): 1167–1207; Grégoire Webber and Paul Yowell, "Introduction: Securing Human Rights Through Legislation," in *Legislated Rights: Securing Human Rights Through Legislation*, ed. Bradley W. Miller et al. (Cambridge: Cambridge University Press, 2018), 1–26; Francisco J. Urbina, "How Legislation Aids Human Rights Adjudication," in *Legislated Rights: Securing Human Rights Through Legislation*, ed. Bradley W. Miller et al. (Cambridge: Cambridge University Press, 2018), 153–80. For arguments that the universalism of rights have been, or can be, employed to the end of self-determinative claims, see Adom Getachew, *Worldmaking After Empire: The Rise and Fall of Self-Determination* (Princeton, NJ: Princeton University Press, 2019); Emma Stone Mackinnon, "The Right to Rebel: History and Universality in the Political Thought of the Algerian Revolution," in *Time, History, and Political Thought*, ed. John Robertson (Cambridge: Cambridge University Press, 2023), 285–307.

87. Scholars have argued that even in the work of John Rawls we can see a preference for the priority of individual rights and negative freedoms. For Rosenblatt, Rawls argued in *A Theory of Justice* that "liberalism based on individualism and self-interest would,

in fact, logically entail the welfare state" but also that the welfare state could happen in the absence of any "deliberate promotion of the common good" (Rosenblatt, *The Lost History*, 273). Danielle Allen has also recently argued that Rawls's deep liberal commitment to the freedom of the individual betrays his claim to value negative and positive freedoms equally. See Danielle Allen, *Justice by Means of Democracy* (Chicago: University of Chicago Press, 2023). See also Katrina Forrester's work on Rawls's relationship to the development of contemporary liberalism: Katrina Forrester, *In the Shadow of Justice: Postwar Liberalism and the Remaking of Political Philosophy* (Princeton, NJ: Princeton University Press, 2019).

88. Thomas Paine, *The Rights of Man* (London: J. S. Jordan, 1791), 122.

89. Paine, *The Rights of Man*, 122–23.

90. Alexis de Tocqueville, *The Old Regime and the French Revolution*, trans. Stuart Gilbert (New York: Anchor, 1955), book 2, chapter 14, 157.

91. Tocqueville, *The Old Regime*, book 1, chapter 3, 13.

92. Berlin, "The Counter-Enlightenment," 8. For an excellent and not at all caricatured account of Hamann, see Robert Alan Sparling, *Johann Georg Hamann and the Enlightenment Project* (Toronto, ON: University of Toronto Press, 2011). Garrard also sees "the Enlightenment's two first opponents as Rousseau and Hamann" (Garrard, *Counter-Enlightenments*, 19). Hamann, he writes, "favored a more organic conception of social and political life, a more vitalistic view of nature, and an appreciation for beauty and the spiritual life of man that, they thought, had been neglected in the eighteenth century" (Garrard, *Counter-Enlightenments*, 3).

93. Berlin, "The Counter-Enlightenment," 21.

94. Berlin, "The Counter-Enlightenment," 24.

95. Berlin, "The Counter-Enlightenment," 24–25.

96. Arthur McCalla, "Evolutionism and Early Nineteenth-Century Histories of Religions," *Religion* 28, no. 1 (1998): 36.

97. McCalla, "Evolutionism," 29.

98. Arthur McCalla, "*Palingénésie philosophique* to *Palingénésie sociale*: From a Scientific Ideology to a Historical Ideology," *Journal of the History of Ideas* 55, no. 3 (1994): 431.

99. McCalla, "*Palingénésie*," 433.

100. McCalla, "*Palingénésie*," 434.

101. McCalla, "*Palingénésie*," 437. See also Arthur McCalla, *A Romantic Historiosophy: The Philosophy of History of Pierre-Simon Ballanche*, Brill's Studies in Intellectual History (Boston: Brill, 1998).

102. See Manon Mathias, "Pre-Darwinian Species Change: Reincarnation and Transformism in George Sand's *Évenor et Leucippe*," *Journal of Literature and Science* 11, no. 1 (2018).

103. Rosenblatt, *The Lost History*, 104.

104. Karl Marx, "On the Jewish Question," in *The Marx-Engels Reader*, ed. Robert C. Tucker (New York: W. W. Norton, 1978), 42.

105. Marx, "On the Jewish Question," 42.

106. Marx, "On the Jewish Question," 42.

107. Marx, "On the Jewish Question," 43.

108. Marx, "On the Jewish Question," 46.

109. Marx, "On the Jewish Question," 46.

110. Kevin Duong, *The Virtues of Violence: Democracy Against Disintegration in Modern France* (Oxford: Oxford University Press, 2020), 139.

111. Duong, *The Virtues of Violence*, 138.

112. Duong, *The Virtues of Violence*, 129.

113. Henri Bergson, *Creative Evolution*, trans. Arthur Mitchell (New York: Henry Holt, 1911), 182.

114. Bergson, *Creative Evolution*, x.

115. See Paul-Antoine Miquel, "Bergson and Darwin: From an Immanentist to an Emergentist Approach to Evolution," *SubStance* 36, no. 3 (2007): 42–56; Magda Costa Carvalho and M. Patrão Neves, "Building the 'True Evolutionism': Darwin's Impact on Henri Bergson's Thought," *Revista Portuguesa de Filosofia* 66, no. 3 (2010): 635–42.

116. Bergson, *Creative Evolution*, 268–69.

117. Bergson, *Creative Evolution*, 106.

118. Bergson, *Creative Evolution*, 266.

119. Bergson, *Creative Evolution*, 7.

120. Bergson, *Creative Evolution*, 7.

121. Bergson, *Creative Evolution*, 163.

122. Bergson, *Creative Evolution*, 37.

123. Bergson, *Creative Evolution*, 165.

124. Bergson, *Creative Evolution*, 166.

125. Bergson, *Creative Evolution*, 52.

126. For a recent turn toward Bergson as a source of (liberal) rights, however, see Alexandre Lefebvre, *Human Rights as a Way of Life: On Bergson's Political Philosophy*, Cultural Memory in the Present (Stanford, CA: Stanford University Press, 2013).

127. Duong, *Virtues of Violence*, 140.

128. Duong, *Virtues of Violence*, 142.

129. Duong, *Virtues of Violence*, 157.

130. Duong, *Virtues of Violence*, 160.

131. Duong, *Virtues of Violence*, 160.

132. See Arnaud François and Roxanne Lapidus, "Life and Will in Nietzsche and Bergson," *SubStance* 36, no. 3 (2007): 100–114.

133. See, for example, Don Dombowsky, "The Rhetoric of Legitimation: Nietzsche's 'Doctrine' of Eternal Recurrence," *Journal of Nietzsche Studies*, no. 14 (1997): 26–45.

134. Christopher E. Forth, "Nietzsche, Decadence, and Regeneration in France, 1891–95," *Journal of the History of Ideas* 54, no. 1 (1993): 112.

135. Forth, "Nietzsche," 98.

136. Jorge Dagnino, Paul Stocker, and Matthew Feldman, *The "New Man" in Radical Right Ideology and Practice, 1919–45* (London: Bloomsbury Academic, 2017), 4.

137. Dagnino, Stocker, and Feldman, *The "New Man,"* 3.

138. Ronald Beiner, *Dangerous Minds: Nietzsche, Heidegger, and the Return of the Far Right* (Philadelphia: University of Pennsylvania Press, 2018), 7–8.

139.   Beiner, *Dangerous Minds*, 10.

140.   Beiner, *Dangerous Minds*, 17.

141.   Beiner, *Dangerous Minds*, 13.

142.   Richard Wolin, *The Seduction of Unreason: The Intellectual Romance with Fascism from Nietzsche to Postmodernism*, 2nd ed. (Princeton, NJ: Princeton University Press, 2019), 4.

143.   Wolin, *The Seduction*, 8.

144.   Wolin, *The Seduction*, 12.

145.   Wolin, *The Seduction*, 3.

146.   Laurence Simmons, "Towards a Philosophy of the Polyp," in *Animals and Agency: An Interdisciplinary Exploration*, ed. Sarah McFarland and Ryan Hediger (London: Brill, 2009), 341–71, citing Gilles Deleuze and Félix Guattari, *Anti-Oedipus: Capitalism and Schizophrenia*, trans. Robert Hurley, Mark Seem, and Helen R. Lane (New York: Penguin Classics, 2009), and Gilles Deleuze and Félix Guattari, *A Thousand Plateaus: Capitalism and Schizophrenia*, trans. Brian Massumi (Minneapolis: University of Minnesota Press, 1987).

147.   Simmons, "Towards A Philosophy of the Polyp," 356.

148.   Christine Daigle and Terrance H. McDonald, eds., introduction to *From Deleuze and Guattari to Posthumanism: Philosophies of Immanence* (London: Bloomsbury Academic, 2022), 8.

149.   Daigle draws this image out of Deleuze and Guattari and from an image concocted by Friedrich Nietzsche in *Daybreak*: "I borrow from the powerful metaphor of the polyp that Nietzsche uses in *Daybreak* where he says: 'With every moment of our lives some of the polyp-arms of our being grow and others dry up, depending on the nourishment that the moment does or does not supply . . . all our experiences are, in this sense, types of nourishment.' What does it mean to think of ourselves as polyps? Interestingly, Deleuze and Guattari quote William S. Burroughs's *Naked Lunch* in which he says, 'The human body is scandalously inefficient. Instead of a mouth and an anus to get out of order why not have one all-purpose hole to eat and eliminate?' This corresponds to the polyp." Christine Daigle and Terrance H. McDonald, "Deleuzian Traces: The Self of the Polyp," in *From Deleuze and Guattari to Posthumanism Philosophies of Immanence*, ed. Christine Daigle and Terrance H. McDonald (London: Bloomsbury Academic, 2022), 48.

150.   Daigle and McDonald, "Deleuzian Traces," 41, 47.

151.   Daigle and McDonald, "Deleuzian Traces," 55.

152.   Daigle and McDonald, "Deleuzian Traces," 41.

153.   Guillaume Faye, *Why We Fight: Manifesto of the European Resistance*, trans. Michael O'Meara (London: Arktos, 2011); Sylvia Wynter in Katherine McKittrick, ed., *Sylvia Wynter: On Being Human as Praxis* (Durham, NC: Duke University Press, 2015).

154.   Wynter in McKittrick, *Sylvia Wynter*, 21, 31.

155.   Faye, *Why We Fight*, 162.

156.   This argument is also made by Horkheimer and Adorno: "The Enlightenment committed itself to liberalism." Max Horkheimer and Theodor W. Adorno, *Dialectic of Enlightenment*, trans. John Cumming (New York: Continuum, 1972), 90.

157.   Berlin, *The Roots of Romanticism*, 27.

158. Berlin, *The Roots of Romanticism*, 27–28.

159. René Descartes, *Meditations, Objections, and Replies*, trans. Donald A. Cress (Indianapolis, IN: Hackett, 2006), 63.

160. François d'Escherny, "Éloge de J. J. Rousseau," in *La philosophie de la politique, ou Principes généraux sur les institutions civiles, politiques, et religieuses* (Paris, [1790] 1796), lxxxvi. Translation is my own.

161. Ryan, *The Making of Modern Liberalism*, 35.

6. RESTORING OUR FIRST RIGHT

1. For a relevant and arresting account of the developmental link between the rights of man and the UN Declaration, see Dan Edelstein, *On the Spirit of Rights*, The Life of Ideas (Chicago: University of Chicago Press, 2019). He writes, "The Declaration of Rights may have been heralded as a new set of divine commandments, but it was a god whose time had not yet come" (193)—this was only to materialize in modern international declarations and universals.

2. Lynn Hunt, *Inventing Human Rights: A History* (New York: W. W. Norton, 2008), 17. See also Peter de Bolla, *The Architecture of Concepts: The Historical Formation of Human Rights* (New York: Fordham University Press, 2013); Jonathan Israel, *Revolutionary Ideas: An Intellectual History of the French Revolution from The Rights of Man to Robespierre* (Princeton, NJ: Princeton University Press, 2014).

3. Anne Phillips, *Unconditional Equals* (Princeton, NJ: Princeton University Press, 2021).

4. De Bolla, *The Architecture*, 261, 268. See also Dan Edelstein, "Early-Modern Rights Regimes: A Genealogy of Revolutionary Rights," *Critical Analysis of Law* 26, no. 1 (2016): 221–42; Dan Edelstein, "Enlightenment Rights Talk," *Journal of Modern History* 84, no. 1 (2014): 530–65.

5. James Tully, "Rethinking Human Rights and Enlightenment: A View from the Twenty-First Century," in *Self-Evident Truths? Human Rights and the Enlightenment*, ed. Kate E. Tunstall (New York: Bloomsbury Academic, 2012): 20.

6. Tully, "Rethinking Human Rights," 22.

7. Samuel Moyn, *Christian Human Rights* (Philadelphia: University of Pennsylvania Press, 2015), 8.

8. Samuel Moyn, *Human Rights and the Uses of History*, 2nd ed. (London: Verso, 2017), 108.

9. "Instead of implying colonial liberation and the creation of emancipated nations, human rights most often now meant individual protection against the state." Samuel Moyn, *The Last Utopia: Human Rights in History* (Cambridge, MA: Belknap, 2012), 4.

10. Samuel Moyn, *Liberalism Against Itself: Cold War Intellectuals and the Making of Our Times* (New Haven, CT: Yale University Press, 2023), 19.

11. Samuel Moyn, "Afterword: The Self-Evidence of Human Rights," in *Self-Evident Truths? Human Rights and the Enlightenment*, ed. Kate Tunstall (New York: Bloomsbury, 2012), 260.

12. Samuel Moyn, "Afterword," 260.

13. Wynter in Katherine McKittrick, ed., *Sylvia Wynter: On Being Human as Praxis* (Durham, NC: Duke University Press, 2015), 11.

14. Daniel S. Forrest, *Suprahumanism: European Man and the Regeneration of History* (London: Arktos, 2014), 25, 29.

15. Forrest, *Suprahumanism*, 239.

16. Wynter in McKittrick, *Sylvia Wynter*, 56.

17. Arthur Versluis, "A Conversation with Alain de Benoist," *Journal for the Study of Radicalism* 8, no. 2 (2014): 97.

18. Claude Lefort, "Human Rights and the Welfare State," in *Democracy and Political Theory* (Minneapolis: University of Minnesota Press, 1988), 21–44.

19. Lefort, "Human Rights," 37–38.

20. Lefort, "Human Rights," 38.

21. Lefort, "Human Rights," 43.

22. Sheldon Wolin, "Fugitive Democracy," in *Fugitive Democracy and Other Essays*, ed. Nicholas Xenos (Princeton, NJ: Princeton University Press, 2016), 100. This distinction is also central to Jacques Rancière's work.

23. Wolin, "Fugitive Democracy," 100.

24. Wolin, "Fugitive Democracy," 107.

25. Chantal Mouffe, *The Return of the Political* (London: Verso, 2020), 3.

26. Chantal Mouffe, *The Democratic Paradox* (London: Verso, 2009), 10–11.

27. Mouffe, *The Return of the Political*, 6.

28. Mouffe, *The Return of the Political*, 6.

29. Mouffe, *The Return of the Political*, 13.

30. Mouffe, *The Return of the Political*, 13.

31. Wendy Brown, *Undoing the Demos: Neoliberalism's Stealth Revolution* (New York: Zone, 2017), 222.

32. Wendy Brown, *In the Ruins of Neoliberalism: The Rise of Antidemocratic Politics in the West* (New York: Columbia University Press, 2019), 188.

33. Guillaume Faye, "Metapolitical Dictionary," in *Why We Fight: Manifesto of the European Resistance*, trans. Michael O'Meara (London: Arktos, 2011).

34. Faye, *Why We Fight*, 192.

35. John Bruce Leonard, "Metapolitics and the Right—Part 1," Arktos.com (blog), October 22, 2018, https://arktos.com/2018/10/22/metapolitics-and-the-right-part-1/.

36. Rinaldo Walcott, *The Long Emancipation: Moving Toward Black Freedom* (Durham, NC: Duke University Press, 2021), 2.

37. Walcott, *The Long Emancipation*, 56.

38. Dean Spade, *Normal Life: Administrative Violence, Critical Trans Politics, and the Limits of Law* (Durham, NC: Duke University Press, 2015), 1.

39. Spade, *Normal Life*, 12.

40. Glen Sean Coulthard, *Red Skin, White Masks: Rejecting the Colonial Politics of Recognition* (Minneapolis: University of Minnesota Press, 2014), 3. For a critical yet more sympathetic account of Indigenous peoples' relationship to liberal rights, see Dale A. Turner,

This Is Not a Peace Pipe: Towards a Critical Indigenous Philosophy (Toronto, ON: University of Toronto Press, 2006).

41. Yann Allard-Tremblay, "For Those Who Will Follow; Earth Marred and Renewing Relationships," *Constellations* 30, no. 2 (2023): 108.

42. Allard-Tremblay, "For Those Who Will Follow," 109.

43. Walcott, *The Long Emancipation*, 73.

44. Rinaldo Walcott, *Queer Returns: Essays on Multiculturalism, Diaspora, and Black Studies* (London, ON: Insomniac, 2016), 76.

45. Walcott, *The Long Emancipation*, 5.

46. Aimé Césaire, *Discourse on Colonialism*, trans. Joan Pinkham (New York: Monthly Review, 2001), 73.

47. Judith Butler, *Undoing Gender* (New York: Routledge, 2004), 37.

48. Butler, *Undoing Gender*, 19.

49. Butler, *Undoing Gender*, 38, 39.

50. Charles W. Mills, *Black Rights/White Wrongs: The Critique of Racial Liberalism* (Oxford: Oxford University Press, 2017), 36, 215.

51. Jane Anna Gordon, *Creolizing Political Theory: Reading Rousseau Through Fanon* (New York: Fordham University Press, 2014).

52. Gordon, *Creolizing Political Theory*, 1.

53. Gordon, *Creolizing Political Theory*, 63.

54. Gordon, *Creolizing Political Theory*, 160. Gordon has also edited an important collection of essays with Neil Roberts on the "project of creolizing Rousseau." See Jane Anna Gordon and Neil Roberts, "Introduction: The Project of Creolizing Rousseau," *CLR James Journal* 15, no. 1 (2009): 3–16. In this collection, see especially Charles W. Mills, "Rousseau, the Master's Tools, and Anti-Contractarian Contractarianism," *CLR James Journal* 15, no. 1 (2009): 92–112; Nelson Maldonado-Torres, "Rousseau and Fanon on Inequality and the Human Sciences," *CLR James Journal* 15, no. 1 (2009): 113–34; Paget Henry, "C. L. R. James, Political Philosophy, and the Creolizing of Rousseau and Marx," *CLR James Journal* 15, no. 1 (2009): 178–205. For a recent argument about Rousseau's radicalism, see Kevin Inston, *Rousseau and Radical Democracy* (New York: Continuum, 2010).

55. Frantz Fanon, *Black Skin, White Masks*, trans. Richard Philcox (New York: Grove, 2008), 22.

56. Vincenzo Ferrone, *The Enlightenment: History of an Idea*, trans. Elisabetta Tarantino (Princeton, NJ: Princeton University Press, 2017), xii.

57. Ferrone, *The Enlightenment*, 213, 13.

58. Kenan Malik, *The Meaning of Race: Race, History, and Culture in Western Society* (New York: New York University Press, 1996), 265, 269.

59. Malik, *The Meaning of Race*, 269.

60. Malik, *The Meaning of Race*, 267.

61. Brown, *Undoing the Demos*, 222.

62. Alex Zamalin, *Black Utopia: The History of an Idea from Black Nationalism to Afrofuturism* (New York: Columbia University Press, 2019), 142, 143.

63.   Bernard E. Harcourt, *Critique and Praxis* (New York: Columbia University Press, 2020), 244.

64.   Harcourt, *Critique and Praxis*, 245.

65.   Harcourt, *Critique and Praxis*, 246.

66.   Helena Rosenblatt, *The Lost History of Liberalism: From Ancient Rome to the Twenty-First Century* (Princeton, NJ: Princeton University Press, 2018), 277.

67.   Moyn, *Liberalism*, 7. For a defense of the virtues of Cold War liberalism, see Joshua L. Cherniss, *Liberalism in Dark Times: The Liberal Ethos in the Twentieth Century* (Princeton, NJ: Princeton University Press, 2021).

BIBLIOGRAPHY

Abray, Jane. "Feminism in the French Revolution." *American Historical Review* 80, no. 1 (1975): 43–62.

Allard-Tremblay, Yann. "For Those Who Will Follow; Earth Marred and Renewing Relationships." *Constellations* 30, no. 2 (2023): 108–18.

Allen, Amy. *The End of Progress: Decolonizing the Normative Foundations of Critical Theory.* New Directions in Critical Theory. New York: Columbia University Press, 2016.

Allen, Danielle. *Justice by Means of Democracy.* Chicago: University of Chicago Press, 2023.

——. *Our Declaration: A Reading of the Declaration of Independence in Defense of Equality.* New York: Liveright, 2014.

L'an I des droits de l'homme: Controverses et débats de 1789 autour de la Déclaration des droits de l'homme, ed. Antoine de Baecque. Paris: CNRS, 1988.

Anderson, Lorin. *Charles Bonnet and the Order of the Known.* Studies in the History of Modern Science, vol. 11. Dordrecht: Reidel, 1982.

Archives parlementaires. Accessed via the ARTFL Project of the University of Chicago. https://artfl-project.uchicago.edu/archives-parlementaires. Last accessed January 6, 2024.

Arendt, Hannah. *The Human Condition.* Chicago: University of Chicago Press, 1998.

——. *On Revolution.* New York: Penguin, 2006.

Aristotle. *Generation of Animals.* In *The Basic Works of Aristotle,* ed. Richard McKeon. New York: Random House, 1970.

——. *Posterior Analytics.* In *The Basic Works of Aristotle,* ed. Richard McKeon. New York: Modern Library, 1941.

Augustine. *The City of God,* trans. Marcus Dods. New York: Modern Library, 1950.

Bacot, Jean-François. "L'idéologie de la régénération: Ce legs délétère de la Révolution." *Le philosophoire* 45, no. 1 (2016): 143–68.

Baczko, Bronislaw. "The Social Contract of the French: Sieyès and Rousseau." *Journal of Modern History* 60 (1988): 98–125.

Baecque, Antoine de, ed. *L'an I des droits de l'homme: Controverses et débats de 1789 autour de la Déclaration des droits de l'homme.* Paris: CNRS, 1988.

——. *The Body Politic: Corporeal Metaphor in Revolutionary France, 1770–1800,* trans. Charlotte Mandell. Stanford, CA: Stanford University Press, 1997.

Baker, John R. *Abraham Trembley of Geneva: Scientist and Philosopher, 1710–1784.* London: Edward Arnold, 1952.

Baker, Keith Michael, ed. *Inventing the French Revolution: Essays on French Political Culture in the Eighteenth Century.* Ideas in Context. Cambridge: Cambridge University Press, 1990.

Barroux, Gilles. *Philosophie de la régénération: Médicine, biologie, mythologies.* Paris: Harmattan, 2009.

Barruel, Augustin. *Memoirs, Illustrating the History of Jacobinism: A Translation from the French of the Abbé Barruel,* trans. Robert Clifford. London: T. Burton, 1798.

Becker, Carl L. *The Heavenly City of the Eighteenth-Century Philosophers,* ed. Johnson Kent Wright. New Haven, CT: Yale University Press, 1932.

Beeckman, Daniel. *A Voyage to and from the Island of Borneo in the East-Indies: With a Description of the Said Island: . . . Together with the Re-establishment of the English Trade There, An. 1714 . . . Also a Description of the Islands of Canary, Cape Verd, Java, Madura . . . with Some Remarks Touching Trade, etc. . . . . Illustrated with Several Curious . . . Cuts; with an Account of the Inhabitants, Their Manners, Customs, Religion, Product, Chief Ports, and Trade.* London: Warner, 1718.

Beiner, Ronald. *Dangerous Minds: Nietzsche, Heidegger, and the Return of the Far Right.* Philadelphia: University of Pennsylvania Press, 2018.

Bell, Duncan. *Reordering the World: Essays on Liberalism and Empire.* Princeton, NJ: Princeton University Press, 2016.

——. "What Is Liberalism?" *Political Theory* 42, no. 6 (2014): 682–715.

Benson, Keith R. "Observation Versus Philosophical Commitment in Eighteenth-Century Ideas of Generation and Regeneration." In *A History of Regeneration Research: Milestones in the Evolution of a Science,* ed. Charles E. Dinsmore, 91–100. Cambridge: Cambridge University Press, 1991.

Bergson, Henri. *Creative Evolution,* trans. Arthur Mitchell. New York: Henry Holt, 1911.

Berlin, Isaiah. "The Counter-Enlightenment." In *Against the Current: Essays in the History of Ideas,* 2nd ed., ed. Henry Hardy, 1–32. Princeton, NJ: Princeton University Press, 2013.

——. *The Roots of Romanticism,* 2nd ed., ed. Henry Hardy and John Gray. Princeton, NJ: Princeton University Press, 2013.

——. "Two Concepts of Liberty." In *Four Essays on Liberty,* 118–172. Oxford: Oxford University Press, 1969.

Blanckaert, Claude. "Buffon and the Natural History of Man: Writing History and the 'Foundational Myth' of Anthropology." *History of the Human Sciences* 6, no. 1 (1993): 13–50.

——. "Premier des singes, dernier des hommes?" *Alliage* 7, no. 8 (1991): 113–28.

Boas, George. *The Happy Beast in French Thought of the Seventeenth Century.* Baltimore: Johns Hopkins, 1933.

Bonnet, Charles. *The Contemplation of Nature: Translated from the French of C. Bonnet*, 2 vols. London: T. Longman, 1766.

——. "Essai de psychologie." In *Oeuvres d'histoire naturelle et de philosophie de Charles Bonnet*, vol. 17, 1–444. Neuchatel: Samuel Fauche, 1783.

——. "Lettre de M. Philopolis au sujet du discours de M. J. J. Rousseau de Genève, sur l'origine et fondemens de l'inégalité parmi les hommes." In Jean-Jacques Rousseau, *Oeuvres complètes* (Paris: NRF-Éditions de la Pléiade, 1965–1995), vol. 3, 1383–1386 [1755].

——. *La palingénésie philosophique, ou Idées sur l'état passé et sur l'état futur des êtres vivans*. Geneva: Claude Philibert and Barthélemy Chirol, 1770.

Botting, Eileen Hunt. "The Early Rousseau's Egalitarian Feminism: A Philosophical Convergence with Madame Dupin and 'The Critique of the Spirit of the Laws.'" *History of European Ideas* 43, no. 7 (2017): 732–44.

——. "Rousseau and Feminism." In *The Rousseauian Mind*, ed. Eve Grace and Christopher Kelly, 463–73. New York: Routledge, 2019.

Bowler, Peter J. "Bonnet and Buffon: Theories of Generation and the Problem of Species." *Journal of the History of Biology* 6, no. 2 (1973): 259–81.

Brown, Wendy. *In the Ruins of Neoliberalism: The Rise of Antidemocratic Politics in the West*. New York: Columbia University Press, 2019.

——. *Undoing the Demos: Neoliberalism's Stealth Revolution*. New York: Zone, 2017.

Buffon, Georges-Louis LeClerc, comte de. *Histoire naturelle, générale et particulière, avec la description du Cabinet Du Roy*. Paris: Imprimerie royale, 1749–1789.

——. *Natural History, General and Particular*, trans. William Smellie. London: W. Strahan and T. Cadell, 1781.

Burke, Edmund. *A Letter from the Right Honourable Edmund Burke to a Noble Lord, on the Attacks Made Upon Him and His Pension, in the House of Lords, by the Duke of Bedford and the Earl of Lauderdale*. London: Leopold Classic Library, 1796.

——. *Reflections on the Revolution in France*, ed. F. G. Shelby. London: Macmillan, 1890.

Butler, Judith. *Gender Trouble: Feminism and the Subversion of Identity*. New York: Routledge, 2006.

——. *Undoing Gender*. New York: Routledge, 2004.

Callanan, Keegan. "Liberal Constitutionalism and Political Particularism in Montesquieu's *The Spirit of the Laws*." *Political Research Quarterly* 67, no. 3 (2014): 589–602.

Camus, Jean-Yves. "Alain de Benoist and the New Right." In *Key Thinkers of the Radical Right: Behind the New Threat to Liberal Democracy*, ed. Mark Sedgwick, 73–90. Oxford: Oxford University Press, 2019.

Carvalho, Magda Costa, and M. Patrão Neves. "Building the 'True Evolutionism': Darwin's Impact on Henri Bergson's Thought." *Revista Portuguesa de Filosofia* 66, no. 3 (2010): 635–42.

Cassirer, Ernst. "Newton and Leibniz." *Philosophical Review* 52, no. 4 (1943): 366–91.

——. *The Philosophy of the Enlightenment*, trans. Peter Gay. Princeton, NJ: Princeton University Press, 1951.

——. *The Question of Jean-Jacques Rousseau*, trans. and ed. Peter Gay. Bloomington: Indiana University Press, 1963.

Césaire, Aimé. *The Complete Poetry of Aimé Césaire*, bilingual ed., trans. Clayton Eshleman and A. James Arnold. Middletown, CT: Wesleyan University Press, 2024.

——. *Discourse on Colonialism*, trans. Joan Pinkham. New York: Monthly Review, 2001.

Cherniss, Joshua L. *Liberalism in Dark Times: The Liberal Ethos in the Twentieth Century*. Princeton, NJ: Princeton University Press, 2021.

Coates, Ta-Nehisi. *Between the World and Me*. Melbourne: Text, 2015.

Conti, Gregory. *Parliament the Mirror of the Nation: Representation, Deliberation, and Democracy in Victorian Britain*. Ideas in Context. Cambridge: Cambridge University Press, 2019.

Coulthard, Glen Sean. *Red Skin, White Masks: Rejecting the Colonial Politics of Recognition*. Minneapolis: University of Minnesota Press, 2014.

Crăiuțu, Aurelian. *Liberalism Under Siege: The Political Thought of the French Doctrinaires*. Applications of Political Theory. Lanham, MD: Lexington, 2003.

Cribb, Robert J., Helen Gilbert, and Helen Tiffin. *Wild Man from Borneo: A Cultural History of the Orangutan*. Honolulu: University of Hawai'i Press, 2014.

Curran, Andrew S. *The Anatomy of Blackness: Science and Slavery in an Age of Enlightenment*. Baltimore: Johns Hopkins University Press, 2013.

Dagnino, Jorge, Paul Stocker, and Matthew Feldman. *The "New Man" in Radical Right Ideology and Practice, 1919–45*. London: Bloomsbury Academic, 2017.

Daigle, Christine, and Terrance H. McDonald, eds. *From Deleuze and Guattari to Posthumanism: Philosophies of Immanence*. London: Bloomsbury Academic, 2022.

Davis, Angela Y. *The Meaning of Freedom: And Other Difficult Dialogues*. San Francisco: City Lights, 2012.

Dawson, Virginia P. *Nature's Enigma: The Problem of the Polyp in the Letters of Bonnet, Trembley and Réaumur*. Philadelphia: American Philosophical Society, 1987.

——. "Regeneration, Parthenogenesis, and the Immutable Order of Nature." *Archives of Natural History* 18, no. 3 (1991): 309–21.

De Bolla, Peter. *The Architecture of Concepts: The Historical Formation of Human Rights*. New York: Fordham University Press, 2013.

Deleuze, Gilles, and Félix Guattari. *Anti-Oedipus: Capitalism and Schizophrenia*, trans. Robert Hurley, Mark Seem, and Helen R. Lane. New York: Penguin Classics, 2009.

——. *A Thousand Plateaus: Capitalism and Schizophrenia*, trans. Brian Massumi. Minneapolis: University of Minnesota Press, 1987.

Deneen, Patrick J. *Regime Change: Toward a Postliberal Future*. New York: Sentinel, 2023.

——. *Why Liberalism Failed*. New Haven, CT: Yale University Press, 2018.

Derathé, Robert. *Jean-Jacques Rousseau et la science politique de son temps*. Paris: Vrin, 1970.

Descartes, René. *Selected Philosophical Writings*, trans John Cottingham and Robert Stoothoff. Cambridge: Cambridge University Press, 1988.

——. *Meditations, Objections, and Replies*, trans. Donald A. Cress. Indianapolis, IN: Hackett, 2006.

Dictionnaires d'autrefois. ARTFL Project, University of Chicago. Accessed July 6, 2023. https://artfl-project.uchicago.edu/content/dictionnaires-dautrefois.

Diderot, Denis. "Letter on the Blind." In *Diderot's Early Philosophical Works*, ed. Margaret Jourdain. Chicago: Open Court, 1916.

Dijn, Annelien de. *Freedom: An Unruly History*. Cambridge, MA: Harvard University Press, 2020.

Dinsmore, Charles E. "Animal Regeneration: From Fact to Concept." *Bioscience* 45, no. 7 (1995): 484–92.

Dombowsky, Don. "The Rhetoric of Legitimation: Nietzsche's 'Doctrine' of Eternal Recurrence." *Journal of Nietzsche Studies*, no. 14 (1997): 26–45.

Donnelly, Jack. "Human Rights as Natural Rights." *Human Rights Quarterly* 4, no. 3 (1982): 391–405.

Doron, Claude-Olivier. "Race and Genealogy: Buffon and the Formation of the Concept of 'Race.'" *Humana. Mente Journal of Philosophical Studies* 5, no. 22 (2012): 75–109.

Douglass, Robin. "Free Will and the Problem of Evil: Reconciling Rousseau's Divided Thought." *History of Political Thought* 31, no. 4 (2010): 639–55.

Douthwaite, Julia V. *The Wild Girl, Natural Man, and the Monster: Dangerous Experiments in the Age of Enlightenment*. Chicago: University of Chicago Press, 2002.

Dubois, Laurent. *Avengers of the New World: The Story of the Haitian Revolution*. Cambridge, MA: Belknap, 2005.

Duchet, Michèle. *Anthropologie et histoire au siècle des lumières: Buffon, Voltaire, Rousseau, Helvétius, Diderot*. Paris: Flammarion, 1978.

Dugatkin, Lee Alan. *Mr. Jefferson and the Giant Moose: Natural History in Early America*. Chicago: University of Chicago Press, 2009.

Duong, Kevin. "The People as a Natural Disaster: Redemptive Violence in Jacobin Political Thought." *American Political Science Review* 111, no. 4 (2017): 786–800.

——. *The Virtues of Violence: Democracy Against Disintegration in Modern France*. Oxford: Oxford University Press, 2020.

Durant, Will. *The Age of Voltaire: The Story of Civilization*, vol. 9. New York: Simon and Schuster, 2011.

Dworkin, Ronald. "Rights as Trumps." In *Theories of Rights*, ed. C. L. Ten, 153–67. Burlington, VT: Ashgate, 2006.

——. *Taking Rights Seriously*. Cambridge, MA: Harvard University Press, 1978.

Eddy, John H., Jr. "Buffon's *Histoire naturelle*: History? A Critique of Recent Interpretations." *Isis* 85, no. 4 (1994): 644–61.

Edelman, Lee. *No Future: Queer Theory and the Death Drive*. Durham, NC: Duke University Press, 2004.

Edelstein, Dan. "Early-Modern Rights Regimes: A Genealogy of Revolutionary Rights." *Critical Analysis of Law* 26, no. 1 (2016): 221–42.

——. "Enlightenment Rights Talk." *Journal of Modern History* 84, no. 1 (2014): 530–65.

——. "Nature or Nation? Rights Conflicts in the Age of the French Revolution." In *Rethinking the Age of Revolutions: France and the Birth of the Modern World*, ed. David Bell and Yair Mintzker, 1–40. (Oxford: Oxford University Press, 2018).

——. *On the Spirit of Rights*. The Life of Ideas. Chicago: University of Chicago Press, 2019.

——. *The Terror of Natural Right: Republicanism, the Cult of Nature, and the French Revolution*. Chicago: University of Chicago Press, 2010.

Escherny, François d'. "Éloge de J. J. Rousseau." In *La philosophie de la politique, ou Principes généraux sur les institutions civiles, politiques, et religieuses*. Paris, [1790] 1796.

Falaky, Fayçal. "Reverse Revolution: The Paradox of Rousseau's Authorship." In *Rousseau and Revolution*. Continuum Studies in Political Philosophy, ed. Holger Ross Lauritsen and Mikkel Thorup, 83–97. New York: Continuum, 2011.

Fanon, Frantz. *Black Skin, White Masks*, trans. Richard Philcox. New York: Grove, 2008.

Farr, James. "The Way of Hypotheses: Locke on Method." *Journal of the History of Ideas* 48, no. 1 (1987): 51–72.

Faye, Guillaume. *Why We Fight: Manifesto of the European Resistance*, trans. Michael O'Meara. London: Arktos, 2011.

Fellows, Otis. "Buffon and Rousseau: Aspects of a Relationship." *PMLA* 75, no. 3 (1960): 184–96.

Ferrone, Vincenzo. *The Enlightenment and the Rights of Man*. Liverpool: Voltaire Foundation in association with Liverpool University Press, 2019.

——. *The Enlightenment: History of an Idea*, trans. Elisabetta Tarantino. Princeton, NJ: Princeton University Press, 2017.

Forrest, Daniel S. *Suprahumanism: European Man and the Regeneration of History*. London: Arktos, 2014.

Forrester, Katrina. *In the Shadow of Justice: Postwar Liberalism and the Remaking of Political Philosophy*. Princeton, NJ: Princeton University Press, 2019.

Forst, Rainer. "The Basic Right to Justification: Toward a Constructivist Conception of Human Rights." *Constellations* 6, no. 1 (1999): 35–60.

Forsyth, Murray. *Reason and Revolution: The Political Thought of the Abbé Sieyes*. New York: Holmes and Meier, 1987.

Forth, Christopher E. "Nietzsche, Decadence, and Regeneration in France, 1891–95." *Journal of the History of Ideas* 54, no. 1 (1993): 97–117.

Foucault, Michel. *Madness and Civilization: A History of Insanity in the Age of Reason*, trans. Richard Howard. New York: Vintage, 1965.

——. *The Order of Things: An Archaeology of the Human Sciences*, trans. Alan Sheridan. New York: Vintage, 1994.

François, Arnaud, and Roxanne Lapidus. "Life and Will in Nietzsche and Bergson." *SubStance* 36, no. 3 (2007): 100–114.

Frank, Stephanie. "The General Will Beyond Rousseau: Sieyès' Theological Arguments for the Sovereignty of the Revolutionary National Assembly." *History of European Ideas* 37, no. 3 (2011): 337–43.

Frick, Marie-Luisa. *Human Rights and Relative Universalism*. New York: Palgrave Macmillan, 2019.

Furet, François. *Interpreting the French Revolution*. Cambridge: Cambridge University Press, 1981.

——. "Rousseau and the French Revolution." In *The Legacy of Rousseau*, ed. Clifford Orwin and Nathan Tarcov, 168–82. Chicago: University of Chicago Press, 1997.

Furet, François, and Mona Ozouf. *A Critical Dictionary of the French Revolution*. Cambridge, MA: Belknap, 1989.

Gannier, Odile. "De l'usage des notes dans le *Discours sur l'inégalité* de Rousseau: Récits de voyages et ethnographie." *Loxias* 27, no. 2 (2009), http://revel.unice.fr/loxias/index.html?id=3169.

Garrard, Graeme. *Counter-Enlightenments: From the Eighteenth Century to the Present*. Routledge Studies in Social and Political Thought 44. New York: Routledge, 2006.

——. "Illiberalism and Opposition to the Enlightenment." In *Routledge Handbook of Illiberalism*,
ed. András Sajó, Renáta Uitz, and Stephen Holmes, 33–42. New York: Routledge, 2021.

Gauchet, Marcel. *Robespierre: The Man Who Divides Us the Most*, trans. Malcolm DeBevoise.
Princeton, NJ: Princeton University Press, 2022.

Gaukroger, Stephen. *The Natural and the Human: Science and the Shaping of Modernity,
1739–1841*. Science and the Shaping of Modernity. Oxford: Oxford University Press, 2016.

Geggus, David Patrick, ed. *The Haitian Revolution: A Documentary History*. Indianapolis, IN:
Hackett, 2014.

Getachew, Adom. *Worldmaking After Empire: The Rise and Fall of Self-Determination*. Princeton, NJ: Princeton University Press, 2019.

Geuss, Raymond. "Liberalism and Its Discontents." *Political Theory* 30, no. 3 (2002): 320–38.

Gillespie, Michael Allen. *The Theological Origins of Modernity*. Chicago: University of Chicago
Press, 2009.

Goodale, Mark. *Reinventing Human Rights*. Stanford, CA: Stanford University Press, 2022.

Gordon, Jane Anna. *Creolizing Political Theory: Reading Rousseau Through Fanon*. New York:
Fordham University Press, 2014.

Gordon, Jane Anna, and Neil Roberts. "Introduction: The Project of Creolizing Rousseau." *CLR
James Journal* 15, no. 1 (2009): 3–16.

Gottlieb, Anthony. *The Dream of Enlightenment: The Rise of Modern Philosophy*. New York:
Liveright, 2016.

Gouges, Olympe de. "Declaration of the Rights of Woman." In *The French Revolution and
Human Rights: A Brief Documentary History*, trans. and ed. Lynn Hunt. Boston: Bedford,
1996.

Griffin, Roger. *The Nature of Fascism*. New York: Psychology, 1993.

Habermas, Jürgen. *Between Facts and Norms: Contributions to a Discourse Theory of Law and
Democracy*, trans. William Rehg. Cambridge: Polity, 1996.

Hall, A. Rupert. *Philosophers at War: The Quarrel Between Newton and Leibniz*. Cambridge:
Cambridge University Press, 1980.

Hall, Stuart. "The West and the Rest: Discourse and Power." In *Essential Essays*, vol. 2. Durham,
NC: Duke University Press, 2018.

Hamilton, Alexander. *A New Account of the East Indies, Being the Observations and Remarks
of Capt. Alexander Hamilton, Who Spent His Time There from the Year 1688 to 1723, Trad-
ing and Travelling, by Sea and Land, to Most of the Countries and Islands of Commerce and
Navigation, Between the Cape of Good-Hope, and the Island of Japon*, vol. 1. Edinburgh: John
Mosman, 1727.

Haraway, Donna. *Simians, Cyborgs, and Women: The Reinvention of Nature*. New York: Routledge, 1990.

Harcourt, Bernard E. *Critique and Praxis*. New York: Columbia University Press, 2020.

Harrison, Peter. *The Territories of Science and Religion*. Chicago: University of Chicago Press,
2017.

Hayek, F. A. "The Principles of a Liberal Social Order." In *The Collected Works of F. A. Hayek*, ed. Paul Lewis, vol. 18, *Essays on Liberalism and the Economy*, 272–91. Chicago: University of Chicago Press, 2022.

Helvétius, Claude Adrien. *De l'esprit: Or, Essays on the Mind and Its Several Faculties*. New York: Burt Franklin, 1972.

Henry, Paget. "C. L. R. James, Political Philosophy, and the Creolizing of Rousseau and Marx." *CLR James Journal* 15, no. 1 (2009): 178–205.

Hobbes, Thomas. *Leviathan: With Selected Variants from the Latin Edition of 1668*, ed. Edwin Curley. Indianapolis, IN: Hackett, 1994.

Holbach, Paul Henri Thiry. *The System of Nature: Or, Laws of the Moral and Physical World*, trans. H. D. Robinson, 2 vols. New York: Burt Franklin, 1970.

Holmes, Stephen. *The Anatomy of Antiliberalism*. Cambridge, MA: Harvard University Press, 1993.

Hoquet, Thierry. "Biologization of Race and Racialization of the Human: Bernier, Buffon, Linnaeus." In *The Invention of Race: Scientific and Popular Representations*, ed. Nicolas Bancel, Thomas David, and Dominic Thomas, 17–32. New York: Routledge, 2014.

Horkheimer, Max, and Theodor W. Adorno. *Dialectic of Enlightenment*, trans. John Cumming. New York: Continuum, 1972.

Horowitz, Asher. "'Law and Customs Thrust Us Back Into Infancy': Rousseau's Historical Anthropology." *Review of Politics* 52, no. 2 (1990): 215–41.

Hume, David. *An Inquiry Concerning Human Understanding*. London: Andrew Millar, 1748.

Hunt, Alastair, Samuel Moyn, Stephanie DeGooyer, and Lida Maxwell. *The Right to Have Rights*. London: Verso, 2018.

Hunt, Lynn. *Inventing Human Rights: A History*. New York: W. W. Norton, 2008.

——. "Revolutionary Time and Regeneration." *Diciottesimo Secolo* 1 (2016): 62–76.

Huot, Paul. *Les prisonniers d'Orléans: Épisode révolutionnaire*. Strasbourg: C Decker, 1868.

Inston, Kevin. *Rousseau and Radical Democracy*. New York: Continuum, 2010.

Israel, Jonathan. *Revolutionary Ideas: An Intellectual History of the French Revolution from The Rights of Man to Robespierre*. Princeton, NJ: Princeton University Press, 2014.

Jackson, Zakiyyah Iman. *Becoming Human: Matter and Meaning in an Antiblack World*. New York: New York University Press, 2020.

Jahoda, Gustav. *Images of Savages: Ancient Roots of Modern Prejudice in Western Culture*. New York: Routledge, 1998.

Jaume, Lucien. *La religieux et le politique dans la Révolution française: L'idée de régénération*. Paris: Presses universitaires de France, 2015.

Kadane, Matthew. *The Enlightenment and Original Sin*. Chicago: University of Chicago Press, 2024.

Kant, Immanuel. *What Is Enlightenment?*, trans. Mary C. Smith. [1784] 2014, last updated March 24, 2021. https://www.constitution.org/2-Authors/kant/enlightenment.html.

Kates, Gary. *The Cercle Social, the Girondins, and the French Revolution*. Princeton, NJ: Princeton University Press, 1985.

Kelly, Christopher. "Rousseau's 'Peut-Être': Reflections on the Status of the State of Nature." *Modern Intellectual History* 3, no. 1 (2006): 75–83.

Kelly, George Armstrong. "A General Overview." In *The Cambridge Companion to Rousseau*, ed. Patrick Riley, 8–56. Cambridge: Cambridge University Press, 2001.

Kingston, Rebecca. *Montesquieu and the Parlement of Bordeaux*. Geneva: Librairie Droz, 1996.

Kukathas, Chandran. "Hayek and Liberalism." In *The Cambridge Companion to Hayek*. Cambridge Companions to Philosophy, ed. Edward Feser, 182–207. Cambridge: Cambridge University Press, 2006.

——. *Hayek and Modern Liberalism*. Oxford: Oxford University Press, 1989.

La Mettrie, Julien Offray de. "Man a Machine." In *Machine Man and Other Writings*, trans. Ann Thomson. Cambridge: Cambridge University Press, 1996.

Laclau, Ernesto. *On Populist Reason*. London: Verso, 2007.

Laclau, Ernesto, and Chantal Mouffe. *Hegemony and Socialist Strategy: Towards a Radical Democratic Politics*. London: Verso, 2014.

Lange, Lynda, ed. *Feminist Interpretations of Jean-Jacques Rousseau*. Re-Reading the Canon. University Park: Pennsylvania State University Press, 2002.

Lefebvre, Alexandre. *Human Rights as a Way of Life: On Bergson's Political Philosophy*. Cultural Memory in the Present. Stanford, CA: Stanford University Press, 2013.

Lefort, Claude. *Democracy and Political Theory*. Minneapolis: University of Minnesota Press, 1988.

Leibniz, G. W. *Discourse on Metaphysics and the Monadology*, trans. George R. Montgomery, ed. Albert R. Chandler. Mineola, NY: Dover, [1714] 2005.

Leigh, R. A. *Unsolved Problems in the Bibliography of J.-J. Rousseau*, ed. J. T. A. Leigh. Cambridge: Cambridge University Press, 1990.

Leonard, John Bruce. "Metapolitics and the Right—Part 1." Arktos.com (blog), October 22, 2018. https://arktos.com/2018/10/22/metapolitics-and-the-right-part-1/.

Lévi-Strauss, Claude. "Jean-Jacques Rousseau, Founder of the Sciences of Man." In *Structural Anthropology*, vol. 2, trans. Monique Layton, 33–43. Chicago: University of Chicago Press, 1983.

Liebman, Elizabeth. "Unspeakable Passions: The Civil and Savage Lessons of Early Modern Animal Representation." In *Representing the Passions: Histories, Bodies, Visions*. Issues and Debates, ed. Richard Meyer, 137–62. Los Angeles: Getty Research Institute, 2003.

Linnaeus, Carl. "Letter, 25 February 1747, Uppsala, to Johann Georg Gmelin, St. Petersburg," February 25, 1747. Letter 0783. Uppsala University Library, Linnaean Correspondence.

Locke, John. *An Essay Concerning Human Understanding*. London, 1690.

——. *Second Treatise of Government*, ed. C. B. Macpherson. Indianapolis, IN: Hackett, 1980.

Lovejoy, Arthur O. *The Great Chain of Being: A Study of the History of an Idea*. Cambridge, MA: Harvard University Press, 1976.

——. "The Supposed Primitivism of Rousseau's 'Discourse on Inequality.' " *Modern Philology* 21, no. 2 (1923): 165–86.

Lovejoy, Arthur O., and George Boas. *Primitivism and Related Ideas in Antiquity*. Baltimore: Johns Hopkins University Press, 1997.

Lyon, John. "The 'Initial Discourse' to Buffon's *Histoire naturelle*: The First Complete English Translation." *Journal of the History of Biology* 9, no. 1 (1976): 133–81.

MacIntyre, Alasdair. *After Virtue: A Study in Moral Theory*, 3rd ed. Notre Dame, IN: University of Notre Dame Press, 2007.

Mackinnon, Emma Stone. "The Right to Rebel: History and Universality in the Political Thought of the Algerian Revolution." In *Time, History, and Political Thought*, ed. John Robertson, 285–307. Cambridge: Cambridge University Press, 2023.

MacLean, Lee. *The Free Animal: Rousseau on Free Will and Human Nature*. Toronto, ON: University of Toronto Press, 2013.

Maistre, Joseph de. *Considerations on France*, ed. Richard A. Lebrun. Cambridge: Cambridge University Press, 1994.

——. "Étude sur la souveraineté." In *Collection: Les archives de la Révolution française*. Bibliothèque nationale. Oxford: Pergamon, 1989.

Maldonado-Torres, Nelson. "Rousseau and Fanon on Inequality and the Human Sciences." *CLR James Journal* 15, no. 1 (2009): 113–34.

Malik, Kenan. *The Meaning of Race: Race, History, and Culture in Western Society*. New York: New York University Press, 1996.

Manent, Pierre. *Natural Law and Human Rights: Toward a Recovery of Practical Reason*, trans. Ralph C. Hancock. Notre Dame, IN: University of Notre Dame Press, 2021.

Marks, Jonathan. "Who Lost Nature? Rousseau and Rousseauism." *Polity* 34, no. 4 (2002): 479–502.

Marx, Karl. "On the Jewish Question." In *The Marx-Engels Reader*, ed. Robert C. Tucker. New York: W. W. Norton, 1978.

Mason, Laura. *Singing the French Revolution: Popular Songs and Revolutionary Politics, 1787–1799*. Princeton, NJ: Princeton University, 1990.

Masters, Roger D. "Jean-Jacques Is Alive and Well: Rousseau and Contemporary Sociobiology." *Daedalus* 107, no. 3 (1978): 93–105.

——. *The Political Philosophy of Rousseau*. Princeton, NJ: Princeton University Press, 1968.

Mathias, Manon. "Pre-Darwinian Species Change: Reincarnation and Transformism in George Sand's *Évenor et Leucippe*." *Journal of Literature and Science* 11, no. 1 (2018).

Mbembe, Achille. *Necropolitics*. Durham, NC: Duke University Press, 2019.

McCalla, Arthur. "Evolutionism and Early Nineteenth-Century Histories of Religions." *Religion* 28, no. 1 (1998): 29–40.

——. "*Palingénésie philosophique* to *Palingénésie sociale*: From a Scientific Ideology to a Historical Ideology." *Journal of the History of Ideas* 55, no. 3 (1994): 421–39.

——. *A Romantic Historiosophy: The Philosophy of History of Pierre-Simon Ballanche*. Brill's Studies in Intellectual History. Boston: Brill, 1998.

McDonald, Joan. *Rousseau and the French Revolution, 1762–1791*. London: Athlone, 1965.

McKittrick, Katherine, ed. *Sylvia Wynter: On Being Human as Praxis*. Durham, NC: Duke University Press, 2015.

McMahon, Darrin M. *Enemies of the Enlightenment: The French Counter-Enlightenment and the Making of Modernity*. Oxford: Oxford University Press, 2002.

——. "What Is Counter-Enlightenment?" *International Journal for History, Culture and Modernity* 5, no. 1 (2017): 33–46.

McMullin, Ernan. "The Impact of Newton's Principia on the Philosophy of Science." *Philosophy of Science* 68, no. 3 (2001): 279–310.

Melzer, Arthur M. *The Natural Goodness of Man: On the System of Rousseau's Thought.* Chicago: University of Chicago Press, 1990.

Mendham, Matthew D. "Gentle Savages and Fierce Citizens Against Civilization: Unraveling Rousseau's Paradoxes." *American Journal of Political Science* 55, no. 1 (2011): 170–87.

Mill, John Stuart. *On Liberty and Utilitarianism.* New York: Bantam Classics, 2008.

Miller, Bradley W., Francisco J. Urbina, Grégoire Webber, Maris Köpcke, Paul Yowell, and Richard Ekins, eds. *Legislated Rights: Securing Human Rights Through Legislation.* Cambridge: Cambridge University Press, 2018.

Mills, Charles W. *Black Rights/White Wrongs: The Critique of Racial Liberalism.* Oxford: Oxford University Press, 2017.

——. *The Racial Contract.* Ithaca, NY: Cornell University Press, 1999.

——. "Rousseau, the Master's Tools, and Anti-Contractarian Contractarianism." *CLR James Journal* 15, no. 1 (2009): 92–112.

Miquel, Paul-Antoine. "Bergson and Darwin: From an Immanentist to an Emergentist Approach to Evolution." *SubStance* 36, no. 3 (2007): 42–56.

Moran, Francis, III. "Between Primates and Primitives: Natural Man as the Missing Link in Rousseau's *Second Discourse*." *Journal of the History of Ideas* 54, no. 1 (1993): 37–58.

——. "Of Pongos and Men: *Orangs-Outang* in Rousseau's *Discourse on Inequality*." *Review of Politics* 57, no. 4 (1995): 641–64.

Morel, Jean. "Recherches sur les sources du *Discours de l'inégalité*." *Annales de la Société Jean-Jacques Rousseau* 5 (1909): 119–98.

Mornet, Daniel. "L'influence de J. J. Rousseau au SVIIIe siècle." *Annales de la Société Jean-Jacques Rousseau* 8 (1912): 33–68.

Mouffe, Chantal. *The Democratic Paradox.* London: Verso, 2009.

——. *The Return of the Political.* London: Verso, 2020.

Moyn, Samuel. "Afterword: The Self-Evidence of Human Rights." In *Self-Evident Truths? Human Rights and the Enlightenment*, ed. Kate E. Tunstall, 249–62. New York: Bloomsbury, 2012.

——. *Christian Human Rights.* Philadelphia: University of Pennsylvania Press, 2015.

——. *Human Rights and the Uses of History*, 2nd ed. London: Verso, 2017.

——. *The Last Utopia: Human Rights in History.* Cambridge, MA: Belknap, 2012.

——. *Liberalism Against Itself: Cold War Intellectuals and the Making of Our Times.* New Haven, CT: Yale University Press, 2023.

Muthu, Sankar. *Enlightenment Against Empire.* Princeton, NJ: Princeton University Press, 2003.

——. "On the General Will of Humanity: Global Connections in Rousseau's Political Thought." In *The General Will: The Evolution of a Concept*, ed. James Farr and David Lay Williams, 270–306. Cambridge: Cambridge University Press, 2015.

Neidleman, Jason. "Politics and Tragedy: The Case of Rousseau." *Political Research Quarterly* 73, no. 2 (2020): 464–75.

Nelson, Eric. *The Theology of Liberalism: Political Philosophy and the Justice of God.* Cambridge, MA: Belknap, 2019.

Nelson, William Max. "Colonizing France: Revolutionary Regeneration and the First French Empire." In *The French Revolution in Global Perspective*, ed. Suzanne Desan, Lynn Hunt, and William Max Nelson, 73–85. Ithaca, NY: Cornell University Press, 2013.

——. *The Time of Enlightenment: Constructing the Future in France, 1750 to Year One*. Toronto, ON: University of Toronto Press, 2021.

Neuhouser, Frederick. *Rousseau's Critique of Inequality: Reconstructing the Second Discourse*. Cambridge: Cambridge University Press, 2014.

Newell, Waller R. *Tyranny: A New Interpretation*. Cambridge: Cambridge University Press, 2013.

Newton, Isaac. *Principia*, trans. Andrew Motte, ed. Florian Cajorli. Berkeley: University of California Press, [1726] 1996.

Niekerk, Carl. "Buffon, Blumenbach, Herder, Lichtenberg, and the Origins of Modern Anthropology." In *Johann Friedrich Blumenbach: Race and Natural History, 1750–1850*, ed. Nicolaas Rupke and Gerhard Lauer, 27–52. London: Routledge, 2018.

Nozick, Robert. *Anarchy, State, and Utopia*. New York: Basic Books, 1974.

O'Hagan, Timothy. *Rousseau*. New York: Routledge, 2003.

——. "Taking Rousseau Seriously." *History of Political Thought* 25, no. 1 (2004): 73–85.

Okin, Susan Moller. "Rousseau's Natural Woman." *Journal of Politics* 41, no. 2 (1979): 393–416.

Olson, Kevin. *Imagined Sovereignties: The Power of the People and Other Myths of the Modern Age*. Cambridge: Cambridge University Press, 2016.

Osler, Margaret J. "John Locke and the Changing Ideal of Scientific Knowledge." *Journal of the History of Ideas* 31, no. 1 (1970): 3–16.

Ozouf, Mona. *L'homme régénéré: Essais sur la Révolution française*. Paris: Gallimard, 1989.

——. "Regeneration." In *A Critical Dictionary of the French Revolution*, ed. François Furet and Mona Ozouf. Cambridge, MA: Belknap, 1989.

Pagden, Anthony. *The Enlightenment: And Why It Still Matters*. New York: Random House, 2013.

Paine, Thomas. *The Rights of Man*. London: J. S. Jordan, 1791.

Pateman, Carole. *The Sexual Contract*. Stanford, CA: Stanford University Press, 1988.

Peyre, Henri. "The Influence of Eighteenth Century Ideas on the French Revolution." *Journal of the History of Ideas* 10, no. 1 (1949): 63–87.

Philips, Menaka. *The Liberalism Trap: John Stuart Mill and Customs of Interpretation*. Oxford: Oxford University Press, 2023.

Phillips, Anne. *Unconditional Equals*. Princeton, NJ: Princeton University Press, 2021.

Pinel, Scipion. *Traité complet du régime sanitaire des aliénés*. Paris: Mauprivez, 1836.

Pinker, Steven. *Enlightenment Now: The Case for Reason, Science, Humanism, and Progress*. New York: Viking, 2018.

Pitts, Jennifer. *A Turn to Empire: The Rise of Imperial Liberalism in Britain and France*. Princeton, NJ: Princeton University Press, 2006.

Planinc, Emma. "The Creation of Man: Linguistic Reformation and the Necessity of the State in the Work of Thomas Hobbes." In *Polis, Nation, Global Community*, 47–66. India: Routledge, 2021.

——. "The Figurative Foundations of Rousseau's Politics." *Modern Intellectual History* 20, no. 1 (2023): 1–26.

———. "Homo Duplex: The Two Origins of Man in Rousseau's *Second Discourse.*" *History of European Ideas* 47, no. 1 (2021): 71–90.

———. "Regenerating Humanism." *History of European Ideas* 46, no. 3 (2020): 242–56.

———. "Regeneration on the Right: Visions of the Future, Past and Present." In *Contemporary Far-Right Thinkers and the Future of Liberal Democracy*, ed. Alejandro Castrillon and Jim McAdams. New York: Routledge, 2021.

Pocock, J. G. A. "The Tell-Tale Article: Reconstructing (. . .) Enlightenment." Plenary address to the 29th annual meeting of the American Society for Eighteenth-Century Studies, University of Notre Dame, Notre Dame, IN, April 2, 1998.

Pope, Alexander. "An Essay on Man." In *Moral Essays and Satires*. London: Cassell, [1734] 1891.

Pranchère, Jean-Yves. "The Negative of Enlightenment, the Positive of Order." In *Joseph de Maistre and the Legacy of Enlightenment*. Oxford University Studies in the Enlightenment, ed. Carolina Armenteros and Richard Lebrun, 45–64. Oxford: Voltaire Foundation, 2011.

Prévost, Antoine-François. *Histoire générale des voyages*. Paris, 1746–1789.

Quinlan, Sean. "Physical and Moral Regeneration After the Terror: Medical Culture, Sensibility and Family Politics in France, 1794–1804." *Social History* 29, no. 2 (2004): 139–64.

Rancière, Jacques. *Dissensus: On Politics and Aesthetics*, trans. Steven Corcoran. New York: Continuum, 2010.

———. *Hatred of Democracy*, trans. Steven Corcoran. London: Verso, 2014.

Reill, Peter H. *Vitalizing Nature in the Enlightenment*. Berkeley: University of California Press, 2005.

Reimarus, Hermann Samuel. *The Principal Truths of Natural Religion Defended and Illustrated, in Nine Dissertations: Wherein the Objections of Lucretius, Buffon, Maupertuis, Rousseau, La Mettrie, and Other Ancient and Modern Followers of Epicurus Are Considered, and Their Doctrines Refuted*. London: B. Law, [1755] 1766.

Rials, Stéphane. *La Déclaration des droits de l'homme et du citoyen*. Paris: Hachette, 1988.

Ritvo, Harriet. "At the Edge of the Garden: Nature and Domestication in Eighteenth- and Nineteenth-Century Britain." *Huntington Library Quarterly* 55, no. 3 (1992): 363–78.

Robbins, Louise E. *Elephant Slaves and Pampered Parrots: Exotic Animals in Eighteenth-Century Paris*. Baltimore: Johns Hopkins University Press, 2002.

Roe, Shirley A. *Matter, Life, and Generation: Eighteenth-Century Embryology and the Haller–Wolff Debate*. Cambridge: Cambridge University Press, 1981.

Roger, Jacques. *Buffon: A Life in Natural History*, trans. Sarah Lucille Bonnefoi. Ithaca, NY: Cornell University Press, 1997.

Rogers, G. A. J. "Locke's Essay and Newton's Principia." *Journal of the History of Ideas* 39, no. 2 (1978): 217–32.

Rosenblatt, Helena. *The Lost History of Liberalism: From Ancient Rome to the Twenty-First Century*. Princeton, NJ: Princeton University Press, 2018.

———. *Rousseau and Geneva: From the First Discourse to the Social Contract, 1749–1762*. Ideas in Context. Cambridge: Cambridge University Press, 1997.

Rosenfeld, Sophia. *A Revolution in Language: The Problem of Signs in Late Eighteenth-Century France*. Stanford, CA: Stanford University Press, 2001.

Rosenfield, Leonora Cohen. "The Rights of Women in the French Revolution." *Studies in Eighteenth-Century Culture* 7, no. 1 (1978): 117–37.

Rousseau, Jean-Jacques. *Emile: or On Education*, trans. Allan Bloom. New York: Basic Books, 1979.

——. *Fiction or Allegorical Fragment on Revelation*. In *On Philosophy, Morality, and Religion*, trans. and ed. Christopher Kelly. Hanover, NH: Dartmouth College Press, 2004), 63–72.

——. *Oeuvres complètes*, 5 vols. Paris: NRF-Éditions de la Pléiade, 1965–1995.

——. *The Discourses and Other Early Political Writings*, 2nd ed., trans. and ed. Victor Gourevitch. Cambridge: Cambridge University Press, 2019.

——. *The Social Contract and Other Later Political Writings*, trans. and ed. Victor Gourevitch. Cambridge: Cambridge University Press, 1997.

Rubinelli, Lucia. *Constituent Power: A History*. Ideas in Context. Cambridge: Cambridge University Press, 2020.

Russell, Bertrand. *A History of Western Philosophy and Its Connection with Political and Social Circumstances from the Earliest Times to the Present Day*. New York: Simon and Schuster, 1945.

Ryan, Alan. *The Making of Modern Liberalism*. Princeton, NJ: Princeton University Press, 2012.

Sahlins, Peter. *1668: The Year of the Animal in France*. Brooklyn: Zone, 2017.

Sainson, Katia. " 'Le régénérateur de la France': Literary Accounts of Napoleonic Regeneration 1799–1805." *Nineteenth-Century French Studies* 30, no. 1 (2001): 9–25.

Sales, Delisle de. *De la philosophie de la nature*. Amsterdam: Arkstée & Merkus, 1770.

Schaeffer, Denise. "Moral Motivation and Rhetoric." In *The Rousseauian Mind*, ed. Eve Grace and Christopher Kelly, 267–77. New York: Routledge, 2019.

——. *Rousseau on Education, Freedom, and Judgment*. University Park: Pennsylvania State University Press, 2014.

Schaub, Jean-Frédéric, and Silvia Sebastiani. "Between Genealogy and Physicality: A Historiographical Perspective on Race in the Ancien Régime." *Graduate Faculty Philosophy Journal* 35, no. 1 (2014): 23–51.

Schmidt, James. "Inventing the Enlightenment: Anti-Jacobins, British Hegelians, and the *Oxford English Dictionary*." *Journal of the History of Ideas* 64, no. 3 (2003): 421–43.

——. "What Enlightenment Project?" *Political Theory* 28, no. 6 (2000): 734–57.

Scott, Joan Wallach. "French Feminists and the Rights of 'Man': Olympe de Gouges's Declarations." *History Workshop Journal* 28, no. 1 (1989): 1–21.

Scott, John T. *Rousseau's God: Theology, Religion, and the Natural Goodness of Man*. Chicago: University of Chicago Press, 2023.

——. *Rousseau's Reader: Strategies of Persuasion and Education*. Chicago: University of Chicago Press, 2020.

Scurr, Ruth. *Fatal Purity: Robespierre and the French Revolution*. New York: Metropolitan, 2006.

Sebastiani, Silvia. "La caravane des animaux." In *Mobilités creatrices: Hommes, savoirs et pratiques en mouvement (XVIe–XIXe siècle)*, ed. Catherine Brice. *Diasporas* 29 (2017).

——. "Challenging Boundaries: Apes and Savages in the Enlightenment." In *Simianization: Apes, Gender, Class, and Race*, ed. Wulf D. Hund, Charles W. Mills, and Silvia Sebastiani, 105–37. Zurich: Lit Zurlag, 2015.

——. "Enlightenment Humanization and Dehumanization, and the Orangutan." In *The Rout-ledge Handbook of Dehumanization*. Routledge Handbooks in Philosophy, ed. Maria Kro-nfeldner, 64–82. London: Routledge, 2021.

Séchelle, M. Hérault. "Parallele de J. J. Rousseau et de M. de Buffon." *Journal encyclopédique* 3 (1786): 329–30.

Selinger, William. *Parliamentarism: From Burke to Weber*. Ideas in Context. Cambridge: Cam-bridge University Press, 2019.

Senior, Matthew, ed. *A Cultural History of Animals in the Age of Enlightenment*. Oxford: Berg, 2009.

Sepinwall, Alyssa Goldstein. *The Abbé Grégoire and the French Revolution: The Making of Modern Universalism*. Berkeley: University of California Press, 2005.

Sewell, William H., Jr. *A Rhetoric of Bourgeois Revolution: The Abbé Sieyes and What Is the Third Estate?* Durham, NC: Duke University Press, 1994.

Shanks, Torrey. *Authority Figures: Rhetoric and Experience in John Locke's Political Thought*. University Park: Pennsylvania State University Press, 2014.

Sheehan, Jonathan. *The Enlightenment Bible: Translation, Scholarship, Culture*. Princeton, NJ: Princeton University Press, 2007.

Shklar, Judith N. *After Utopia: The Decline of Political Faith*, ed. Samuel Moyn. Princeton, NJ: Princeton University Press, 2020.

——. *Men and Citizens: A Study of Rousseau's Social Theory*. Cambridge: Cambridge University Press, 1969.

——. "Rights in the Liberal Tradition." *Political Studies* 71, no. 2 (2023): 279–94.

Siedentop, Larry. *Inventing the Individual: The Origins of Western Liberalism*. Cambridge, MA: Belknap, 2014.

Simmons, Laurence. "Towards a Philosophy of the Polyp." In *Animals and Agency: An Inter-disciplinary Exploration*, ed. Sarah McFarland and Ryan Hediger, 341–71. London: Brill, 2009.

Sloan, Phillip R. "Buffon, German Biology, and the Historical Interpretation of Biological Species." *British Journal for the History of Science* 12, no. 2 (1979): 109–53.

——. "The Buffon-Linnaeus Controversy." *Isis* 67, no. 3 (1976): 356–85.

——. "The Idea of Racial Degeneracy in Buffon's *Histoire naturelle*." *Studies in Eighteenth-Century Culture* 3, no. 1 (1974): 293–321.

——. "Metaphysics and Vital Materialism: Émilie du Châtelet and the Origins of French Vital-ism." In *Philosophy of Biology Before Biology*, ed. Cécilia Bognon-Küss and Charles T. Wolfe. London: Routledge, 2019.

Smith, Justin E. H. *Divine Machines: Leibniz and the Sciences of Life*. Princeton, NJ: Princeton University Press, 2011.

——, ed. *The Problem of Animal Generation in Early Modern Philosophy*. Cambridge Studies in Philosophy and Biology. Cambridge: Cambridge University Press, 2006.

——. *Nature, Human Nature, and Human Difference: Race in Early Modern Philosophy*. Prince-ton, NJ: Princeton University Press, 2015.

Spade, Dean. *Normal Life: Administrative Violence, Critical Trans Politics, and the Limits of Law*. Durham, NC: Duke University Press, 2015.

Sparling, Robert Alan. *Johann Georg Hamann and the Enlightenment Project*. Toronto, ON: University of Toronto Press, 2011.

Spary, E. C. "Climate Change and Creolization in French Natural History, 1750–1795." In *Johann Friedrich Blumenbach: Race and Natural History, 1750–1850*, ed. Nicolaas Rupke and Gerhard Lauer, 53–79. New York: Routledge, 2018.

——. *Utopia's Garden: French Natural History from Old Regime to Revolution*. Chicago: University of Chicago Press, 2000.

Spector, Céline. *Rousseau*. Classic Thinkers. Cambridge: Polity, 2019.

Starobinski, Jean. *Transparency and Obstruction*. Chicago: University of Chicago Press, 1998.

Stewart, John Hall. *A Documentary Survey of the French Revolution*. Ann Arbor: University of Michigan Press, 1951.

Stovall, Tyler. *White Freedom: The Racial History of an Idea*. Princeton, NJ: Princeton University Press, 2021.

Strauss, Leo. *Natural Right and History*. Chicago: University of Chicago Press, 1965.

——. *What Is Political Philosophy?* Glencoe, IL: Free Press, 1959.

Swenson, James. *On Jean-Jacques Rousseau: Considered as One of the First Authors of the Revolution*. Stanford, CA: Stanford University Press, 2000.

Taine, Hippolyte. *The Ancient Regime*, trans. John Durand. New York: Henry Holt, 1876.

Talmon, J. L. *The Origins of Totalitarian Democracy*. London: Mercury, 1961.

Tasioulas, John. "Saving Human Rights from Human Rights Law." *Vanderbilt Journal of Transnational Law* 52, no. 5 (2019): 1167–1207.

Taylor, Samuel. "Rousseau's Contemporary Reception in France." *Studies on Voltaire and the Eighteenth Century* 27 (1963): 1545–74.

Tocqueville, Alexis de. *The Old Regime and the French Revolution*, trans. Stuart Gilbert. New York: Anchor, 1955.

Trouillot, Michel-Rolph. "Anthropology and the Savage Slot: The Poetics and Politics of Otherness." In *Global Transformations: Anthropology and the Modern World*, 7–28. New York: Palgrave Macmillan, 2003.

——. *Silencing the Past: Power and the Production of History*. New York: Beacon, 2015.

Tully, James. "Rethinking Human Rights and the Enlightenment: A View from the Twenty-First Century." In *Self-Evident Truths? Human Rights and the Enlightenment*, ed. Kate E. Tunstall, 3–34. New York: Bloomsbury Academic, 2012.

Turner, Dale A. *This Is Not a Peace Pipe: Towards a Critical Indigenous Philosophy*. Toronto, ON: University of Toronto Press, 2006.

Urbina, Francisco J. "How Legislation Aids Human Rights Adjudication." In *Legislated Rights: Securing Human Rights Through Legislation*, ed. Bradley W. Miller, Francisco J. Urbina, Grégoire Webber, Maris Köpcke, Paul Yowell, and Richard Ekins, 153–80. Cambridge: Cambridge University Press, 2018.

Vanpée, Janie. "Performing Justice: The Trials of Olympe de Gouges." *Theatre Journal* 51, no. 1 (1999): 47–65.

Vartanian, Aram. "Review of *Abraham Trembley of Geneva: Scientist and Philosopher* by John R. Baker." *Isis* 44, no. 4 (1953): 387–89.

——. "Trembley's Polyp, La Mettrie, and Eighteenth-Century French Materialism." *Journal of the History of Ideas* 11, no. 3 (1950): 259–86.

Vartija, Devin. *The Color of Equality: Race and Common Humanity in Enlightenment Thought.* Philadelphia: University of Pennsylvania Press, 2021.

——. "Revisiting Enlightenment Racial Classification: Time and the Question of Human Diversity." *Intellectual History Review* 31, no. 4 (2021): 603–25.

Vaughan, C. E., ed. *The Political Writings of Jean-Jacques Rousseau.* New York: John Wiley, 1962.

Velkley, Richard. "The Measure of the Possible: Imagination in Rousseau's Philosophical Pedagogy." In *The Challenge of Rousseau*, ed. Eve Grace and Christopher Kelly, 217–29. Cambridge: Cambridge University Press, 2013.

Versluis, Arthur. "A Conversation with Alain de Benoist." *Journal for the Study of Radicalism* 8, no. 2 (2014): 79–106.

Vyverberg, Henry. *Human Nature, Cultural Diversity, and the French Enlightenment.* Oxford: Oxford University Press, 1989.

Walcott, Rinaldo. *The Long Emancipation: Moving Toward Black Freedom.* Durham, NC: Duke University Press, 2021.

——. *Queer Returns: Essays on Multiculturalism, Diaspora, and Black Studies.* London, ON: Insomniac, 2016.

Webber, Grégoire. "Rights and Persons." In *Legislated Rights: Securing Human Rights Through Legislation*, ed. Bradley W. Miller, Francisco J. Urbina, Grégoire Webber, Maris Köpcke, Paul Yowell, and Richard Ekins, 27–54. Cambridge: Cambridge University Press, 2018.

Webber, Grégoire, and Paul Yowell. "Introduction: Securing Human Rights Through Legislation." In *Legislated Rights: Securing Human Rights Through Legislation*, ed. Bradley W. Miller, Francisco J. Urbina, Grégoire Webber, Maris Köpcke, Paul Yowell, and Richard Ekins, 1–26. Cambridge: Cambridge University Press, 2018.

Weheliye, Alexander G. *Habeas Viscus: Racializing Assemblages, Biopolitics, and Black Feminist Theories of the Human.* Durham, NC: Duke University Press, 2014.

Weiss, Penny A. *Gendered Community: Rousseau, Sex, and Politics.* New York: New York University Press, 1993.

Williams, D. F. "On So-Called 'Palingenetic Ultra-Nationalism'—Part 1." Arktos.com (blog), September 25, 2019. https://arktos.com/2019/09/25/on-so-called-palingenetic-ultra-nationalism-part-1/.

Williams, David Lay. *Rousseau's Platonic Enlightenment.* University Park: Pennsylvania State University Press, 2007.

Winston, Michael E. *From Perfectibility to Perversion: Meliorism in Eighteenth-Century France.* New York: P. Lang, 2005.

Wokler, Robert. "The *Discours sur l'inégalité* and Its Sources." PhD diss., University of Oxford, 1976.

——. "From *l'homme physique* to *l'homme moral* and Back: Towards a History of Enlightenment Anthropology." *History of the Human Sciences* 6, no. 1 (1993): 121–38.

——. "Perfectible Apes in Decadent Cultures: Rousseau's Anthropology Revisited." *Daedalus* 107, no. 3 (1978): 107–34.

Wolin, Richard. *The Seduction of Unreason: The Intellectual Romance with Fascism from Nietzsche to Postmodernism*, 2nd ed. Princeton, NJ: Princeton University Press, 2019.

Wolin, Sheldon. "Fugitive Democracy." In *Fugitive Democracy and Other Essays*, ed. Nicholas Xenos, 100–113. Princeton, NJ: Princeton University Press, 2016.

Zamalin, Alex. *Black Utopia: The History of an Idea from Black Nationalism to Afrofuturism*. New York: Columbia University Press, 2019.

INDEX

www.ingramcontent.com/pod-product-compliance
Lightning Source LLC
LaVergne TN
LVHW090044010225
802671LV00001B/117